LEARN
BRAZILIAN
PORTUGUESE

LEARN BRAZILIAN PORTUGUESE

Speak, Write, and Understand Portuguese in No Time

Fernanda L. Ferreira, Ph.D.

FALL RIVER PRESS

New York

To my spouse Jane, who has inspired me to complete this project, and to our cats BeeBee, Liza, and Tessa, who make life interesting

FALL RIVER PRESS

New York

An Imprint of Sterling Publishing Co., Inc.
1166 Avenue of the Americas
New York, NY 10036

ISBN 978-1-4351-6760-5

For information about custom editions, special sales, and premium and corporate purchases, please contact Sterling Special Sales at 800-805-5489 or specialsales@sterlingpublishing.com.

Manufactured in China
2 4 6 8 10 9 7 5 3 1

sterlingpublishing.com

Cover design by Igor Satanovsky

Contents

Introduction

Y OU PICKED UP THIS BOOK because you might have already watched a Brazilian movie, listened to a *bossa nova* song, or learned what *capoeira* means. Perhaps you already know that Brazilians love soccer and that they have won the World Cup five times. But you might still struggle with the Portuguese language, even if the Brazilian dialect sounds fascinating to you. *Boas notícias!* (Good news!). This book will help you in your journey to become more fluent in this beautiful language.

There are twenty chapters in this book that cover everything from the origins of the Portuguese language to accent marks, formal greetings, various verb forms and conjugations, and Brazilian cinema, cuisine, and music. The chapters on more discrete grammatical points are replete with practical, easy-to-follow exercises. The Answer Key (Appendix C at the back of the book) is available so you can check your work and evaluate your progress as you move through the chapters. There is no particular order in which you should read this book, although grammar topics are introduced in an increasing level of difficulty. That said, the instructions are easy enough that any reader should be able to grasp the content without having to refer constantly to previous pages.

A very attractive part of this book is the CD that accompanies the text. You will hear a native speaker from Brazil reading important examples of vocabulary and pronunciation. Some of the book exercises require that you listen to the CD in order to complete them. This will boost your confidence and make this experience more enjoyable.

Learners face many challenges as they try to master a new language. The most important element to remember is motivation. Research into second language acquisition has shown time and again that motivation is a crucial part of learner success. And that the establishment of clear goals from the beginning will also contribute to your success. Once you have decided what you want to get from this experience, devise a clear game plan, and set out to get it! Don't forget that practice makes perfect, so study for shorter time periods but study often!

As the author of *Learn Brazilian Portuguese*, I hope that after you finish reading it you will have a better grasp of the intricacies of the Portuguese language, its pitfalls for the English speaker, and its unexpected beauty. At the same time, I hope that you will have a better understanding of what makes Brazilians who they really are.

CHAPTER 1

Introducing the Portuguese Language

NOT MANY PEOPLE know that Portuguese is spoken in Brazil, one of the few Latin American countries where Spanish is not the official language. In fact, Portuguese is spoken in far-reaching parts of the globe, such as Goa (India), Macau (China), Guinea, Bissau, Angola, and Mozambique, among other countries. So what are the origins of this language? How is it similar or different from Spanish? What makes Brazilian Portuguese different from European Portuguese? And why should we learn it?

Why Learn Portuguese?

Have you ever listened to a *bossa nova* love song and wondered what the lyrics mean? Perhaps you have always been intrigued by fascinating exotic places such as the Amazon jungle or Copacabana beach. Maybe your grandparents emigrated from the Azores, Madeira, or Portugal, and you always wanted to write to them in their language. Or you might be interested in learning Portuguese to communicate with your coworkers.

Many people in the world (close to 200 million) speak Portuguese. You might be interested to know that many African and Asian countries have Portuguese as their official language. In addition, there is a growing Portuguese-speaking population in the United States. Because it is an uncommonly taught language, being fluent in it will probably serve you well when you look for a job! Also, learning Portuguese will help you understand the lyrics of famous *bossa nova* songs, the lines in Oscar-nominated Brazilian films, and the prose of an incredibly diverse body of literature.

Whatever the reason, be it reclaiming your heritage, learning more about the diversity of Latin America, or discovering new worlds of cuisine, literature, and history, learning Portuguese is a great step in your life. So put on your *samba* shoes and let's get started!

Portuguese: A Romance Language

Portuguese is a Romance language, which does not mean that it is full of loving words, but simply that it originated from Latin, the language of the Roman Empire. Along with other Romance languages, Portuguese came from Vulgar Latin, which simply meant that it was the "common," everyday speech of soldiers, farmers, settlers, and slaves of the Roman Empire.

Romance languages include Italian, French, Spanish, Galician, Romanian, and Catalan. There are also minority languages such as Occitan, Provençal, Friulian, and Ladin among many other tongues whose origins can be traced back to Latin. With the decline of the Roman Empire in the fifth century, Vulgar Latin began to change slowly, taking on the diverse features and styles of the localities where it was spoken, thus generating the incredible array of

Romance languages. The Visigoths, a group of barbaric tribes that invaded the Iberian Peninsula, added to the development of Portuguese and Spanish.

Portuguese is becoming more and more popular in Asia. The number of Portuguese speakers has grown in particular in Macau, China, due to the region's increase in diplomatic and economic relations with Portugal and other Lusophone countries. Similarly, there have been reports of an increase in East Timor's Portuguese-speaking population in recent years.

In the seventh century, the Moors, an Arabic ethnic group of northern Africa, invaded the south of Spain and Portugal. The effect of the Arabic language is still found today in Portuguese and Spanish words, such as *arroz* (rice) and *algodão* (cotton). With colonization efforts by Spain, Portugal, and France starting in the early fifteenth century, Romance languages began to be spoken in many different parts of the world. Today, two-thirds of Romance language speakers live outside of Europe. In the case of Portuguese, approximately eighty percent of its speakers are concentrated in Brazil.

Similarities to Spanish

Portuguese and Spanish can be called "sister languages" due to their intrinsic similarities. After all, they both derive from spoken Latin. The following table shows the similarities in orthography between these languages.

Comparing Portuguese to Spanish: Part I

Portuguese	Spanish	English
classe	*clase*	class
casa	*casa*	house
livro	*libro*	book
caderno	*cuaderno*	notebook

However, these similarities should not fool the serious Portuguese student. When using your knowledge of Spanish to help with your Portuguese, be mindful that these are different languages, and similarity in orthography does not always mean similarity in pronunciation. Always learn how to pronounce the "sounds" of Portuguese instead of relying on your Spanish. What about differences in words and meanings? The following list shows how these languages can vary significantly:

Comparing Portuguese to Spanish: Part II

Portuguese	Spanish	English
cedo	temprano	early
desenvolvimento	desarrollo	development
envelope	sobre	envelope
irmã	hermana	sister

If that wasn't enough, there are some tricky words which are commonly referred to as "false cognates." These words sound similar to English or Spanish but mean something completely different in your target language, in this case, Portuguese. The novice student needs to watch out for these "false friends."

False Cognates

Portuguese	Spanish
cuchilo (nap)	cuchillo (knife)
tirar (to take)	tirar (to throw away)
escritório (office)	escritorio (desk)
embaraçada (confused, ashamed)	embarazada (pregnant)

The trick here is to use a good Portuguese-English dictionary and always make sure you are saying the correct word, depending on the social situation. Some awkward moments may occur, but most of the time native speakers will understand and help you out.

European Portuguese Versus Brazilian Portuguese

When the Portuguese arrived in Brazil in the early sixteenth century, they found many speakers of different Native American languages already living there. It has been estimated that there were more than 1,000 indigenous languages spoken in Brazil at the time of the Portuguese arrival. With the advancement of white populations into the coastal areas of Brazil, these populations were slowly decimated by disease or genocide, so that nowadays we are left with about 170 different Native Brazilian languages in Brazil.

The development of Brazilian Portuguese is a complex one, but one that is fascinating nonetheless. Portuguese colonization in Brazil really started in 1548 with the introduction of a system of *capitanias* or territories awarded to Portuguese officials on a hereditary basis. Most of these territories failed economically, except for São Vicente (today's São Paulo state) and Pernambuco. Later, there was a system of governorships that responded directly to the King of Portugal. With the invasion of Portugal by Napoleon, the Portuguese Royal family transferred to Rio de Janeiro. This transatlantic move had a significant impact on the Portuguese educational policy in Brazil, especially with regard to the development of language instruction.

The path followed by Brazil since it became independent in 1822 was very different from that followed by other Portuguese colonies such as Angola and Mozambique. In these countries, the Portuguese-speaking community is a learned minority. In Brazil, Portuguese has been spoken by many generations of Brazilians, given it a distinctly Brazilian flavor. Also, one has to account for linguistic contact with the Brazilian indigenous population, whose languages, including Tupi Guarani and others, also contributed words to the Brazilian dialect.

In 2002, the city of São Gabriel da Cachoeira, a municipality in the state of Amazonas, passed a law making the indigenous languages Nheengatu, Tukano, and Boniwa official languages along with Portuguese.

In addition, one cannot forget the influence of millions of black Africans who were forcibly brought to Brazil to work in the sugarcane fields, gold mines, and the homes of Portuguese masters. These Bantu and Kwa language speakers offered a unique twist to the way Portuguese is spoken in Brazil.

TRACK 1

Words of Indigenous Origin in Brazilian Portuguese

Brazilian Portuguese	English
plants	
abacaxi	pineapple
caju	cashew fruit
animals	
piranha	piranha
sucuri	anaconda
arara	macaw
place names	
Guanabara	
Jacarepaguá	
Tijuca	
personal names	
Araci	
Iracema	
supernatural beings	
Tupã	supreme being of the Tupi people
Curupira	human-like creature whose feet are backwards; brings bad luck or death to those who see him

Not all scholars agree with the extent to which or even the very idea that African languages influenced Brazilian Portuguese. Some think that these languages simply added to the richness of vocabulary, while others think that the influence can be felt to the core of the language. For these scholars, Brazilian Portuguese might have changed so much, it could even be considered a semi-creole! The jury is still out on this issue, but the fact remains that Brazilian Portuguese has characteristics that clearly show that it evolved differently from European Portuguese in significant ways.

TRACK 2

Words of African Origin in Brazilian Portuguese

Brazilian Portuguese	English
senzala	slave quarters
caçula	youngest offspring
moleque	young boy; pejorative
mucama	young slave girl who fetches things
quilombo	village of marooned slaves
tanga	very short bikini or loincloth
berimbau	one-stringed African instrument

Tips on Learning Portuguese

First remember that the longest journey starts with the first step. And, as you begin traveling down this road, you must come prepared. Remember that just as on any other journey, there are incremental steps, and that you cannot expect to get to the end of it without following a well-traveled path. The following are helpful tips in the incredible linguistic expedition of acquiring Portuguese.

Relax!

Studies have shown that students do better with a language when they are less stressed about learning. Give yourself a break and don't expect to know and blurt out everything perfectly after you have heard it only once. Language learning takes time and effort, but it can be incredibly rewarding.

Use What You Learn

When learning Portuguese, concentrate on the variations of phrases or expressions instead of individual words. Don't just translate each word from/to English. Concentrating on the target language rather than on the translation will also boost your learning. Instead of lists and lists of words, try to place expressions in subcategories, according to their situation, such as "greetings," "introductions," or "ordering food."

> Consider buying a good Portuguese-English dictionary. There are several excellent options on the market that can help you; you can choose according to your learning style. Learn how to "decode" the various symbols in the dictionary ("n" for noun, "a" for adjective, etc.) and always double-check the English-Portuguese side of the dictionary to make sure you have the correct idiom.

Once you have learned a new word or phrase, you should use it immediately and often, preferably in a real situation. But don't worry about saying it as a native speaker from the start. The message, or what you say, is more important than the native-sounding pronunciation, at least at first. Remember that we all have accents, even the so-called native speaker; it's just a question of degree.

Picture It

Many successful language learners use pictures to remember words in the target language. Instead of long translated lists, try creating a set of flashcards with stick-figure drawings or pictures of common vocabulary items cut out of magazines. You don't have to be an artist; just draw clearly enough for you to get the message.

Another nice idea is to simply "label" every appliance and piece of furniture in your home with adhesive labels. After a while, you will notice that you won't need the labels anymore, and the word will come to you immediately.

Study Often and in Short Bursts

Learning a new language can be tiring. It is a known fact that students who study for shorter periods of time (fifteen to twenty minutes per day, five days a week) acquire more language than those who cram their studies in one day, and only do this once in a blue moon. If you feel that you can study for a longer period of time, don't forget to take short breaks.

Use the Web

It is just incredible the wealth of information easily available to you at your fingertips. There are millions of sites written in Portuguese, with information on the culture, cuisine, entertainment, sports, and famous celebrities of Portuguese-speaking countries. Also consider joining newsgroups or checking out blogs in Portuguese or about Brazil. You will learn a lot by exchanging information with Portuguese speakers electronically.

Concentrate on Your Interests

Combine what you like about sports, cuisine, and music with your desire to learn Portuguese. Learn the vocabulary of your favorite pastimes in this newfound mode of communication. The same goes for your profession. Whether you are an architect, artist, photographer, musician, or lawyer, there are specific words in Portuguese that relate to your area of expertise. Learning those will not only make you more marketable, but will also give you a sense of connection to colleagues in the global arena.

Immerse Yourself

Try out your own version of an immersion program. If available in your area, taste a *churrasco* at a Brazilian restaurant, take *samba* or *lambada* dancing lessons, learn how to play *capoeira*, and listen to Brazilian music. In some American markets, there are cable channels in Portuguese, such as *Globo* and *RTP*. Any good bookstore or local library will have travel books about Portuguese-speaking countries. Take one home and become inspired by the sites and images of exotic places. Your local video store should have at least a couple of more recent Oscar-nominated Brazilian movies. Watch with the subtitles and be amazed at how much you already know in Portuguese. Movies are also an incredible window into the culture of a country; try to find the similarities, not just the differences from your own. If you are a religious person or are curious about religious culture, try to go to a Catholic church in an area with a large Brazilian population. Because of the increase in the Brazilian population in the United States, more and more American dioceses have masses celebrated in Portuguese.

Recognizing What You Already Know

Because both Portuguese and English are Indo-European languages, some words in Portuguese have a similar spelling to English, and thus it is easy to identify them and guess their meaning. Look at the following list and see how many words you are already familiar with. Then listen to how the words sound when spoken on the CD.

TRACK 3

- *acidente*
- *ator*
- *adorável*
- *animal*
- *automóvel*
- *bagagem*
- *catedral*
- *central*
- *ciclista*
- *condutor*
- *conversível*
- *criatura*
- *crime*
- *cruel*
- *elefante*
- *famoso*
- *favor*
- *físico*
- *futebol*
- *hospital*

- *hotel*
- *humor*
- *idéia*
- *importante*
- *inevitável*
- *informação*
- *inventar*
- *local*
- *motor*
- *música*
- *natural*
- *plano*
- *popular*
- *potente*
- *presidente*
- *rádio*
- *respeitável*
- *sinistro*
- *táxi*
- *telefone*

Aside from the interesting ways that some of these words end, they can be easily associated with the same word in English. You can figure out their meanings as you read them because they are *cognates*. Later, you will learn how to pronounce them in Portuguese.

You must have noticed that a few words have the exact same spelling as in English, such as *favor, hotel, local, motor*. These are true pure cognates because they are orthographically identical and have the same meaning in both languages. Others on the list have close to the same spelling, and also have the same meaning, such as *adorável* (adorable), *bagagem* (baggage), *rádio* (radio), and *telefone* (telephone). These are called true cognates, meaning that they have similar but not identical spelling.

The way languages evolve led to orthographic as well as semantic (i.e., meaning-related) changes throughout the ages. These changes inadvertently created pairs of words that have similar spelling but different or closely related meanings in both languages. Don't be misled by these "false" cognates. Here is a short list, which you can add to as you learn Portuguese.

False Cognates

Portuguese	English
assistir	to attend or to watch, **not** to assist
constipado	congested, when suffering from a cold, **not** constipated
delito	crime, **not** delight
futebol	soccer, **not** football
recordar	to remember, **not** to record

Common Suffixes

As you learn to decipher words in Portuguese, some "clues" may help you along the way. Pay attention to the endings of words and related them to corresponding endings in English. This technique makes your life easier when learning new words, and it will help you guess the meaning of words, as well as their grammatical class.

Common Suffixes and Their Meanings

Suffix	Meaning
–al	
(pertaining or related to; an extension of; a place)	
fenomenal	phenomenal, pertaining to a phenomenon
bambuzal	plantation of bamboo trees
usual	usual, or an extension of use
–ável /–ível	
(having the ability or aptitude to or capacity of)	
adorável	adorable, capable of being adored
conversível	convertible, capable of being converted
–or	
(agents that are or do; abstractions)	
inventor	inventor, one who invents
amor	love, abstract noun

These endings are referred to as suffixes. These suffixes often enlighten you as to the meanings of the words. A complete list of examples would be too long, but here are a few:

Portuguese Cognates with Suffixes –ável/–ível, –al, and –or

–ável /–ível	–al	–OR
acessível	*abdominal*	*ardor*
biodegradável	*cordial*	*destruidor*
compreensível	*emocional*	*fervor*

Portuguese Cognates with Suffixes *–ável/–ível,* **–al, and** *–or*

–ável /–ível	*–al*	*–or*
durável	*federal*	*instrutor*
evitável	*fundamental*	*mentor*
falsificável	*ilegal*	*pastor*
incomparável	*nacional*	*professor*
lamentável	*normal*	*protetor*
miserável	*oficial*	*refletor*
negociável	*original*	*rumor*

There are also other types of cognates that are similar to English, though not identical:

Suffixes Similar to English

TRACK 6

Portuguese Example	English Translation
–agem	
(pertaining to, particularly broadened to a collection; similar to English "–age")	
bagagem	baggage, luggage
–ano/–ana	
(pertaining to origin, location; relating to beliefs and affiliations; similar to English "–an")	
americano	American
republicano	Republican
–ante/–ente	
(related to an event, the nature of, or an agent; similar to "–ant" and "–ing" in English)	
acidente	accident, an unexpected event
importante	important, something of great effect
potente	potent, of powerful nature
presidente	president, one who presides

Suffixes Similar to English (continued)

Portuguese Example	English Translation
−ção/−são	
(abstraction of an act or state of being; similar to the English "−tion" and "−sion")	
atenção	attention
informação	information
−ico/−ica	
(relating to; being similar to; similar to the English "−ic" and "−al")	
físico	physical, physicist
idêntico	identical
−ista	
(pertaining to one who does; similar to English "−ist")	
artista	artist, one who creates art
ciclista	cyclist, one who rides a bicycle
−oso/−osa	
(relating to possession or characteristic; similar to English "−ous," "−ful," and "−y")	
curioso	curious
famoso	famous
−ura	
(abstraction of an act or state of being; similar to English "−ture," "−ure," and "−ness")	
criatura	creature
cultura	culture
−ário/−ária	
(pertaining to the subject; relating to an act or thing; similar to English "−ary")	
milionário	millionaire
voluntário	voluntary, volunteer

—ncia

(relating to an act or state; result of an action; abstraction; similar to English "—nce" and "—ncy")

abstinência	abstinence
elegância	elegance
insistência	insistence

—dade

(relating to an abstraction and a state of being; similar to English "—ty," "—ness," and "—hood")

brevidade	brevity
claridade	clarity
felicidade	happiness

—ismo

(pertaining to an action or practice; state or condition; principles similar to "—ism")

atletismo	athleticism
idealismo	idealism

—mente

(pertaining to the manner, the timing, and the place of an action; similar to "—ly")

felizmente	fortunately
claramente	clearly

Congratulations! You were just able to read a great number of words in Portuguese, and you probably understood most of them. Try to see the patterns of similar words as you encounter them in the language. Go back to these words often and try to incorporate them into your active Portuguese vocabulary. If you feel that some of them are too obvious, then you know you don't have to look them up again in the dictionary.

EXERCISE: SUFFIXES

Now, try your best to complete this short suffix challenge! Write down the Portuguese translations of the following English words. Check your answers in Appendix C.

1. incident: _____
2. mechanical: _____
3. identity: _____
4. unfortunately: _____
5. resistance: _____

CHAPTER 2

The Sounds of Portuguese

I T'S NOW TIME to learn about the Portuguese alphabet and all the different sounds in the language. How do you pronounce the vowels? What about the nasal sounds? What are nasal diphthongs? How do you pronounce consonant combinations such as *–nh–* and *–lh–*? What is the typical stress pattern in Portuguese? In this chapter you will learn all of this plus how to write electronic documents in Portuguese using all the accent marks.

The Portuguese Alphabet

Like almost all Romance languages, Portuguese follows the Latin alphabet and incorporates six diacritics, or special characters. There are the three accents (acute: ó; circumflex: ê; and grave: à), plus the cedilla ç, the tilde ã, and the dieresis ü. The written system also has three letters (k, w, and y) that are part of the official alphabet but are very rarely used, mostly appearing in foreign words (windsurf, kitsch) and personal names (Wagner, Darcy, Yaracilda). The following are the Portuguese letters and the way they are pronounced.

TRACK 7

The Portuguese Letters

Letter	Portuguese Name	Pronunciation	Example	Approximate English Sound
a	a	AH	casa	father
b	bê	BEH	berço	basement
c	cê	SEH	centro	cent
			com	comb
d	dê	DEH	dado	dance
e	é or ê	EH	ele	cake
f	efe	E-fee	fala	fact
g	gê	JHEH	gente	measure
h	agá	a-GAH	hóspede	[silent]
i	i	EE	cinco	seek
j	jota	JOH-tah	já	pleasure
k	ká	KAH	kiwi	kitchen
l	ele	EH-lee	lavar	loud
m	eme	EH-mee	mesa	mouse
n	ene	EH-nee	não	never
o	ó or ô	AW or OH	óbvio	awe
p	pê	PEH	pão	paint

The Portuguese Letters

Letter	Portuguese Name	Pronunciation	Example	Approximate English Sound
q	quê	KEH	quinze	key
r	erre	EH-hee	Rio	heap
			carrego	unhappy
			caro	butter
s	esse	EH-see	santo	simple
t	tê	TEH	tempo	steak
u	u	OOH	caju	juice
v	vê	VEH	veja	very
x	xis	SHEES	roxo	shoe
w	dáblio	DAH-blee-oo	watt	water
y	ípsilon	EEP-see-laun	Yara	year
z	zê	ZEH	zinco	zebra

There are also special letters and combinations of letters that make up unexpected sounds in Portuguese:

TRACK 8

Special Letters and Combinations of Letters

Letter(s)	Portuguese Example	English Translation	Pronunciation
–ç–	caça	hunt	like English s
–nh–	tamanho	size	a little softer than the Spanish ñ
	façanha	feat	
–lh–	filho	son	like the middle sound in "medallion"
	trabalho	work	
–ch–	chá	tea	pronounce as in "shovel"

Accent Marks

The accent marks in Portuguese help with the correct pronunciation of words. They indicate to the reader where to put the emphasis on the word, or even if a vowel is more "open" or "closed." Become familiar with these special diacritic marks of the language.

Accent Marks

Marks	Name in English	Name in Portuguese
á, é, í, ó, ú	acute	*acento agudo*
ê, ô	circumflex	*acento circunflexo*
à	grave	*acento grave*
ã, õ	tilde	*til*
ü	dieresis	*trema*

It is important to remember that accent marks are not immediately intuitive to the second-language learner. When learning Portuguese, give yourself a while to learn where to include these accents. However, as you read more and more materials in Portuguese, keep track of the accents and where they usually go on the word. Familiarity with the written word will boost your confidence and spelling accuracy in Portuguese!

Listening Practice 1

Read the following pairs of words and circle the one you hear on the CD. Check your answers in Appendix C.

TRACK 9
1. *avô* (grandfather)   *avó* (grandmother)
2. *galho* (branch)   *ganho* (I win)
3. *hesitar* (to hesitate)   *recitar* (to recite)

4. *cá* (here)　　　　　　*chá* (tea)
5. *canção* (song)　　　　*cancão* (species of bird)
6. *híspido* (hairy)　　　*ríspido* (curt, rude)
7. *bingo* (Bingo)　　　　*pingo* (drop)
8. *broa* (type of bread)　*proa* (part of a ship)

A Closer Look at the Portuguese Consonants

Sometimes the same sound in a language can be expressed by different letters. This is the case in English, as with the [f] sound that is pronounced using the upper teeth and the bottom lip and can happen at the beginning of a word like *fact* or at the end of a word like *enough*! The same happens in Portuguese. The same [s] sound can be heard in words such as *simples* (simple) or *cartaz* (poster), *cinema* (movie), or even in *excelente* (excellent). Similarly, the same letter can refer to very different sounds. In the next few tables we will cover the major pitfalls of spelling and pronunciation in Portuguese, letter by letter.

The Letter C

Before vowels *e* or *i* this letter has a "soft" [s] sound as in the English word "force." Examples are *centro* (center) and *cinco* (five). However, before vowels *a, o, u,* and most consonants, the letter has a "hard" [k] sound as in the English word "coat." Some examples are *casa* (house), *comida* (food), *cuidado* (care), *crédito* (credit), or *clínica* (clinic).

The Letter G

This letter often stands in for a sound that does not appear at the beginning of English words, but can be found in the middle of the word "measure." In Portuguese it appears at the beginning of words when the vowels *e* or *i* follow it, such as in *gente* (people) and *ginásio* (gym). It has a "hard" sound when it appears before vowels *a, o, u,* and other consonants, as in the English word "game." Examples are *gato* (cat), *gota* (drop), *guri* (young boy), and *grande* (big).

The Letter S

This letter can stand in for two different but closely related sounds. The first sound is very similar to the sound in English words "**s**ink" and "ca**s**t." The Portuguese examples are *sopa* (soup), *esse* (this one), and *lápis* (pencil). The second is a raspier [z] sound as in the English words "tho**s**e," "wi**s**dom," and "tran**s**it." The counterpart examples in Portuguese are *casada* (married), *desde* (since), and *trânsito* (traffic).

The Letter Z

This letter is very similar to the English letter, especially in the start of words. As with the English word "**z**ebra," the same sound is found in Portuguese with *zero* (zero) and *prazer* (pleasure). However, this letter has a sound similar to the English word "cook**s**" at the end of segments, such as in the Portuguese example *cartaz* (poster).

The Letter T

In some dialects of Brazilian Portuguese, such as the *carioca* (the name of the dialect of Rio de Janeiro), this letter can have a much unexpected sound. Before the vowels *i* and sometimes *e* if unstressed and at the end of a word, it will sound as in the English word "*cheer*!" So Portuguese words such as *tipo* (type) and *elefante* (elephant) will sound like CHEE-poh and eh-leh-FAHN-chee. This does not happen in all contexts. In the case of the letter appearing before other vowels and consonants, it sounds as in the English word "**t**ime" (without the added aspiration). Portuguese examples are *terra* (earth) and *trem* (train).

The Letter D

As with the previous letter, the a similar unexpected sound appears when in close contact with the letter *i*. So, much like the sound in the English word "**j**eans," the Portuguese word *dia* (day) might be pronounced like JEE-ah. Before all other contexts, the letter behaves like the English word "**d**en," yielding Portuguese examples such as *dar* (to give) and *droga* (drug).

Because these curious sounds with the letters *t* and *d* before *i* are pronounced by speakers of Rio de Janeiro, a more economically developed area, they are seen as more prestigious pronunciations. However, for most of the north, northeast, and south of Brazil, they are mostly ignored and speakers communicate successfully pronouncing the *t* and the *d* similarly to the English letters.

The Letter R

This letter has two basic sounds, which are very different from the English *r*. First, it is pronounced like the [h] as in the English word "**h**eat." Portuguese examples are *rua* (street), *dor* (pain), *guardanapo* (napkin), *carro* (car), and *genro* (son-in-law). Second, this letter in Portuguese is pronounced similarly to the *r* at the end of English words "lette**r**" or "late**r**." It can be found in Portuguese words such as *caro* (expensive) and *branco* (white).

You will notice that Brazilians will leave out the r sound at the ends of words, such as *amor* (love) or *chamar* (to call). This is not seen as a reflection of uneducated speech or laziness, but rather an evolution of the language. The same happened with French, whose final consonants are never pronounced! So, to sound more native, make sure to drop the end-word *r* in Portuguese!

The Letter L

The one thing to remember about this letter is that at the end of words the *l* sounds like a *w* as in the English word "no**w**." So the Portuguese word *Brasil* sounds like BRAH-zeew. The letter behaves like the English letter *l* at the beginning of words.

The Letters M and N

As you might have noticed, Portuguese has a good many nasal sounds. The letters *m* and *n*, when appearing at the end of a word or syllable, are an indication that the previous vowel is nasalized. Thus, the combination of vowel plus *m* or *n* should not be perceived as two different sounds (vowel plus consonant) but actually a nasal-sounding vowel. Portuguese words such as *sim* (yes) and *bom* are pronounced by making more air to come out of your nostrils and avoiding putting your lips together at the end. The letters behave like English letters when they come at the beginning of a word such as *mesa* (table) and *nome* (name).

The Letter X

Amazingly, there are four different sounds that could be uttered when this letter appears in Portuguese words. The first is similar to the English word "**sheep**." Portuguese examples are *xadrez* (chess) and *lixo* (trash). The second sound is similar to the English word "**fix**," as in the Portuguese *complexo* (complex). Thirdly, this letter can sound like a normal [s], as with the English word "feast." Portuguese examples are *excluir* (to exclude) and *excepcional* (exceptional). Finally it is very common to hear a [z] sound as in the English word "amazing." Portuguese examples are *exótico* (exotic) and *roxo* (purple).

Listening Practice 2

Read the following items and circle the word or sound that you hear on the CD. Check your answers in Appendix C.

TRACK 10

1. *dó* (pity)   *dor* (pain)

2. *guia* (guide)   *gia* (small frog)

3. *roxo* (purple):   [ks]   [sh]   [s]

4. *anexo* (attached): [ks]   [sh]   [s]

5. *cansada* (tired):   [sh]   [s]   [z]

Stress Pattern in Portuguese

The study of the vowels and the stress pattern in a language are intimately connected. That is because the "stress," or the emphasis that one puts on a word, normally happens on the vowel. In order to sound "native" in Portuguese, the student should learn how to put the correct amount of force or stress on the center of the correct vowel, that is, on the right syllable.

In Portuguese words are usually stressed on the next-to-last syllable, though there are also words that are stressed on the last syllable or the third-to-last syllable. Here are some examples:

TRACK 11

Word Stress

Next-to-Last Syllable	Last Syllable	Third-to-Last Syllable
piloto (pilot)	*café* (coffee)	*capítulo* (chapter)
imagem (image)	*baú* (chest)	*código* (code)
contente (happy)	*caquí* (kind of fruit)	*árvore* (tree)
fácil (easy)	*dominó* (domino)	*fósforo* (match)

All verbs in infinitives ending in –r, such as *amar* (to love), have the stress on the next-to-last syllable. When a nasal diphthong ends a word, such as *irmão* (brother), the stress is on the last syllable.

Oral and Nasal Vowels

The vowel system of Portuguese is a little more complex than that of Italian or Spanish, which could be considered "phonetic" languages (what you see is what you get). There are twelve distinct vowel sounds in Portuguese, including oral and nasal vowels. Oral vowels are what English speakers are normally familiar with, and nasal vowels are partially produced with the nasal tract. The difference between a vowel and a consonant is that vowels are produced without obstructions from the vocal tract, with air flowing freely and some minor constriction of the lips or opening of the mouth. Consonants, on the other hand, are produced by the interplay of air flow and obstructions produced by the lips, teeth, or the back of the throat, as well as other parts of the vocal and nasal tract. The following is a detailed account of the vowels in Portuguese.

The Vowel A

TRACK 12

Type	English Word	Portuguese Examples
Stressed	father, cot	*garfo* (fork), *caro* (expensive)
Unstressed	tuba	*porta* (door), *filha* (daughter)
Nasal	before nasal consonants or with tilde	*banho* (bath), *irmã* (sister)

The Vowel E

Type	English Word	Context	Portuguese Examples
Open	net	written with the acute é	*café* (coffee)
Closed		written with a circumflex ê	*pêssego* (peach)
Longer	me	at the end of a word	*filme* (movie)
		at end of one-syllable word	*de* (of); *e* (and)
Nasal		before nasal consonants	*senha* (code), *bem* (well)

The Vowel I

Type	English Word	Context	Portuguese Examples
Longer	see	at the end of syllable	*saí* (I left), *país* (country), *raiz* (root)
Shorter	say	at the end of the word	*pai* (father), *leite* (milk)
Nasal		before nasal consonants	*tinha* (he had), *sim* (yes)

The Vowel O

Type	English Word	Context	Portuguese Examples
Open	saw	written with the acute ó	*dominó* (domino)
Closed		written with a circumflex ô	*complô* (scheme)
Longer	glue	at the end of a word	*pato* (duck)
		at the end of one-syllable word	*do* (of the), *o* (the)
Nasal		before nasal consonants	*sonho* (dream), *com* (with)

The Vowel U

Type	English Word	Context	Portuguese Examples
Longer	tooth	at the end of syllable/word	*caju* (cashew fruit), *tu* (you), *grúa* (forklift)
Shorter	bow	at the end of the word	*pau* (wood, stick), *nau* (boat)
		in the combinations qua and gua	*quadro* (board), *guarda* (policeman)
Nasal		before nasal consonants	*punha* (he would put), *um* (one)

The vowel U is silent when used in the combinations *que*, *qui*, *gue*, and *gui*. In these cases only pronounce the "hard" consonants, as in *queijo* (cheese), *quinze* (fifteen), *guerra* (war), and *guitarra* (electric guitar).

Listening Practice 3

TRACK 13

Read the pairs of words and circle the one you hear on the CD.

1. *cinto* (belt)   *cito* (I cite)

2. *canto* (I sing)   *cato* (I look for [colloquial])

3. *anjo* (angel)   *ajo* (I act)

4. *sim* (yes)   *si* (himself/herself)

5. *funga* (he/she sniffs)   *fuga* (escape)

Diphthongs

Diphthongs are combinations of two vowels pronounced together in one syllable. There can be oral or nasal diphthongs in Portuguese. Some of them do not have a corresponding English sound, but you will be able to say them in no time.

TRACK 14

Oral Diphthongs

Approximate English Sound	Portuguese Examples
my	*pai* (father)
cow	*autor* (author)
	papéis (papers)
hay	*rei* (king)
	deus (god)
	céu (sky)
	oi (hi)
coy	*dói* (it hurts)
	viu (she saw)
	cuidado (careful)

TRACK 15

Nasal Diphthongs

Portuguese	English
mãe	mother
cão	dog
põe	she puts

There are some nasal diphthongs that are not expressed orthographically with the ~ (tilde) but rather with nasal consonants. This is the case with words ending with *–em* or *–en* as in *porém* (but) and *podem* (they can). In addition, there is one special nasal diphthong that starts with a nasal consonant: *muito* (many, very).

Hiatus

A hiatus is a combination of vowels that are in separate syllables. While diphthongs are two graphic vowels together, one pronounced longer and slower than the other, the hiatus expresses two strong vowels said very clearly. Here are some examples:

- *tia* (**aunt**)
- *rua* (**street**)
- *caos* (**chaos**)
- *rio* (**river**)

Typing in Portuguese

When writing electronically, it is important to add the accent symbols and diacritics that are part of the Portuguese language. There is a big difference between an accented vowel *é* (is) and one without an accent *e* (and). The following table shows how to add these accents into your electronic documents.

Window Keys	Result
Control + ' [apostrophe], then any vowel	á, é, í, ó, ú
Control + ` [grave], then a	à
Control + Shift + ~ [tilde], then vowel	ã, õ
Control +, [comma], then c	ç

Apple Keys	Result
Option + e, then any vowel	á, é, í, ó, ú
Option + ` [grave], then a	à
Option + n, then vowel	ã, õ
Option + c	ç

Now practice writing the following words in your computer: *maçã* (apple), *sofá* (sofa), *às quatro* (at four), and *corações* (hearts).

CHAPTER 3

Beginning Conversation

TRAVELING ABROAD CAN be stressful, but you'll probably find it a lot easier if you know some basic survival phrases. In this chapter you will learn how to say hello, introduce yourself, bid goodbye, and greet people over the phone. You will also learn some important emergency words that may come in handy when visiting a foreign country. You will make a great first impression with your Portuguese after reading this chapter.

Greetings

This might be the easiest communication strategy you will learn in a second language. Go ahead and start by greeting people in Portuguese when traveling to Brazil. Brazilians will appreciate your efforts in trying to speak their language, and help you along. Start by greeting the doorman at the hotel, salespeople, and taxi drivers. Use this list of common greetings:

TRACK 16

Greetings in Portuguese

Portuguese	English
Olá!	Hello!
Oi!	Hi!
Alô!	Hello! (when answering the phone)
Bom dia!	Good morning
Boa tarde!	Good afternoon
Boa noite!	Good evening!/Good night!
Como vai?	How are you?
Bem, obrigada (for women).	Fine, thanks.
Bem, obrigado (for men).	Fine, thanks.
Tudo bem?/Tudo bom?	How is it going?
Tudo bom!/Tudo bem!	Everything's great!

There are many colloquial ways of saying "How are you?" in Brazilian Portuguese. From *tudo jóia* (literally "everything's a jewel") to *tudo legal* meaning exactly what it appears, that everything is "legal," so nothing bad at all. Also, when answering the question *tudo bem?* you can reply with *tudo bom* or vice versa.

Talking on the Phone

You might have guessed that talking on the phone in your second language is actually harder than it appears. Since you cannot rely on visual cues, such as hand gestures, facial expressions, or lip movements, it is a lot more complicated to decode what people are saying on the other line. So don't be discouraged; just keep on trying and ask for a lot of repetition. A common telephone dialogue would go as follows:

Q: José: *Alô?* (Hello?)
A: Luci: *Alô, posso falar com Fernando?* (Hello, may I speak to Fernando?)

Q: José: *Quem quer falar com ele?* (Who wishes to talk to him?)
A: Luci: *Aqui é a Luci, ele está em casa?* (This is Luci, is he at home?)

Q: José: *Não, ele não se encontra, quer deixar recado?* (No, he's not in, do you want to leave a message?)
A: Luci: *Sim, por favor, diga para ele que a Luci ligou.* (Yes, please tell him that Luci called.)

Q: José: *Tá certo.* (Okay.)
A: Luci: *Obrigada, tchau!* (Thanks, bye!)

Q: José: *Tchau.* (Bye.)

Most people who live in big cities in Brazil have a traditional landline, but the sale of cell phones has increased tremendously in Brazil and Latin America as a whole. Part of the reason is that telephone lines are very expensive, and it takes a long time (sometimes months) to have a line bought through the official channels. Some people buy landlines from other people who have them and advertise their sale in the newspaper. After they buy the line privately, they have their names transferred and installation happens rather quickly. However, the advantages and ease of buying a cell phone, especially a prepaid one, have generated a virtual boom in wireless telephony in Brazil.

When taking your cell phone with you to Brazil, make sure it is compatible. Some popular U.S. carriers do not carry telephones that are usable in Latin America. Always check with your wireless service to verify if your cell phone will work in Brazil or, if possible, add international service to your plan before traveling.

Even though using a telephone is a convenient way to talk, most Brazilians still prefer face-to-face communication. So don't be surprised if people say very little on the phone and arrange to meet with you right away. It's just another cultural difference that underscores Brazilians' love of the *bate-papo* or a friendly chat!

Quick Introductions

Once you have learned how to greet someone, the next best thing to do is to introduce yourself. Here are some common ways to do that in Portuguese:

Common Introductions

TRACK 17

Portuguese	English
Eu me chamo Laura.	My name is Laura.
Meu nome é Fabíola.	My name is Fabíola.
Muito prazer.	Nice to meet you.
Igualmente.	Same here.
Esse é o meu marido, João.	This is my husband, João.
Essa é a minha esposa, Clara.	This is my wife, Clara.
Como é (o) seu nome?	What is your name?
Como o senhor se chama?	What is your name (sir)? [formal]
Como a senhora se chama?	What is your name (ma'am)? [formal]
De onde você é?	Where are you from?
O que você faz?	What do you do?
O que você estuda?	What do you study?

Notice that there are formal ways of addressing people in Portuguese. This is more common in the European rather than in the Brazilian Portuguese dialect, but nevertheless it is part of Latin American courtesy. When Brazilians are speaking to someone who is older or of a higher social class, or to someone that they simply are not acquainted with, Brazilians will normally use the phrases *o senhor* for a man and *a senhora* for a woman. Social distance can be measured in many different ways—age, social class, level of education, and familiarity, among other social cues. After getting to know someone, you may switch to the more colloquial pronoun *você* (you).

> A good general rule is to use *o senhor* and *a senhora* until they give you permission to call them by *você*. Since Brazilians are normally pretty informal, that might happen right away! As far as how Brazilians address their parents, not very long ago children were required to use *o senhor* and *a senhora*. But nowadays, this has become obsolete.

What about hugs and kisses? And what do you when you are introduced for the first time? In the south of Brazil (in big cities like São Paulo), it is common for women to kiss on one cheek once. In Rio de Janeiro and in other parts of Brazil, such as northeastern cities of Recife and Salvador, women normally give each other two kisses, one on each cheek. This may happen every time you see each other, if you are friendly acquaintances. For closer relationships, such as cousins, sisters, or close friends, this is not common. Men and women will do the same, one or two kisses, while men will pat each other on the back and shake hands warmly.

EXERCISE: WHAT TO SAY?

Fill in the blanks with the best words in the following dialogues. Check your answers in Appendix C.

1. Marcos: *Olá, meu _____ é Marcos.*

2. Fabíola: *Eu me _____ Fabíola. Muito _____*

3. Marcos: *Igualmente. De _____ você é?*

4. Fabíola: *_____ sou do Rio de Janeiro.*

Saying Goodbye

You've learned the most common ways of greeting people and introducing yourself. But what about when you have to say goodbye? Instead of just leaving the room without being noticed, try and use these words to bid farewell to your newfound Brazilian friends. It will earn you positive points on the social scale, which will help you out next time you see them.

TRACK 18

Saying Goodbye

Portuguese	English
Tchau!	Bye!
Até logo./Até breve.	See you soon.
Até mais.	See you later.
Até amanhã!	See you tomorrow!
Tudo de bom.	All the best.
Boa viagem.	Have a good trip.
Vou nessa.	I'm leaving./I have to go. [very informal]
Volte sempre.	Come back always./Come again.
Amanhã a gente se fala.	We'll talk tomorrow.
Me diverti muito!	I had a lot of fun!
Boa noite!	Good night!

As far as saying goodbye, the same kissing rules apply: one or two kisses for women, warm handshakes for men. Don't be surprised if a Brazilian will kiss you three times and say *três pra casar*, meaning "three times so you can get married." This is sort of a little play with the two-kiss rule, and one which can lead to closer friendships.

EXERCISE: GOODBYE!

Now test what you've learned about saying goodbye in Portuguese. Fill in the blanks in the dialogue below, according to the context. Check your answers in Appendix C.

1. Lúcia: *Olá, Seu Ivanildo,* _____ *vai o* _____?

2. Seu Ivanildo: *Vou bem,* _____, *Lúcia. E você?*

3. Lúcia: _____ *bom. Tchau!*

4. Seu Ivanildo: *Até* _____.

Other Vocabulary You May Need

Unfortunately, you might find yourself in a situation where you'll need some emergency words. If you lose your checkbook, your car breaks down, or worse, you will need to know words that will help you communicate your predicament. You might also want to learn a list of helpful words and question that will aid you in learning Portuguese. First, let's start with some helpful vocabulary items that may be essential in a sticky situation.

TRACK 19

Emergency Vocabulary

English	Portuguese
an accident	*um acidente*
arrest, to	*prender, pôr na cadeia*
attorney	*o advogado, a advogada*
bag	*a bolsa*
billfold	*a carteira*
consulate	*o consulado*
documents	*os documentos*
dollars	*os dólares*
help!	*socorro!*
judge	*o juiz*
key, keys	*a chave, as chaves*
money	*o dinheiro*
necklace	*a corrente, o colar*

Emergency Vocabulary

English	Portuguese
police	*a polícia*
traveler's checks	*os cheques de viagem*

The following is a quick guide that might help you in getting important information in Portuguese. This list of questions and expressions can be a great reference.

TRACK 20

Helpful Words and Expressions in Portuguese

Portuguese	English
Por favor.	Please.
Com licença.	Excuse me. [before you do something]
Desculpe!/Perdão!	I'm sorry! [after you do something]
Desculpe, não entendi.	Sorry, I didn't get that./I didn't understand.
Poderia repetir, por favor?	Could you repeat that, please?
Você fala inglês?	Do you speak English?
Falo um pouquinho (de português).	I speak a little bit (of Portuguese).
Como se diz isso em português?	How do you say that in Portuguese? [as you point to it]

Although not exhaustive, this list of expressions can really be handy as you interact with Portuguese speakers in Brazil. Hopefully, this brief chapter helped you with an initial understanding of the Portuguese language and the way Brazilians talk and interact with each other. These helpful hints and vocabulary terms should be practiced often and consistently so that you may master them in a timely fashion.

EXERCISE: CHAPTER REVIEW

Now let's review what you've learned! Write the word that you would say in Portuguese depending on the situation presented. Check your answers in Appendix C.

1. After you stepped on somebody's foot inside a crowded bus.

   _____

2. When you want to get through as you walk a busy street.

   _____

3. You would like to thank someone.

   _____

4. Somebody said something, but you didn't quite catch it.

   _____

5. You want to tell someone that you speak a little Portuguese.

   _____

6. You want to know the name of a fruit you see in a street market.

   _____

CHAPTER 4

Nouns, Articles, and Contractions

WHAT MAKES A word feminine or masculine in Portuguese? How are plurals formed? How many ways can you say "the"? What is the difference between "definite" and "indefinite" articles? In this chapter you will find out all about singular and plural nouns, articles, demonstratives, and those common contractions in Portuguese.

Nouns: Persons, Places, and Things

One of the first things you learn while in grade school is that nouns refer to persons, places, and things. When learning a second language, you will find that copious lists of nouns make up most of the words you learn in the beginning. It is also easier to learn nouns because most of them refer to something concrete. However, they also refer to abstract elements, ideas, and qualities. You will notice that in Portuguese the nouns fall under two categories: masculine and feminine. So, the words *mesa* (table), *bolsa* (bag), and *chave* (key) belong to the feminine gender, while *caderno* (notebook), *livro* (book), and *pente* (comb) are masculine. Most of the time you can tell by the ending of the word which gender it belongs to. However, there are some tricky examples, as you might expect, as in the examples that end in *–e* above (*chave* and *pente*), which can be either feminine or masculine. Here is a list of common nouns and their gender classification.

TRACK 21

Portuguese Nouns

Masculine	Feminine
livro (book)	*mochila* (backpack)
tio (uncle)	*tia* (aunt)
espelho (mirror)	*escola* (school)
quadro (blackboard)	*mesa* (table)
título (title)	*página* (page)
gesto (gesture)	*janela* (window)

What are the basic rules that you can follow in order to find out the gender of a noun? The first thing you should keep in mind is that nouns that end in *–o* are almost always masculine, as in the examples above. Second, nouns that end in (unstressed) *–a* are normally feminine, as in the examples. What if a noun does not end in either of those vowels? Here are some general rules:

TRACK 22

Nouns Ending in the Consonants –*l*, –*r*, and –*z*, the Vowel –*u*, and the Letters –*ume* Are Masculine

Portuguese	English
hotel	hotel
casal	married couple
mar	sea
professor	teacher, professor
rapaz	young man
cartaz	poster
peru	turkey
tatu	armadillo
ciúme	jealousy
legume	vegetable

Aside from the most common unstressed -*a* ending for feminine nouns, there are other nouns with suffixes that are typically feminine. The following table outlines those endings with some examples.

TRACK 23

Nouns Ending in the Suffixes –*dade*, –*agem*, and –*ção* Are Normally Feminine

Portuguese	English
identidade	identity, ID card
liberdade	liberty
garagem	garage
viagem	trip
comunicação	communication
atenção	attention

You will have noticed that nouns that end in –*dade* usually translate to a word in English that ends in "–ty," while a Portuguese word that ends in –*agem* most of the time compares to English words ending in "–age." Finally,

Portuguese words ending in *–ção* are often translated into words that end in "–tion" in English, and are mostly feminine in Portuguese. But be careful! Some very common words that end in *–(ç)ão* are masculine. These are *coração* (heart) and many words related to transportation, such as *avião* (airplane) and *caminhão* (truck).

> Most nouns that end in a stressed *–á* are masculine. For example, *chá* (tea) and *sofá*, as well as the names of countries such as *Canadá* and *Panamá*. The best way to learn the gender of these words is to write them down with the article as in *o chá* (the tea). As you learn more words, continue adding them to your list.

Another very tricky set of words are the ones that end in an unstressed vowel *–a*, but are unexpectedly masculine as well. This happens because these words are originally from Greek, so they are not Latin-based. Here is a list of common examples:

TRACK 24

Masculine Words of Greek Origin Ending in *–a*

Portuguese	English
o cinema	movie theater
o mapa	map
o planeta	planet
o problema	problem
o programa	program
o telefonema	phone call

You will notice that most of them end in the combination of *–ma*. If you can identify that combination as you read or hear the word, then you can guess that it is masculine. Finally, there are some words that have the same ending for the masculine and feminine forms. You can say that *Maria é uma ótima pianista* (Maria is a great pianist) while *Mário é um grande jornalista* (Mario is a great reporter). These words generally refer to professions, so they are easy to spot. The following is a list of examples.

TRACK 25

Nouns that End in –*ista* (both masculine and feminine forms)

Portuguese	English
artista	artist
dentista	dentist
especialista	expert
jornalista	journalist
pianista	pianist
tenista	tennis player

Practicing with Gender

In the next set of words, write the article "the" in Portuguese before each one: use *o* for masculine and *a* for feminine. If the word has the same spelling for masculine or singular, write *o/a*. Check your answers in Appendix C.

1. _____ *caderno* (notebook)

2. _____ *contagem* (act of counting)

3. _____ *caminhão* (truck)

4. _____ *armazém* (storage facility)

5. _____ *amor* (love)

6. _____ *ação* (action)

7. _____ *socialista* (socialist)

8. _____ *avental* (apron)

9. _____ *crachá* (identification tag)

10. _____ *alfândega* (customs)

11. _____ *esquema* (scheme, plan)

12. _____ *liberdade* (liberty)

Although gender is an important part of the Portuguese grammar, it is not immediately mastered by speakers whose native language does not include these categories. In English, some gender is still reflected when objects such as ships or boats are referred to as "she" (i.e., "Before the Titanic sank, **she** was considered an unsinkable ship"). More to the point, grammatical gender can be seen in the English possessive pronouns "his" and "hers." Simply think of gender in Portuguese as that "gender quality" found in English pronouns, only extended to all nouns. Unfortunately, there is no hidden key to grammatical gender; there is no rhyme or reason for *garfo* (fork) to be masculine and *faca* (knife) to be feminine. You just have to learn its gender!

One tip for learning the gender of nouns is to write them together in categories. With any list of vocabulary that you learn, you should find ways in which words can be connected (be it "school objects," "home appliances," or "my favorite clothes"). Think of your brain as a "closet" that is organized in "drawers" or categories. If you put socks and shirts in their own designated places, it will be easier to retrieve them later. The same happens with Portuguese words!

From Nouns to Pronouns

Saying the same noun every time you had to refer to something in normal discourse could get really repetitive. It would sound somewhat like this: "I went to **the movies** with **Robert**, but **Robert** got to **the movies** late, then we watched **the movie**, and **Robert** and I liked **the movie**, but **Robert** and I did not like the popcorn at **the movies**." Notice that the words in bold are repeated at least twice, which makes the entire utterance sound too repetitive, almost silly. Normally, we would replace the words "Robert" for "he," "Robert and I" for "we," "the movie" for "it," and finally "the movies" for "there." The same happens in Portuguese, where we substitute nouns for pronouns, which are words that are used in place of nouns. The following is a list of personal pronouns in Portuguese.

TRACK 26

Personal Pronouns in Portuguese

Singular	Plural
eu (I)	*nós/a gente* (we)
tu/você (you)	*vocês* (you, y'all, you guys)
ele (he)	*eles* (they)
ela (she)	*elas* (they)

You will notice that there are two basic ways of referring to "we" in Brazilian Portuguese: *nós*, which is a little less used and more formal; and *a gente*, which is more common and more colloquial. The important rule to follow when using these two personal pronouns is to conjugate the verb in the plural when using *nós* and in the singular when using *a gente*. It might seem counterintuitive, but *a gente* literally means "we the people," so it is grammatically singular, even though it refers to more than one person.

> You might notice that more traditional Portuguese grammars include the plural form *vós* for "you" plural or "y'all." This form is archaic and never used in Brazilian Portuguese. You might hear the words *convosco* (with you [pl.]) in church (for example, *O Senhor esteja convosco* [May God be with you]), and the possessive forms *vosso, vossa* (yours) uttered by many speakers from Portugal, but not in Brazil.

There are two forms for "you" in Portuguese. Here you just have to learn what the Brazilians are saying and follow along. Some of this variation is dialectal, based on the geographical regions. In the south of Brazil, in states such as Rio Grande do Sul and Santa Catarina, the *tu* form is regularly used, with its separate verb conjugation. In the big urban and cultural centers such as Rio de Janeiro and São Paulo, and the state of Minas Gerais, you might hear the form *você* as well as its reduced form *cê*. Finally, in many places in the northeast of Brazil, such as in the cities of Recife and Fortaleza, the familiar *tu* is used, albeit with similar verb conjugations belonging to the *você* form. Although this might be daunting at first, if you cannot go wrong if you stick to using *você* for "you." They will all understand you and respond accordingly.

What about the levels of formality? Although this is not as ingrained in the grammar as in Spanish, Brazilians will show a certain level of respect as they address different people. When first introduced to an older gentleman or woman, use *o senhor* and *a senhora* respectively. This form of address might be used always with such persons, unless they indicate that they do not mind being addressed with the *você* form. When referring to people in the third or second person, it might be common to hear *Seu José* for "Mr. José" and *Dona Maria* for "Mrs. Maria" as a form of respect. Here is a sample dialogue:

> **Q:** Robert: *Olá, Seu José, como vai?* (Hello Mr. José, how are you?)
> **A:** José: *Bem, obrigado, Robert, e você?* (Fine, thanks, Robert, and you?)
> **Q:** Robert: *Tudo bem, e como vai sua esposa, Dona Maria?* (Great, and how is your wife, Mrs. Maria?)
> **A:** José: *Ela vai muito bem, obrigado.* (She's very well, thanks.)

EXERCISE: ADDRESSING OTHERS

Now it's time to see what you've learned! Write the word você next to the people that you should address in a more familiar tone, and the words o senhor or a senhora (for men and women, respectively) if they require a higher level of formality. Check your answers in Appendix C.

1. your cousin: _____

2. the local shopkeeper (male): _____

3. your grandfather: _____

4. your best friend: _____

5. your classmate: _____

6. the librarian (female): _____

Definite and Indefinite Articles

How many ways are there to say "the" in Portuguese? What about using "a/an" or "some"? The answer to these two questions has to do with the agreement system of the language, that is, the fact that all nouns have masculine and feminine forms, as well as singular and plural variants. First, let's talk about the definite articles. By "definite" we mean that the referent refers to a specific thing. So, use it when you mean specifically "the Portuguese book," not "the French book." In addition, you might want to say, for example, *o livro* meaning "the book," the one that you had mentioned before, not any old book. The following table presents the Portuguese definite articles:

Definite Articles

Number	Masculine	Feminine
singular	*o livro* (the book)	*a mesa* (the table)
plural	*os livros* (the books)	*as mesas* (the tables)

As you can see, there are four ways of saying "the" in Portuguese, depending on the gender and number of the noun. In Portuguese, we use the definite article more often than in English. For example, when referring to general things, such as "friends and family," we say *os amigos* ([the] friends) and *a família* ([the] family), using these definite articles. The same goes for set expressions such as the English "love is blind," which would be translated in Portuguese as *o amor é cego*, again, using the definite article to start the sentence. Definite articles are so often used that they are even common when referring to proper names. It is common to hear people address others in some parts of Brazil by adding a definite article such as in *o Paulo*, meaning "Paul," or literally "the Paul" to refer to someone. Finally, one of the most interesting features of Portuguese is the fact that we might opt to say *o meu livro*, literally "(the) my book" when using the possessive pronouns. We will discuss the possessives in detail in Chapter 7.

What about indefinite pronouns? These are used when we refer to things that are nonspecific or that we mention for the first time in discourse. They also follow the agreement rule in Portuguese. Here they are:

Portuguese Indefinite Articles

Number	Masculine	Feminine
singular	*um livro* (a book)	*uma mesa* (a table)
plural	*uns livros* (some books)	*umas mesas* (some tables)

The important thing to remember is that indefinite articles are used for nonspecific things, so you might say *Eu li um livro* for "I read a book," while you might say *Eu li o livro de português* for "I read the Portuguese book," which is more specific. As far as pronunciation goes, the nasal consonants are there to indicate that the vowels are nasalized, and are not really pronounced as the English *m* or *n*.

EXERCISE: DEFINITE OR INDEFINITE?

Now you give it a try. Fill in the blanks with a form of the definite article (o, os, a, as) or the indefinite article (um, uns, uma, umas), depending on the context. Check your answers in Appendix C.

1. *Eu tenho* _____ *lápis,* _____ *caderno e* _____ *caneta.*

2. *Cláudio tem* _____ *livro de português.*

3. *Essas são* _____ *suas canetas?*

4. *Os amigos chamaram* _____ *José para a festa.*

5. *Não coma muito, você pode ter* _____ *ataque cardíaco!*

Demonstratives

When speaking your own language, it is often common for you to refer to things and people by including a demonstrative, such as "this" or "that" before it, depending on the relative or perceived distance involved. In Portuguese the same is true, although speakers also follow the familiar system of gender and number agreement. The following chart summarizes the demonstrative system.

Demonstratives in Portuguese

Number	Masculine	Feminine	English
singular	*este/esse*	*esta/essa*	this
plural	*estes/esses*	*estas/essas*	these
singular	*aquele*	*aquela*	that
plural	*aqueles*	*aquelas*	those

In some Portuguese textbooks you will find the explanation that the *este* group is used for things that are closer to the speaker, while the *esse* group is used for referents that are close to the listener or hearer. But what if something is located between the two speakers at the same relative distance? It is safe to say that Portuguese speakers do not follow those distinctions too closely, interchanging between *esse* and *este* quite frequently, regardless of the fact that some grammar and textbooks will translate them consistently—*este* (this) and *esse* (that)—without making allowances for variation. In fact, the *este* group is losing ground to the *esse* group in colloquial speech. So, a non-native speaker of Portuguese will more frequently use the demonstrative *esse* (this) when referring to almost all things that are relatively closer. What is definitely clear in the Portuguese grammar is that *aquele*, meaning "that" or "that over there," refers to things that are a bit far away or remote from everyone.

> In written language, *este* and its variations are used when referring to things that follow in the text. So, in the sentence *Ele disse estas palavras* (He uttered these words), the comment will follow the sentence. By the same token, if the sentence is *Ele disse essas palavras* (he uttered these words), the comment would have been placed before it.

When you use demonstratives for the first time in discourse, they are followed by a noun, which of course determines the form of the demonstrative. So, you say *essas janelas* (these windows) and *esta porta* (this door).

However, once the noun has been said, it can be omitted in subsequent interactions, such as in the dialogue that follows.

> **Q:** Maria: *Ai, que frio! Fecha essa janela.* (Wow, it is cold! Close this window.)
> **A:** Marcos: *Qual? Essa?* (Which one? This one?)
> **Q:** Maria: *Sim, essa mesmo.* (Yes, this very one.)

There are also neutral forms that are used when the referent is unknown or not determined by gender. So, use the words *isto* and *isso* (this) and *aquilo* (that) by themselves when referring to unknown concepts. These are very handy words to know, especially when you want to know what things are in Portuguese. Look at the following dialogue.

> **Q:** Vinícius: *O que é isso?* (What is that?)
> **A:** Chico: *Isso é um sapo.* (That's a frog.)
> **Q:** Vinícius: *E o que é aquilo que ele está comendo?* (And is that thing that he's eating?)
> **A:** Chico: *É uma mosca.* (It's a fly.)

Common Contractions

When using prepositions ("to" and "from") followed by determiners (the articles and demonstratives we have just learned), interesting things happen in Portuguese. Saying these groups of words together causes them to "contract" or combine in order to form a different, shorter word. Here are some common contractions in Portuguese:

Using *De* + Definite Article in Portuguese

Preposition + Definite Article	Contraction	English
de + o	*do*	from the
de + a	*da*	from the
de + os	*dos*	from the
de + as	*das*	from the

When would you have to use these contractions? Frequently, as they are required and very common in everyday conversation, such as when you say sentences that refer to your origin, for example, *Eu sou dos Estados Unidos* (I am from the United States). Thus, when saying *Ele é do Brasil* you are literally saying "He is from 'the' Brazil." Some examples of common contractions are included in the following dialogue.

Q: Roberto: *Eu sou do Brasil, e você?* (I am from Brazil, how about you?)
A: Jennifer: *Eu sou dos Estados Unidos. E a Ana?* (I am from the United States. And Anna?)
Q: Roberto: *Ela é da França.* (She's from France.)
A: Jennifer: *É mesmo? E o Jacques? De onde ele é?* (Really? And Jacques? Where's he from?)
Q: Roberto: *Eu acho que ele é do Canadá.* (I think he's from Canada.)
A: Jacques: *Não, eu sou das Filipinas!* (No, I'm from the Philippines!)

Again, you will notice that even countries have gender and number, and thus must follow the same gender/number system spelled out in previous sections. You would have to know the "gender" of the country, and whether it takes a definite article, in order to say these sentences correctly.

Some countries do not require the use of the definite article (*o, a, os, as*), so there is no contraction, just the bare preposition. The most noted examples are *Ela é de Portugal* (She's from Portugal), *Ele é de Moçambique* (He's from Mozambique), and *Eles são de Cuba* (They are from Cuba).

Another common contraction is between the preposition *em* (in, on, at) and the definite articles. Here are the examples.

Using *Em* + Definite Article in Portuguese

Preposition + Definite Article	Contraction	English
em + o	*no*	in the

LEARN BRAZILIAN PORTUGUESE

Using *Em* + Definite Article in Portuguese

Preposition + Definite Article	Contraction	English
em + a	*na*	in the
em + os	*nos*	in the
em + as	*nas*	in the

When would you use these contractions? How about when talking about where you live? Here is a sample dialogue that includes some of these contractions.

Q: Anita: *Rogério, onde você mora?* (Rogério, where do you live?)
A: Rogério: *Eu moro no estado do Amazonas, no Brasil.* (I live in the state of Amazonas, in Brazil.)
Q: Anita: *Nossa, e você, Nilda?* (Wow, and you, Nilda?)
A: Nilda: *Eu moro na ilha da Madeira, Portugal.* (I live in the island of Madeira, Portugal.)
Q: Rogério: *Eu adoraria visitar vocês dois.* (I would love to visit both of you.)
A: Anita: *Você será sempre bem-vinda na nossa casa!* (You are always welcome in our house!)

What about indefinite articles, do they contract? Sure! The common contraction involving the preposition *em* (in, on) and the indefinite articles *um, uma* (a/an) is summarized below.

Using *Em* + Indefinite Article in Portuguese

Preposition + Indefinite Article	Contraction	English
em + um	*num*	in a
em + uma	*numa*	in a
em + uns	*nuns*	in some
em + umas	*numas*	in some

Again, in order to express indefinite ideas, a speaker could use those indefinite pronouns. For example, one could say *Eu vivo num bairro elegante* (I live in an elegant neighborhood), or *Eu estudo numa universidade muito cara* (I study in a very expensive university). Notice that in these two examples, the places were not specifically mentioned. In this chapter you learned some basic building blocks of Portuguese grammar. In the next chapter you will be able to use some of these words with some basic verbs.

EXERCISE: CONTRACTIONS

Now let's test what you've learned about contractions. Write in the missing contractions in the following translated sentences. Check your answers in Appendix C.

1. I am **from the** United States.

   Eu sou _____ *Estados Unidos.*

2. I live **in a** dorm.

   Eu moro _____ *residência estudantil.*

3. She is **from** Cuba.

   Ela é _____ *Cuba.*

4. They are **from the** Island of Madeira.

   Eles são _____ *Ilha da Madeira.*

5. I study **in a** big university.

   Eu estudo _____ *universidade grande.*

CHAPTER 5

Who Are You? Introducing *Ser*

FIRST IMPRESSIONS COUNT! As you learn Portuguese, you will notice that the verb *ser* (to be) is used a lot, especially as you talk about yourself, your physical and emotional characteristics, and your occupation. Finally, you will see that *ser* is used for counting and telling time. Read on and you will see how important *ser* really is.

Expressing Identity: *Ser*

If someone were to ask you about yourself, how would you answer? Look at the following examples and notice how Mário Rodrigues describes himself.

Meu nome é Mário Rodrigues. (My name is Mário Rodrigues.)
Sou médico. (I am a medical doctor.)
Sou simpático, de estatura mediana. (I am friendly, of average height.)
Sou de Campinas. (I am from Campinas.)

You will notice that Mário Rodrigues has indicated his name, his profession, his physical and emotional characteristics, and his place of origin. All of these traits are part of his identity, and are not likely to change. These somewhat permanent characteristics are expressed using the verb *ser* (to be) in Portuguese.

TRACK 27

The Verb *Ser* in the Present Tense

Portuguese	English
eu sou	I am
você é	you are
ele/ela é	he/she/it is
nós somos	we are
vocês são	you (plural) are
eles/elas são	they are

Remember that there is also the *tu* form which is used in some parts of Brazil, and is conjugated as *tu és* for "you are." Also remember that often Brazilians will use the phrase *a gente* for the first person plural or "we," so you would say *a gente é* for "we are." If you want to be more formal, use the second person *o senhor* and *a senhora* for "you sir/ma'am are…" and conjugate it with the conjugated form *é*.

Place of Origin

As mentioned above, use the verb *ser* to talk about place of origin, such as your nationality. Here is a sample dialogue.

> **Q:** *De onde você é?* (Where are you from?)
> **A:** *Sou dos Estados Unidos.* (I am from the United States.)
> **Q:** *Então, você é americana?* (So, you are American?)
> **A:** *Sim, sou americana!* (Yes, I'm American!)
> **Q:** *Muito prazer!* (Nice to meet you!)

What follows is a list of some nationalities in Portuguese. The first form is the masculine, followed by the feminine form. If only one form is listed, the adjective can be used for both masculine and feminine referents.

TRACK 28

Countries and Nationalities

Country	Nationality
Angola	angolano, angolana
Alemanha	alemão, alemã
Argentina	argentino, argentina
Austrália	australiano, australiana
Áustria	austríaco, austríaca
Bélgica	belga
Brasil	brasileiro, brasileira
Canadá	canadense
Chile	chileno, chilena
China	chinês, chinesa
Colombia	colombiano, colombiana
Costa Rica	costa-ricense
Ecuador	equatoriano, equatoriana
Egito	egípcio, egípcia

França	francês, francesa
Grã-bretanha	britânico, britânica
Grécia	grego, grega
Haiti	haitiano, haitiana
Holanda	holandês, holandesa
India	indiano, indiana
Inglaterra	inglês, inglesa
Irã	iraniano, iraniana
Iraque	iraquiano, iraquiana
Irlanda	irlandês, irlandesa
Israel	israelense
Itália	italiano, italiana
Jamaica	jamaicano, jamaicana
Japão	japonês, japonesa
México	mexicano, mexicana
Nicarágua	nicaragüense
Panamá	panamenho, panamenha
Polônia	polonês, polonesa
República Checa	checo, checa
Suécia	sueco, sueca
Suíça	suíço, suíça
Tailandia	tailandês, tailandesa
Venezuela	venezuelano, venezuelana

You can use these forms as an adjective; for example, *Ele é um médico japonês* (He is a Japanese doctor), or as a noun, as in *Ele é japonês* (He is Japanese). As far as the plural of these forms goes, most of the time you will use the masculine and add an *–s* at the end, so *americano > americanos*, and *canadense > canadenses*. Feminine plural forms do exist, but only with the adjectives that end in *–o* in the masculine singular, which changes to *–as*, as in *americano > americanas*.

EXERCISE: NAME THE NATIONALITIES

Now let's practice with an exercise. Indicate the nationalities of the following people. Check your answers in Appendix C.

1. *Stefi Graff é de Berlim. Ela é* _____ .

2. *Pelé é de São Paulo, Brasil. Ele é* _____ .

3. *O senhor Putin e a senhora Stakhnevich são de Moscou.*

   Eles são _____ .

4. *Sofia Loren e Marcelo Mastroiani são de Roma.*

   Eles são _____ .

5. *O senhor Takenaka é de Tóquio. Ele é* _____ .

Characteristics

What do you look like? What are your major, unchangeable characteristics? The adjectives that reflect this part of your identity are expressed also using the verb *ser* (to be). The following is a list of adjectives that go with this verb.

TRACK 29

Common Characteristics

Portuguese	English
alto, alta	tall
baixo, baixa	short
barato, barata	cheap
bonito, bonita	pretty
burro, burra	stupid
careca	bald
doce	sweet
elegante	elegant

Common Characteristics (continued)

Portuguese	English
engraçado, engraçada	funny
estudioso, estudiosa	studious
famoso, famosa	famous
feio, feia	ugly
forte	strong, stocky
gordo, gorda	fat
idoso, idosa	elderly
inteligente	intelligent
jovem	young
louro, loura	blond
magro, magra	thin
moreno, morena	dark-skinned
pobre	poor
ruivo, ruiva	redheaded
sério, séria	serious
velho, velha	old

If only one word is given on the list, the same form can be used for both masculine and feminine, as in *inteligente* (intelligent). Otherwise, the masculine is written first, followed by the feminine form.

Occupations

Your occupation can hardly be considered a permanent characteristic; however, it immediately identifies you to others. For example, if you want to say that you are a doctor, you should use the verb *ser* (to be). By the same token, if you want to say that you are a student, you should also use *ser*, even if your status as a student is not a permanent condition!

Listen to Track 30 to hear a few examples.

TRACK 30

Qual é sua profissão?
(What is your profession?)

O que você faz?
(What do you do?)

Eu sou médica.
(I'm a doctor.)

Eu sou engenheiro.
(I'm an engineer.)

Notice that in Portuguese there is no need to add the indefinite article "a" or "an" before the profession, as we do in English. So you are saying, literally, "I am doctor." And, if you say *Eu sou um médico* (I am a doctor), you are actually saying that you are "one doctor," as opposed to two! The only time when you might have to say *um* or *uma* before a profession or a noun, is when you give a description afterwards. In other words, you should say *Eu sou um estudante inteligente* (I am an intelligent student).

Here is a list of some well-known professions in Portuguese:

TRACK 31

Profissões e Ocupações (Professions and Occupations)

Portuguese	English
advogado, advogada	lawyer
ator, atriz	actor, actress
analista	psychotherapist
analista de sistemas	systems analyst
arquiteto, arquiteta	architect
bancário, bancária	bank teller
cantor, cantora	singer
consultor, consultora	consultant
contador, contadora	accountant
costureiro, costureira	clothes designer, dressmaker
diretor, diretora	director
empregado, empregada	employee, maid
engenheiro, engenheira	engineer
estudante	student
farmacêutico, farmacêutica	pharmacist
fotógrafo, fotógrafa	photographer
garçom, garçonete	waiter, waitress
gerente	manager
jornalista	reporter, journalist
juiz, juíza	judge
operário, operária	factory worker
músico, música	musician
pianista	pianist
professor, professora	teacher, professor
vendedor, vendedora	salesperson
vendedor ambulante, vendedora ambulante	street vendor

Unless it is not specifically listed, the feminine form is the same as the masculine form, such as in *gerente* (manager) and *pianista* (pianist).

EXERCISE: **NAME THAT PROFESSION!**

Now give an exercise a try. Fill in the blanks with a word that describes the person's profession or occupation. Check your answers in Appendix C.

1. He plays the piano beautifully.   *Ele é* _____ .

2. She teaches at a high school.   *Ela é* _____ .

3. He works in a bank, as a teller.   *Ele é* _____ .

4. She makes decisions in court.   *Ela é* _____ .

5. She helps customers with their purchases.   *Ela é* _____ .

Personal Relationships

As you can see, the verb *ser* is not only used for permanent characteristics and occupations, but also for describing relationships between people! It would be hard to try to fit all types of relationships into a category defined as "permanent." That is why the best description for the uses of this verb is "identification." As you say *Eu sou o irmão dela* (I am her brother), you are identifying yourself and describing your relationship to someone. Here are some other examples:

> *Carolina é amiga de Raul.* (Carolina is Raul's friend.)
> *As duas alunas são companheiras.* (The two students are friends/partners.)
> *Marcos e José são sócios.* (Marcos and José are business partners.)
> *José e João são concorrentes.* (José and João are competitors.)
> *Helena é filha de Orlando.* (Helena is Orlando's daughter.)
> *Eu sou filha de Iracema.* (I am Iracema's daughter.)
> *Minha irmã e eu somos filhas de Eraldo.* (My sister and I are Eraldo's daughters.)

Note that not all personal relationships have to do with family. Many relationships are of close friendships, competitors, or even business associations. They all have to be described using this verb. To learn more about the vocabulary of "family," check out upcoming chapters.

Numbers and *Ser*

The verb *ser* is very versatile; it is also used when dealing with numbers and counting. You could explain the usage of *ser* with numbers by associating it with truthful, immutable descriptions. Thus, two plus two is always four, so *dois e dois são quatro*. For a complete overview of numbers, refer to Chapter 8. What follows is series of sentences that describe mathematical operations.

$3 \times 4 = 12$	*três vez quatro são doze*
$2 + 2 = 4$	*dois mais dois são quatro*
$9 - 1 = 8$	*nove menos um são oito*
$6 \div 2 = 3$	*seis dividido por dois são três*

If you would like to ask for the bill at a restaurant, simply say *Quanto foi a conta?* (How much was the bill?). Because it related to activities in the past, the verb *ser* is expressed in the past tense, *foi* (was). The answer to your question could be *São vinte reais* (It is twenty reais). Notice that when dealing with numbers, the verb is in the plural form in Portuguese.

When referring to cost of products and services, you should use *ser*, as in *Um quilo de arroz é dois reais* (One kilogram of rice is two reais). *Real* is the Brazilian currency, and *reais* is its plural form. More commonly, Portuguese speakers will use the verb *custar* (to cost) to deal with prices and costs. An example of a typical sentence would be *Quanto custa a pedicure?* (How much is the pedicure?); in other words, how much does it cost?

CHAPTER 6

How Are You? Introducing *Estar*

Now that you have mastered the use of *ser* (to be) we will move on to another "to be" verb: *estar*. While we associate *ser* with physical characteristics and identity, *estar* is associated with physical states, mental conditions, and location in space. Now let's see where you are in your progress.

States of Being: *Estar*

Use *estar* to help you communicate how you are at a certain point in time. This verb is also used to express the location of someone or something, and the (frequently temporary) states of being. Here are some examples:

A senhora está bem? (How are you, ma'am?)
Estou bem, obrigada. (I am well, thanks.)
Onde você está? (Where are you?)
Estou na escola. (I am at school.)

For the other forms of *estar*, refer to the following table.

TRACK 32

The Verb *Estar* in the Present Tense

Portuguese	English
eu estou	I am
você está	you are
ele/ela está	he/she/it is
nós estamos	we are
vocês estão	you (plural) are
eles/elas estão	they are

It is important to pronounce the forms *estou* (*eu* form) and *estão* (*vocês/eles* form) very clearly, since they might sound similar at the beginning. Practice these two forms out loud, especially the first person singular, which you might have to use more frequently.

When Brazilians are talking, they will very often cut off the first syllable, *es–*, of these verb forms. Be prepared to hear *tou, tá, tamo(s), tão* in spoken conversation. You might even start saying them too!

Many grammars of Portuguese use the distinction "temporary" states for *estar* versus "permanent" aspects for *ser*. This is a good general rule, but it does not tell the whole story. For example, you should say *Eu sou estudante* (I am a student) even though this is (hopefully!) not a permanent condition, but rather just a way of identifying yourself. You should also say *O gato está morto* (The cat is dead), even though being dead is not temporary, but rather a change in physical state.

As clearly put by the well-known Portuguese linguist Mário Perini, *ser* introduces qualities that are seen as inherent to the subject, while *estar* captures qualities that are seen as transitory or otherwise nonessential. More information about other uses of *estar*—specifically, its use with physical states—is presented in the next section.

Physical States

Use a form of the verb *estar* with the adjectives and adverbs in the following table to express how people feel, look, or seem. Don't forget that some adjectives and adverbs need to "match" their respective subjects, especially if the masculine form ends in *–o*. For example: *Ele está cansado* (He is/looks tired); *Ela está cansada* (She is/seems tired). As you can see, sometimes we can translate the verb *estar* (to be) for the verbs "to seem," "to appear," or "to feel" in English, because they reflect not an immutable physical characteristic, but rather a condition or state. The following are some common physical states that are used with the verb *estar*.

Vocabulary: Describing How You Feel

Portuguese	English
acordado	awake
bêbado	drunk
bem	well
cansado	tired

Vocabulary: Describing How You Feel

Portuguese	English
descansado	rested
doente	sick
dormindo	asleep
enjoado	sick, bored, boring
fraco	weak
limpo	clean
mais ou menos	so-so
ocupado	busy
pálido	pale
sóbrio	sober

Here is a sample dialogue where a lot of these words may be used:

Q: *Oi, Roberto, como estás?* (Hi, Roberto, how are you?)
A: *Estou bem, mas um pouco cansado.* (I'm fine, but a little tired.)
Q: *Estás bêbado ainda?* (Are you still drunk?)
A: *Não, estou sóbrio, mas de ressaca!*
(No, I'm sober, but I'm hungover.)
Q: *Eu sei, e hoje eu vou estar super ocupado.* (I know, and today I will be very busy.)
A: *Eu também, e só agora estou acordado.* (Me too, and only now am I awake.)
Q: *E a casa, 'tá limpa?* (And the house, is it clean?)
A: *Eh... mais ou menos!* (Hmm... sort of!)

Mental States

Besides physical conditions, there are also mental states that should be expressed with *estar*. Look at some sample vocabulary used to aid you in communicating how you feel mentally or emotionally.

Vocabulary: Describing How You Feel

Portuguese	English
amedrontado	scared
animado	excited
ansioso	anxious
apaixonado	in love
contente	happy
envergonhado	embarassed
estupefato	stunned
excitado	aroused
feliz	happy
impressionado	impressed
irritado	irritated
louco	crazy
nervoso	nervous
preocupado	worried
satisfeito	satisfied
tranqüilo	calm
triste	sad

Take a look at the following dialogue, which includes many of the adjectives you just reviewed.

Q: *E então, Maria, foi ver o Roberto Carlos?* (So, Maria did you go see Roberto Carlos?)

A: *Sim, ele é lindo e maravilhoso!* (Yes, he is so handsome and wonderful!)

Q: *Nossa, você está apaixonada, não?* (Wow, you are really in love, huh?)

A: *Claro, eu estou louca de amor por ele.* (You bet, I am crazy in love with him.)

Q: *Você está mesmo animada. Eu estou estupefata!* (Yes, you look really excited. I am stunned!)

A: *Assim é o amor!* (That's how love is!)

Location

The verb *estar* can express where something is in a particular place at a particular time. So, if you ask *Onde você está?* (Where are you?) you can answer, *Estou em casa* (I'm at home). Physical location usually refers to something or someone that is only temporarily located in a place, such as a book on a table, or a person at a bank, for example.

> In order to describe where places (buildings, cities, etc.) are located, Portuguese speakers use the verb *ficar* (to be located). For example, *Onde fica o supermercado?* (Where is the supermarket?); *Fica na esquina da Rua Quinze* (It's at the corner of Fifteenth Street).

Here are some words that help locate things or persons when using the verb *estar* with physical location.

Expressing Location with Prepositional Phrases

Portuguese	English
embaixo de	under
em cima de	on top
dentro de	inside
fora de	outside
perto de	close to
longe de	far from
debaixo de	under
sobre	over, on top
atrás	behind
em frente de	in front of
detrás de	behind of
defronte de	facing, in front of

You can also use the verb *estar* to indicate a location that is not necessarily associated with space, but rather time. You can say *Estou no meu segundo dia de prova* (I am on my second day of exams), meaning that you are in certain place in a process of being tested.

Estar in the Present Progressive Tense

The present progressive is the verb tense you use when you want to express actions or feelings that are continuous or ongoing. This tense is comparable to the English progressive, which is done by using the verb "to be" plus an "–ing" ending, as in "I am writing." By comparison, in Brazilian Portuguese we use the verb *estar* plus the *–ndo* ending, as in *Estou falando* (I am talking). Here is how this verb tense is constructed.

Present Progressive Tense

Type of Verb	estar + –ndo	English
–ar verbs	*estou estudando*	I am studying
–er verbs	*estou escrevendo*	I am writing
–ir verbs	*estou assistindo*	I am watching

As far as the use of progressive tenses, English speakers use the "–ing" structures more often. For example, you use the "present" progressive in the sentence "I'm flying tomorrow" even though it is about the future. This particular usage is not permitted in Portuguese. We would instead use the regular present tense, as in *Eu viajo amanhã* (I fly tomorrow). Most commonly, the present progressive tense in Portuguese is used to reflect ongoing actions or to reflect situations at the moment of speech. As with many other structures in the language, it does not have to be describing an action; it could denote a non-action, as in *Eu estou pensando* (I'm thinking). Here are some other examples of action and non-action present progressive sentences:

> *Eu estou falando português.* (I am speaking Portuguese.)
> *Ela está comendo feijão com arroz.* (She is eating rice and beans.)
> *Ele está bebendo cerveja.* (He is drinking beer.)
> *Nós estamos assistindo à televisão.* (We are watching television.)

Eles estão andando no parque. (They are walking in the park.)
Elas estão refletindo sobre a proposta. (They are reflecting on the proposal.)

Ser or *Estar*?

It might be tricky to decide whether to use *ser* or *estar* in Portuguese, since it is all the same in English—that is, you use the verb "to be" for most instances. But there are some very clear distinctions, as can be seen in the following chart.

Guidelines for Using *Ser* and *Estar*

Uses of *Ser*	Uses of *Estar*
Identification	**Physical States**
Eu sou estudante. (I'm a student.)	*Eu estou doente.* (I am/feel sick.)
Place of Origin/Nationality	**Mental States**
Você é do Brasil. (You are from Brazil.)	*Você está contente.* (You are/feel happy.)
Você é canadense. (You are Canadian.)	
Physical Traits	**Point of Location**
Ele é alto. (He is tall.)	*Ele está em casa.* (He is at home.)
Profession/Occupation	**Present Progressive**
Ela é médica. (She is a doctor.)	*Ela está trabalhando.* (She is working.)
Ela é estudante. (She is a student.)	
Personal Relationships	
Nós somos irmãs. (We are sisters.)	
Nós somos sócios. (We are business partners.)	
General Statements	
O amor é cego. (Love is blind.)	
Numbers and Time	
Dois mais dois são quarto. (Two plus two is four.)	
São doze horas. (It is twelve o'clock.)	

Peculiar Uses

When talking about geographical location, there are at least three possibilities in Portuguese, all grammatically acceptable: (a) *São Paulo é no Brasil*; (b) *São Paulo está no Brasil*; and (c) *São Paulo fica no Brasil*, all of which are all translated as "São Paulo is (located) in Brazil." Although *ser* would be the logical choice here, since the fact that a city is located in a particular country is inherent to it, both *estar* and *ficar* seem to be gaining ground in such cases.

There are some adjectives that are used with both *ser* and *estar* resulting in different interpretations of meaning, and thus different translations in English. If we say *Ele é gordo* (He is fat), we mean that being fat is this person's intrinsic quality. Another example of this is in the sentence *Os elefantes são grandes* (Elephants are big); it is clear that this being big is part and parcel of being an elephant. On the other hand, if we say *Ele está gordo!* (He is fat!), we mean that he looks or appears to be fat, because perhaps he has gained a lot of weight recently, and in demonstrating this recent change of state, we use *estar* to express surprise. The following are a series of examples with *ser* and *estar* and their translations.

Using Both *Ser* and *Estar*

Portuguese	English
Ele é louco.	He's crazy. (He should be committed.)
Ele está louco.	He's crazy. (He did something crazy, at that moment.)
A professora é chata.	The teacher is boring. (She is always boring.)
O filme está chato.	The film is boring. (The statement is the speaker's impression; it is not necessarily true.)
Eles são magros.	They are skinny. (That's their intrinsic quality.)
Eles estão magros.	They are skinny. (They lost a lot of weight.)
Eu sou feliz.	I am happy. (That's how I am in general, a happy person.)
Eu estou feliz.	I am happy. (Something happened that made me happy; I am happy at the moment.)
Isso é difícil.	This is difficult. (It's an intrinsically difficult subject.)
Isso está difícil.	This is difficult. (It's more difficult than expected.)

Think you've got a handle on all this? Give it a try with the following exercises.

CHOOSING *SER* OR *ESTAR*

Decide whether ser or estar belongs in the following sentences. Check your answers in Appendix C.

1. *Clarice é/está no hospital.* (Clarice is in the hospital.)
2. *Ela é/está médica pediatra.* (She is a pediatrician.)
3. *Ela é/está uma pessoa contente por natureza.* (She is a happy person by nature.)
4. *Clarice e Kadu são/estão brasileiros.* (Clarice and Kadu are Brazilian.)
5. *Agora eles são/estão no Rio de Janeiro.* (Now they are in Rio de Janeiro.)
6. *Kadu é/está estudante de medicina.* (Kadu is a medical student.)
7. *Ele é/está nervosa com os exames.* (He is nervous about exams.)

NOW YOU CONJUGATE!

Write in the correct verb form, using either ser or estar. Check your answers in Appendix C.

1. *Meus pais _____ na Europa.* (My parents are in Europe.)

2. *O vermelho _____ uma cor linda.* (Red is a beautiful color.)

3. *Meu amigo Jonas _____ engenheiro civil.* (My friend Jonas is a civil engineer.)

4. *O livro de português _____ em cima da mesa.* (The Portuguese book is on top of the table.)

5. *Fortaleza _____ no Nordeste do Brasil.* (Fortaleza is located in the northeast of Brazil.)

6. *_____ sete horas da noite.* (It's seven o'clock at night.)

7. *Nós _____ muito contentes com os nossos filhos.* (We are very happy with our children.)

EXERCISE: **TIME TO TRANSLATE**

Translate the following sentences into Portuguese. Check your answers in Appendix C.

1. She looks thin. _____

2. They are teachers. _____

3. He is furious. _____

4. We are Cuban. _____

5. You are in the city. _____

Agreement Rules

One important concept that students of Portuguese must learn is the fact that all the elements of the noun phrase need to "agree with" or be in the same gender and number as the noun. So, Portuguese speakers say *um cantor famoso* for "a famous singer" who is male and *uma cantora famosa* for "a famous singer" who is female. By the same token, if there is more than one element, the nouns and adjectives also have to "agree" in terms of number. Speakers say *uns cantores famosos* for famous singers like the Beach Boys and *umas cantoras famosas* for the Dixie Chicks. Here are some more examples of nouns phrases in Portuguese where the agreement is clearly at play.

> *um cartaz bonito* (a pretty poster)
> *uns livros interessantes* (some interesting books)
> *uma janela aberta* (an open window)
> *umas alunas engraçadas* (some funny [female] students)

You'll find out more details about gender and plural agreement in the next few sections.

Plurals in Nouns and Adjectives

In formal written Portuguese and very formal speech, number agreement is followed pretty strictly. This does not happen in colloquial or less careful speech. Some words are easy to guess the plural, and others either follow a predetermined rule or are exceptions and must be learned by heart. Here are the rules for forming plural nouns in Portuguese.

First, as a general rule: add an –s to the singular form.

gato (cat)	*gatos* (cats)
mesa (table)	*mesas* (tables)
chave (key)	*chaves* (keys)
mão (hand)	*mãos* (hands)

All the plural words in Portuguese end in –s. However, there might be changes to the previous vowels or consonants that come before. The plural formation depends on the stress of the words and whether diphthongs are found at the end.

If the word ends in –l, drop –l and add –is. If the result is –iis, drop one –i.

jornal (newspaper)	*jornais* (newspapers)
papel (paper)	*papéis* (papers)
fuzil (rifle)	*fuzis* (rifles)

If the word ends in –l but the last syllable is not stressed, drop –l and add –eis.

fóssil (fossil)	*fósseis* (fossils)
réptil (reptile)	*répteis* (reptiles)

If the word ends in –s or –x, and the last syllable is not stressed, the plural is identical.

lápis (pencil)	*lápis* (pencil)
clímax (climax)	*clímax* (climaxes)

If the word ends in *–m*, drop *–m* and add *–ns*.

jovem (youngster)	*jovens* (youngsters)
bombom (bonbons)	*bombons* (bonbons)

If the word ends in a consonant, add *–es*.

licor (liqueur)	*licores* (liqueurs)
cartaz (poster)	*cartazes* (posters)

The words in the next group end in *–ão* in the singular and have three different possibilities in the plural. Here is how this works:
If the word ends in *–ão*, and the last syllable is not stressed, add *–s*.

órgão (organ)	*órgãos* (organs)

If the word ends in *–ão* and the last syllable is stressed, add *–s*, or *–ões*, or *–ães*:

irmão (brother)	*irmãos* (brothers)
melão (melon)	*melões* (melons)
capitão (captain)	*capitães* (captains)

The first example (*irmãos*) shows the simple "add an –s" rule. However, this is not the most common plural for words ending in *–ão*. The second example (*melões*) is actually the most common result for the singular words that end in *–ão*. If one had to guess the plural of a word ending in *–ão*, this would be the best guess. Finally, the last example (*capitães*) is the least common case. There are only a handful of words in Portuguese that have this plural ending, including *pães* (breads) and *alemães* (Germans). Even though it might seem daunting at first, plurals are manageable in Portuguese once you learn the general rules.

EXERCISE: **WHAT'S THE PLURAL FORM?**

Now let's see what you've learned about singular and plural forms of words in Portuguese. Write the plural forms of the following words in Portuguese. Check your answers in Appendix C.

1. *coração* (heart): _____

2. *canil* (kennel): _____

3. *pincel* (paintbrush): _____

4. *pão* (bread): _____

5. *órfão* (orphan): _____

6. *difícil* (difficult): _____

7. *cantor* (singer): _____

8. *tórax* (thorax): _____

CHAPTER 7

Describing People and Things in Portuguese

IN THE PREVIOUS chapter, you learned that nouns and adjectives need to agree in gender and number in Portuguese. In this chapter you will learn how to arrive at the plural of nouns, how to determine the correct order of elements in a noun phrase, how to make comparisons, how to talk about the "best" and the "worst," and how to express ownership and possession.

From Nouns to Adjectives

What are adjectives? Adjectives modify the nouns that they are attached to. The masculine form is usually accepted as the "default" form, from which the feminine is somehow "derived." This is one reason that when new words enter the language they are generally masculine. Whichever the gender, the fact remains that all elements in the noun phrase must match. How do you get from the masculine to the feminine forms? If the masculine ends in –*o*, you should drop the –*o* and add –*a* to get the feminine form. If the masculine word ends in –*u* or –*ês*, simply add the –*a* to the word to create the feminine counterpart. The following are some examples of masculine and feminine descriptive adjectives, which have to agree with the nouns.

TRACK 33

Masculine and Feminine Adjectives

Masculine	Feminine	English
amarelo	*amarela*	yellow
bonito	*bonita*	pretty
cru	*crua*	raw
freguês	*freguesa*	customer
vermelho	*vermelha*	red

Some adjectives have the same form for feminine and masculine. This happens often with adjectives that end in –*e*, such as *inteligente* (intelligent), *doente* (sick), and *contente* (happy). There are also a good number of adjectives that end in consonants that have the same form for both masculine and feminine, such as *azul* (blue), *capaz* (able), *familiar* (familiar), *internacional* (international), *marrom* (brown), and *virgem* (virgin). It is easy to see the changes in masculine and feminine adjectives by looking at a list of common nationalities. As you learn Portuguese, you might want to communicate your citizenship, or refer to people of various nationalities. Here is a short list of adjectives of nationality:

TRACK 34

Masculine and Feminine Nationalities

Masculine	Feminine	English
americano	americana	American
brasileiro	brasileira	Brazilian
mexicano	mexicana	Mexican
inglês	inglesa	English
canadense	canadense	Canadian
alemão	alemã	German

You will notice that *canadense* ends in –*e* and therefore has the same form for both masculine and feminine. For masculine words that end in –*ão*, the feminine form is derived by removing the –*o* and leaving the nasalized vowel –*ã* at the end, as in the word *alemão*, *alemã* (German). There are some nationalities that do not change in form, regardless of gender. These are *hindu* (Hindu) and *zulu* (Zulu), among others.

Additionally, words ending in –*eu* in the masculine change to –*éia* in the feminine, such as in the word *hebreu*, *hebréia* (Hebrew).

Nationalities are not written with capital letters in Portuguese, as they are in English. They follow the same rule of other adjectives and begin with lower-case letters.

EXERCISE: TRANSFORMING ADJECTIVES

Now let's see what you've learned about transforming adjectives. Make the appropriate changes so that the masculine form will become the feminine one. Check your answers in Appendix C.

1. *francês* (French): _____

2. *indiano* (Indian): _____

3. *nu* (naked): _____

4. *ateu* (Atheist): _____

5. *jornaleiro* (newspaper seller): _____

6. *japonês* (Japanese): _____

7. *israelense* (Israelite): _____

8. *colombiano* (Colombian): _____

The Order of Modifiers

As with any language, Portuguese has a certain order that must be followed by the elements of the noun phrase. Modifiers are all the parts of the phrase that influence and change the meaning of the noun. You can say "**the** book," "**a** book," or "**good** book," and all those phrases have different meanings. That is because those modifiers (the, a, good) modify or add to the noun "book." In Portuguese, some modifiers precede the noun, while others (usually descriptive adjectives) follow the noun. First, let's look at the list of common modifiers that precede the noun:

Order of Modifiers Occurring Before the Noun

Group I	Group II	Group III
predeterminers	determiners	quantifiers/possessives/numerals
todos (all)	*o* (the)	*poucos* (few)
ambos (both)	*um* (a/an)	*muitos* (many)
	este/esse (this)	*vários* (several)
	aquele (that)	*tantos* (so many)
	algum (some)	*meus, seus, etc.* (my, your, etc.)
	dois, três, quatro (two, three, four)	

Other possibilities such as the words *qualquer* (any) and *tal* (such) are also part of group III, but are not mentioned here for the sake of simplicity. Suffice to say that the examples in the previous table are very common in spoken as well as written language. The following are some examples of noun phrases that include a combination of modifiers:

TRACK 35

Todos	meus	amigos	All (of) my friends
I	II	[noun]	
Ambas	as	blusas	Both (of) the blouses
I	II	[noun]	
As	poucas	explicações	The few explanations
II	III	[noun]	
Meus	dois	amigos	My two friends
III	III	[noun]	
Meus	muitos	amigos	My many friends
III	III	[noun]	

As you can see, it is common to have phrases that include elements from groups I and II, as well as combinations that include elements from groups II and III. And, as can be seen from the fourth and fifth examples in the previous table, it is possible to have at least two items from group III, most commonly when a possessive is followed by another modifier from the same group.

Descriptive Adjectives

Descriptive adjectives are modifiers that usually follow the noun in Portuguese. In Portuguese we say the noun first, and then we give it qualifications. So, unlike in English, you say um carro vermelho, literally "a car red." Imagine how hard it would be for simultaneous interpreters translating a long description from English to Portuguese: They would have to wait until all the adjectives were said, keep them in mind, then translate the noun, and only then add all the adjectives in Portuguese!

In Chapter 5, you learned a lot of descriptive adjectives for physical characteristics. In this section you will put all of these adjectives in the correct order.

EXERCISE: PUT IT ALL IN ORDER

Read the jumbled words in each item and rewrite the noun phrase using the correct order of modifiers. Check your answers in Appendix C.

1. *vermelho um carro* (a red car): _____

2. *casas novas umas* (some new houses): _____

3. *amigos os todos meus* (all my friends): _____

4. *aluno o inteligente* (the intelligent student): _____

5. *laranja blusa uma* (an orange blouse): _____

6. *livros ambos os* (both of the books): _____

7. *a amiga minha* ([the] my friend): _____

8. *carro um novo* (a new car): _____

Making Comparisons

Sometimes it is not enough to simply describe something; you need to compare it with something else in order to give a clearer idea of what you are talking about. There are two main kinds of comparisons: ones in which unequal elements are being compared and ones in which equal elements are being compared.

Comparing Unequal Elements

Comparing unequal elements is simple. Whenever you say that one thing is bigger, better, stronger, heavier, and so forth, than another thing, you are saying that these two things are unequal. You probably make comparisons of inequality in English all the time; now let's see how to do it in Portuguese.

TRACK 36

Comparison of Unequal Elements

X	verb	mais (more)	ADJECTIVE	(do) que (than)	Y
Brad Pitt	é	mais	bonito	que	Will Ferrell.
Brad Pitt	is	more	handsome	than	Will Ferrell.

X	verb	mais (more)	ADJECTIVE	(do) que (than)	Y
A minha casa	é	menos	confortável	que	a sua casa.
My house	is	less	comfortable	than	your house.

X	verb	mais (more)	NOUN	(do) que (than)	Y
José	*tem*	*mais*	*amigos*	*que*	*o irmão dele.*
José	has	more	friends	than	his brother.

X	verb	mais (more)	NOUN	(do) que (than)	Y
João	*tem*	*menos*	*dinheiro*	*que*	*José.*
João	has	less	money	than	José.

In spoken language, the particle *do* is usually not heard. But it is possible to see it written as in *João tem mais paciência **do** que José* (João has more patience than José). Although most comparisons follow the formulas you saw in the table, there are some irregular comparatives that should be noted. The adjective *bom* (good) has the comparative *melhor* (better), and the adjective *ruim* (bad) has the comparative *pior* (worse). Some examples are *Rita é melhor estudante que Pedro* (Rita is a better student than Pedro) and *Teresa é pior atleta que Jacinto* (Teresa is a worse athlete than Jacinto).

EXERCISE: COMPARING UNEQUAL ELEMENTS

Now you give it a try. Read the information below about the people and write a comparative sentence. Here's an example: Pedro, eighteen years old/Jacinto, seventeen years old. > *Pedro é mais velho que Jacinto.* (Pedro is older than Jacinto). Check your answers in Appendix C.

1. Rita, IQ = 120/Teresa, IQ = 110.

   _____

2. Marta, forty-three years old/Rodrigo, forty-six years old.

   _____

3. Amaro, 1m 70c in height/Cláudio 1m 80c in height.

   _____

4. Jorge, 90 kilos in weight/Maria, 63 kilos in weight.

   _____

5. Bill Gates $$$$/Donald Trump $$.

   _____

Comparing Equal Elements

Just as you commonly need to compare things that are unequal, you also need to compare things that are equal in nature. The following table demonstrates how to do this in Portuguese.

TRACK 37

Comparison of Equal Elements

X	verb	tão	ADJECTIVE	quanto	Y
Martha	*é*	*tão*	*famosa*	*quanto*	*Donald.*
Martha	is	as	famous	as	Donald.
Dave	*é*	*tão*	*engraçado*	*quanto*	*Jay.*
Dave	is	as	funny	as	Jay.

X	verb	tão	NOUN	quanto	Y
Jacinto	*tem*	*tanto*	*dinheiro*	*quanto*	*Pedro.*
Jacinto	has	as much	money	as	Pedro.
Eu	*tenho*	*tanta*	*paciência*	*quanto*	*a minha esposa.*
I	have	as much	patience	as	my wife.
Eu	*tenho*	*tantos*	*amigos*	*quanto*	*a minha irmã.*
I	have	as many	friends	as	my sister.
Rita	*tem*	*tantas*	*canetas*	*quanto*	*Teresa.*
Rita	has	as many	pens	as	Teresa.

As you can see from the examples on the table above, the expression *tanto...quanto* (as much/many as) in Portuguese can have four different forms depending on the noun: *tanto, tantos, tanta, tantas.* Always keep in mind these four categories, which intersect: singular, plural, masculine, and feminine.

EXERCISE: COMPARING EQUAL ELEMENTS

Now give it a try. Fill in the blanks with the correct words in these comparative sentences. Check your answers in Appendix C.

1. *Jorge é* _____ *feio* _____ *Vicente.* (Jorge is as ugly as Vincent.)

2. *Martha é* _____ *rica* _____ *Donald.* (Martha is as rich as Donald.)

3. *O Porsche tem* _____ *potência* _____ *o Ferrari.* (The Porsche has as much power as the Ferrari.)

4. *Meu computador tem* _____ *problemas* _____ *o seu.* (My computer has as many problems as yours.)

5. *Gilberto tem* _____ *talento* _____ *Chico.* (Gilberto has as much talent as Chico.)

Superlatives: The Best of the Best

TRACK 38

Now that you know how to compare two individuals or things, we can talk about comparing individuals or things to a whole group to which they belong. Superlatives are a way to make this comparison. Imagine that you are Goldilocks and you have come into the bears' house. If you had to compare the three beds, you would make a decision between the best one of the three. And if Goldilocks spoke Portuguese, she would say *Esta é a cama mais confortável das três* (This is the most comfortable bed of the three). Here is a summary of how superlatives are expressed in Portuguese.

Superlatives in Portuguese

[individual/thing]	is	the [category]	mais/menos de [quality]	[group]
Guga	*é*	*o tenista*	*mais famoso*	*do Brasil.*
Guga is the most famous tennis player of Brazil.				
São Paulo	*é*	*a cidade*	*mais populosa*	*da América do Sul.*
São Paulo is the most populated city in South America.				
Joaquim	*é*	*o aluno*	*menos aplicado*	*da classe.*
Joaquim is the least dedicated student of the class.				

Notice that the usage of the preposition *de* (of) + definite article results in a contraction such as *do* and *da* (of the) in Portuguese. Although most superlatives follow the structure above, there are some irregular superlatives in Portuguese. These are *o melhor* (the best), *o pior* (the worst), *o maior* (the biggest), and *o menor* (the smallest). Now, let's see if you have mastered the art of the superlatives!

EXERCISE: FILL IN THE SUPERLATIVE

Fill in the blanks with the best answer in the superlative sentences. Check your answers in Appendix C.

1. *O futebol é o esporte* _____ *popular* _____ *Brasil.* (Soccer is the most popular sport in Brazil.)

2. *Brasília é a capital* _____ *moderna* _____ *América Latina.* (Brasília is the most modern capital of Latin America.)

3. *Amália Rodrigues é a* _____ *canora de Fado* _____ *Portugal.*
(Amália Rodrigues is the best Fado singer of Portugal.)

EXERCISE: WRITE SUPERLATIVE SENTENCES

Use the elements given and write a superlative sentence (it doesn't matter if it's not true!). For example: *O Ferrari/carro/rápido/Europa* > *O Ferrari é o carro mais rápido da Europa.*

1. *O MacIntosh/computador/caro/mundo*

   _____

2. *Conan/comediante/engraçado/Estados Unidos*

   _____

3. *A feijoada/comida/famosa/Brasil*

   _____

Ownership and Possession

Possessives are words that explain who "owns" or "possesses" things. In English they are commonly used and also follow a gender and number system, at least for third person (notice the words "his," "her," and "their"). The Portuguese possessive system does the same, with some intricacies. First, let's present the possessives for first and second persons:

First and Second Person Possessives in Portuguese

Person	Pronoun	Possessive Forms	English
First Singular	eu	(o) meu [noun], (os) meus [noun]	"my"
		(a) minha [noun], (as) minhas [noun]	
Second	você	(o) seu [noun], (os) seus [noun]	"your"
		(a) sua [noun], (as) suas [noun]	
Second	tu	(o) teu [noun], (os) teus [noun]	"your"
		(a) tua [noun], (as) tuas [noun]	
First Plural	nós	(o) nosso [noun], (os) nossos [noun]	"our"
		(a) nossa [noun], (as) nossas [noun]	

The definite articles in parentheses are optional in Brazilian Portuguese.

Although it might seem overwhelming at first, you will soon realize that it all depends on the thing "owned," not the person who "owns" it, and the whole systems becomes much clearer. Since the form of the possessive depends on the noun that comes afterwards, it makes sense that there would be four forms, masculine and feminine, singular and plural, as in *meu, meus, minha, minhas* for "my." Also notice that the table gives both the *tu* and the *você* forms which refer to the second person singular pronoun "you." You might come across someone in Brazil asking you *Como é **teu** nome?* (What is your name?) and you can respond easily by starting with ***Meu** nome é...!*

EXERCISE: **WHO OWNS IT?**

Now try your hand at an exercise. Translate the following noun phrases using the correct first and second person possessive pronouns. Check your answers in Appendix C.

1. my pen: _____

2 your book: _____

3. my friends: _____

4. our parents: _____

5. your backpack: _____

6. our house: _____

7. your notebooks: _____

8. my sisters: _____

More Possessive Pronouns

Now let's turn our attention to the remaining possessive pronouns. These are somewhat different because they refer to the third person (he, she, it, they), and follow more colloquial rules. Here is a summary:

Third Person Possessive Pronouns in Portuguese

Pronoun	Possessive Forms	English
ele (he)	*o* [noun] *dele*	his [noun]
	a [noun] *dele*	his [noun]
	os [noun] *dele*	his [noun]
	as [noun] *dele*	his [noun]
ela (she)	*o* [noun] *dela*	her [noun]
	a [noun] *dele*	her [noun]
	os [noun] *dele*	her [noun]
	as [noun] *dele*	her [noun]

Third Person Possessive Pronouns in Portuguese

Pronoun	Possessive Forms	English
eles (they [men])	*o* [noun] *deles*	their [noun]
	a [noun] *deles*	their [noun]
	os [noun] *deles*	their [noun]
	as [noun] *deles*	their [noun]
elas (they [women])	*o* [noun] *delas*	their [noun]
	a [noun] *delas*	their [noun]
	os [noun] *delas*	their [noun]
	as [noun] *delas*	their [noun]

Notice that the position of the noun with respect to the possessive pronoun changes, as compared to the first and second person. When you talk about the third person (he, she, it, they) possessives, you are literally saying "the book of his" (e.g., *o livro dele*) and not "his book." Notice also that each "person" can own singular or plural things. Thus, we can say *os livros dele*, meaning "the books of his" or better yet "his books," as well as *o livro delas* (their books). With time you will be able to tackle this complex system and become a master at it! Let's see how much of it you have already understood.

EXERCISE: **TRANSLATION**

Translate the following noun phrases using the correct third person possessive pronouns. Check your answers in Appendix C.

1. Their (female) classes: _____

2. His computer: _____

3. Her pencil: _____

4. Their (male) house: _____

5. Her books: _____

6. Their (female) car: _____

7. His glasses: _____

8. Her purse: _____

CHAPTER 8

The Vocabulary of Numbers

NUMBERS ARE PERHAPS one of the first things you tackle when learning a new language. In this chapter you will become familiar with cardinal numbers (one, two, three, etc.) and ordinal numbers (first, second, third, etc.) in Portuguese. You will also see how these are important when you learn the days of the week and how to tell time. And don't forget the months and the seasons; these are all vocabulary of time.

Cardinal Numbers

These numbers are used for counting and expressing quantities. In Portuguese, the number one has two forms: *um* for masculine and *uma* for feminine. The same is true for the number two: *dois* and *duas*. The basic number sequence that you must learn is zero through fifteen. See the following table.

TRACK 39

Numbers Zero to Fifteen

zero	zero	ZEH-roh
one	um, uma	UHN, UHN-ah
two	dois, duas	DOY-sh, DOO-ahsh
three	três	TREYSH
four	quatro	KWA-troh
five	cinco	SIN-koo
six	seis	SEYSH
seven	sete	SEH-tchee, SHE-tee
eight	oito	OY-too
nine	nove	NOH-vee
ten	dez	DEH-ish
eleven	onze	OHN-zee
twelve	doze	DOH-zee
thirteen	treze	TREH-zee
fourteen	catorze	kah-TOHR-zee
fifteen	quinze	KEEN-zee

Notice that the number *sete* (seven) has variable pronunciation in different regions of Brazil. The speakers from the southeast, especially those from Rio de Janeiro, will have a more palatal variant (SEH-tchee), which is heard with the combinations *te* and *ti*, such as the word *tia* (aunt), pronounced TCHEE-ah. Now the next set of numbers is a combination of "ten" plus a unit number. See the following table:

TRACK 40

Numbers Sixteen to Nineteen

sixteen	*dezesseis*	deh-zeh-SEYSH
seventeen	*dezessete*	deh-zeh-SEH-tchee
eighteen	*dezoito*	deh-ZOY-too
nineteen	*dezenove*	deh-zeh-NOH-vee

Notice that the combination of *–ss–* indicates a soft pronunciation of an [s] sound in English, not a [z] sound that is associated with a *–s–* that is common between vowels. The next set of numbers is from *vinte* (twenty) to *cem* (one hundred). When we need to express the combination of tens and units, we simply use the word *e* (and) in between the numbers. See the following examples.

TRACK 41

Numbers Twenty to One Hundred

twenty	*vinte*	VEEN-tchee
twenty-one	*vinte e um, uma*	VEEN-tchee-ee-UHN, -UHN-ah
twenty-two	*vinte e dois, duas*	VEEN-tchee-ee-DOYSH, - DOO-ahsh
twenty-three	*vinte e três*	VEEN-tchee-ee-TREYSH
thirty	*trinta*	TREEN-tah
forty	*quarenta*	kwa-REHN-tah
fifty	*cinqüenta*	sin-KWEN-tah
sixty	*sessenta*	seh-SEHN-tah
seventy	*setenta*	seh-TEHN-tah
eighty	*oitenta*	oy-TEHN-tah
ninety	*noventa*	noh-VEHN-tah
one hundred	*cem*	SEH-in

After *cem* (one hundred), any combination of 100 plus another unit, such as 101, results in a change to *cento* (hundred) plus the word *e* followed by the unit. The same is repeated after each case. See the following examples.

one hundred and one	*cento e um, uma*	SEHN-too-ee-UHN, -UHN-ah
one hundred and ten	*cento e dez*	SEHN-too-ee-DEYSH
one hundred and eleven	*cento e onze*	SENH-too-ee-OHN-zee
one hundred and twenty-one	*cento e vinte e um, uma*	SEHN-too-ee-VEEN-tchee-ee-UHN, -UHN-ah

Starting at two hundred and up to nine hundred, the numbers have a masculine and a feminine form. These depend on what follows, if it is a masculine or a feminine noun. So, "two hundred students" could be *duzentos alunos* (two hundred [male] students) or *duzentas alunas* (two hundred [female] students). And don't forget that the rule for one and two still applied, with two forms. So, there could be *duzentas e trinta e uma páginas* (two hundred and thirty-one pages), where the word "page" is feminine, and thus the number one is expressed in the feminine form. See the next set of numbers below.

Numbers Two Hundred to Nine Hundred

TRACK 42

two hundred	*duzentos, duzentas*	doo-ZEHN-toos, doo-ZEHN-tahs
three hundred	*trezentos, trezentas*	treh-ZEHN-toos, treh-ZEHN-tahs
four hundred	*quatrocentos, quatrocentas*	kwa-troh-ZEHN-toos, kwa-troh-ZEHN-tahs
five hundred	*quinhentos, quinhentas*	keen-NHEN-toos, keen-NHEN-tahs
six hundred	*seiscentos, seiscentas*	seys-SEHN-toos, seys-SEHN-tahs
seven hundred	*setecentos, setecentas*	seh-the-SEHN-toos, seh-the-SEHN-tahs
eight hundred	*oitocentos, oitocentas*	oy-too-SEHN-toos, oy-too-SEHN-tahs
nine hundred	*novecentos, novecentas*	noh-vee-SEHN-toos, noh-vee-SEHN-tahs

After those, the number *mil* (one thousand) shows no variation; that is, there is no feminine counterpart. However, if the number ends in one, such as in one thousand and one, there is the normal feminine form of one, depending on the noun. An example is *mil e uma páginas* (one thousand and one pages), where the word "page" is feminine. See more examples below.

one thousand nine hundred	*mil e novecentos*
	meel-ee-noh-vee-SEHN-toos
one thousand nine hundred and two	*mil novecentos e dois*
	meel-noh-vee-SEHN-toos-ee-DOYSH
one thousand nine hundred and twenty-two	*mil novecentos e vinte e dois*
	meel-noh-vee-SEHN-toos-ee-VEEN-tchee-ee-DOYSH

Notice that if there is a need to use *e* (and) after the hundreds then the first *e* is dropped. Remember that in the case of the years that relate to the last millennium, we don't say "nineteen hundred" but rather "one thousand, nine hundred," and so forth.

In Portuguese (and in most other languages), a period is used after the thousands. So the number 1,400 in English is expressed as 1.400 in Portuguese. The reverse also happens in the case of fractions. The number *pi* is expressed as 3,1416 . . . with a comma, not a period, in Brazil!

You might not use the words *um milhão* (one million) or *um bilhão* (one billion) in Brazil, since inflation has been curbed in the past decades. But you might need to use them when referring to populations. These words match the English closely, unlike in Spanish dialects, where one billion is expressed as "one thousand million." Make sure to use the preposition *de* after these words and before nouns, such as in *dois milhões **de** pessoas* (two million people).

EXERCISE: TRANSLATION USING NUMBERS

Now let's try some practice. Write in the numbers in Portuguese followed by a translation of the words. Check your answers in Appendix C.

1. 15 notebooks:

    _____

2. 83 books:

    _____

3. 379 professors:

    _____

4. 761 female students:

    _____

5. 1.006 cars:

    _____

6. 432.578 people:

    _____

Ordinal Numbers

Ordinal numbers are used when you want to talk about sequences, such as first, second, third, and so on. Use these numbers to refer to kings, emperors and popes, such as D. Pedro II, pronounced *Dom Pedro segundo* (Pedro the Second), the second emperor of Brazil. The following are the ordinal numbers in Portuguese:

Ordinal Numbers

TRACK 43

Portuguese	English
primeiro	first
segundo	second
terceiro	third

Portuguese	English
quarto	fourth
quinto	fifth
sexto	sixth
sétimo	seventh
oitavo	eighth
nono	ninth
décimo	tenth
décimo-primeiro	eleventh
décimo-segundo	twelfth
vigésimo	twentieth

You might also hear *trigésimo* (thirtieth) and *quadragésimo* (fortieth) in more elevated sequences. As you can see from the table, at the eleventh number, you start with the word *décimo*, add a dash, and then add the ordinal number of the corresponding unit, such as in *décimo-quinto* (fifteenth). Make sure to match the ordinal number to the noun(s) it modifies, depending on gender. So, you should say *décimo-sexto andar* for (sixteenth floor), which is masculine and *décima-sexta cláusula* for (sixteenth clause), which refers to feminine noun.

The common abbreviations used for ordinal numbers (1st, 2nd, and 3rd) are different in Portuguese, as can be expected. When expressing abbreviated ordinal numbers, use the superscripts 1° (*primeiro*) or 1ª (*primeira*) depending on the gender or the noun. Use the same symbols for all sequences, 2° (*segundo*) and 2ª (*segunda*), and so on.

EXERCISE: **USING ORDINAL NUMBERS**

Okay, now let's see how you fare with an ordinal numbers exercise. Rewrite the expressions using the numbers for the following items. Check your answers in Appendix C.

1. *A 7ª maravilha do mundo* (the seventh wonder of the world)
2. *O 4° ciclo do inferno* (the fourth ring of hell)
3. *A 1ª lição* (the first lesson)
4. *A 5ª dinastia* (the fifth dynasty)
5. *O 20° tenista do ranking mundial* (the twentieth tennis player of the world ranking.)

Days of the Week

One of the most unique aspects of the Portuguese language has to do with the names of weekdays. We express the days of the week by using ordinal numbers followed by the word *feira*. The following table more clearly explains the origin of the names of the weekdays.

TRACK 44

Weekdays

English	Portuguese	Origin	Literal Translation
Sunday	*domingo*	Domenica	Day of the Lord
Monday	*segunda-feira*	Feria Secunda	Second Holy Day
Tuesday	*terça-feira*	Feria Tertia	Third Holy Day
Wednesday	*quarta-feira*	Feria Quarta	Fourth Holy Day
Thursday	*quinta-feira*	Feria Quinta	Fifth Holy Day
Friday	*sexta-feira*	Feria Sexta	Sixth Holy Day
Saturday	*sábado*	Shabbat	The Sabbath

This distinctive way of expressing weekdays came about because of a very influential bishop named Martinho de Dume, also known as Martinho de Braga. During his tenure as a Bishop of Braga, he considered it undignified for good Christians to say the names of weekdays by their original pagan names—*Lunae dies* (Day of the Moon), *Martis dies* (Day of Mars), *Mercurii dies* (Day of Mercury), *Jovis dies* (Day of Jovis or Jupiter), *Veneris dies* (Day of Venus), *Saturni dies* (Day of Saturn), and *Solis dies* (Day of the Sun). So, starting from Sunday, he devised the names *Prima Feria*, *Secunda Feria*, and so forth, for the days of the Holy Week. The current word *feira* is a linguistic corruption of *Feria*, which meant "Holy Day" or holiday, a day on which people should not work. Later, the first day (*Prima Feria*) or Sunday, was changed to *Domenica*, which is Latin for the "Day of the Lord." This meaning is also kept in Spanish, Italian, and French.

To form the plural of the days of the week, you should add an –s to both parts of the word: for example, *segundas-feiras* (Mondays) and *quartas-feiras* (Wednesdays). In spoken Portuguese it is very common to drop the word –*feira* and simply say *Eu estudo português nas terças e quintas* (I study Portuguese on Tuesdays and Thursdays).

To know what day it is you should ask *Que dia (da semana) é hoje?* (What day [of the week] is today?). The answer could be *É sexta!* (It's Friday!). Also when referring to a specific day of the week when asked *Quando você vai à igreja?* (When do you do to church?), the answer could be *no domingo* (on Sunday). For the other days of the week use the contraction *na* for the weekdays, as in *na segunda*, *na terça*, *na quarta*, and so on. And use *no sábado* to express "on Saturday."

Talking about Time

Que horas são? is the expression used to ask what time is it in Portuguese. If you are answering about a singular time (that is, if it's a certain hour, on the dot), you should say *São _____ horas*. We use the verb *são* (are) because the noun *horas* (hours) is in the plural form. But between 1:00 P.M. and 1:59 P.M. you should say *É uma hora* plus any minutes. Also use *É* if the time is noon or midnight.

Here are some examples.

TRACK 45

Telling Time in Portuguese

English	Portuguese
It's (twelve) noon.	*É meio-dia.*
It's (twelve) midnight.	*É meia-noite.*
It's 1:00 p.m.	*É uma hora (em ponto).*
It's 2:00 p.m.	*São duas horas.*
It's 2:15 p.m.	*São duas e quinze.*
It's 2:20 p.m.	*São duas e vinte.*
It's 6:30 p.m.	*São seis e meia./São seis e trinta.*
It's 6:40 p.m.	*São vinte para as sete./São seis e quarenta.*
It's 6:45 p.m.	*São quinze para as sete./São seis e quarenta e cinco.*

Notice that it is not necessary to say *horas* or *minutos* when telling time. In order to say that it's the time "on the dot," say *em ponto*. In addition, it is possible to say either "it's twenty minutes to four" or "it's three forty"; both ways are acceptable in colloquial speech. In Portuguese, speakers do not use the symbols A.M. and P.M., so they need to indicate the time of the day by using some extra words.

da manhã (in the morning)
da tarde (in the afternoon)
da noite (in the evening)
da madrugada (in the small hours of the morning)

It is also very common to use the 24-hour clock, or what is commonly known as "military time," instead of the added phrases *de manhã*, *da tarde*, and so on, in order to avoid confusion between morning, afternoon, and evening hours. Here are some examples:

The concert starts at 2200. (*O concerto começa* **às** *vinte e duas horas.*)
The movie starts at 3:30 P.M. (*O filme começa* **às** *quinze e trinta.*)
The class ends at 5:45 P.M. (*A aula termina* **às** *dezessete e quarenta e cinco.*)

As you can see from these examples, to say when something ends or starts you have to use the contraction *às* (at) plus the time. If it's one o'clock, use the singular *à* (at) plus the time. For example, to answer the question *Quando começa a peça de teatro?* (When does the play start?) a person might answer *Começa às vinte horas* (It starts at 8 P.M.).

The Months and Seasons

The months or *os meses* in Portuguese are very easy to learn because they sound a lot like their English equivalents. See the following list below:

TRACK 46

The Months

Portuguese	English
janeiro	January
fevereiro	February
março	March
abril	April
maio	May
junho	June
julho	July
agosto	August
setembro	September
outubro	October
novembro	November
dezembro	December

Notice that the months are not written in capital letters, as they are in English. All except the first of the month—*É primeiro de agosto* (It's the first of August)—are expressed with the verb *são* as in *São vinte e seis de julho* (It's July 26th). Also notice that even though the day in English is expressed in ordinal numbers (first, second, 26th, and so on), they are normal cardinal numbers in Portuguese. And, the day comes first, followed by the month, which is how you might answer the question *Que dia é hoje?* (What day is today?).

The months are usually associated with seasons, and since Brazil is below the equator, these happen in different months as compared to the United States. See below.

The Seasons in Brazil

TRACK 47

Season	English	Months
o verão	the summer	*dezembro, janeiro, fevereiro*
o outono	the fall	*março, abril, maio*
o inverno	the winter	*junho, julho, agosto*
a primavera	the spring	*setembro, outubro, novembro*

Since parts of Brazil are very tropical, the changing of the seasons is not nearly as evident as in countries such as the United States or Canada. In fact, sometimes in the northeastern parts of Brazil there is basically a raining or monsoon season, followed by a drought or dry season. When traveling abroad to countries below the equator, always check with the available online resources to find out which "season" they are in.

Practice with Numbers

Now that you've learned all about using numbers to talk about time, days, months, and seasons, let's see what you remember. The following three exercises will test your knowledge; you can check your answers in Appendix C at the back of the book.

EXERCISE: DO YOU HAVE THE TIME?

TRACK 48

Listen to the time said on the audio CD and circle the written equivalent below.

1. 2:30   12:30

2. 6:40   7:20

3. 7:10   1710

4. 12 A.M.   12 P.M.

EXERCISE: WHAT IS THE DATE?

TRACK 49

Listen to the CD and circle the date that you hear.

1. 01/04   01/05

2. 11/08   08/11

3. 07/06   06/07

4. 31/03   31/05

EXERCISE: HOLIDAYS

Write out the dates in Portuguese for the following holidays.

1. *O Dia da Indenpendência dos Estados Unidos* (Independence Day):

_____

2. *O Dia dos Namorados* (Valentine's Day):

_____

3. *O dia de São Patrício* (Saint Patrick's Day):

_____

4. *O (Dia de) Natal* (Christmas Day):

_____

CHAPTER 9

First Conjugation Verbs

THE VERBS ARE one of the most important parts of the grammar of a language. Once you learn how to conjugate the basic verbs, you will start making a lot of sense. In this chapter you will learn the first conjugation, or the formation of verbs that end in *–ar* in the infinitive. We will start with regular verbs and move on to verbs with prepositions. Using all those verbs with the vocabulary of "going places" will help you form great sentences in Portuguese!

Regular –*AR* Verbs

There are four main categories of verbs in Portuguese, and the first and most important one of them is the group of verbs that end in –*ar* in the infinitive (for example, *falar* [to speak]). The infinitive can be understood as the "default" form of the verb, or the form that can change depending on the grammatical person. In English, this is comparable to the "to" form, as in "to walk" or "to speak." The other categories are the verbs that end in –*er* (*comer* [to eat]),–*ir* (*dormir* [to sleep]), and a smaller category of verbs that end in –*or* (*compor* [to compose]). We will review these other categories in the next chapters. For now, look at the conjugation below which is the model that should be followed for all verbs that end in –*ar*, in the present tense.

TRACK 50

Falar (to speak) in the Present Tense

Portuguese	English
eu falo	I speak
você fala	you speak [one person]
ele/ela fala	he/she speaks
nós falamos	we speak
vocês falam	you (all) speak [more than one person]
eles/elas falam	they speak

Notice that *elas* refers to "they" as in all females, and *eles* refers to all males or a mixed group of persons. The conjugation for the *tu* is not mentioned above (*tu falas* [you speak]) because if you use *você* (you) in order to address one person you will be understood by all speakers. You might hear the *tu* form, and people will probably conjugate it using the *você* ending: *tu f'ala* (you speak), though this is considered ungrammatical by many educated speakers. Here is a list of common verbs that end in –*ar*:

TRACK 51

Common Verbs Ending in –AR

Portuguese	English
acabar	to finish
achar	to find, to think
ajudar	to help
colocar	to put, to place
começar	to start
comprar	to buy
descansar	to rest
estudar	to study
ficar	to be (situated), to stay
jogar	to play (a sport or a game)
morar	to live
pagar	to pay
tocar	to play (an instrument), to touch
tomar	to drink
trabalhar	to work
viajar	to travel

In order to learn these verbs, try to first memorize them by putting the verbs into lists or categories. Can you divide the above list into "things that I do often" and "things that I rarely do"? How about dividing the list into "action verbs" and "mental verbs"? Whatever categories you chose to organize the verbs, the important thing is that you find a way to process and arrange these new pieces of information in your brain. Once you have done this, it will be easier to retrieve the information later.

EXERCISE: FILL IN THE BLANK

Complete the blanks with the correct form of the verb, depending on the subject. Check your answers in Appendix C.

1. *A criança* _____ *futebol.* (The child plays soccer.)

2. *Os jovens* _____ *clarinete.* (The youngsters play clarinet.)

3. *Nós* _____ *português e inglês.* (We speak Portuguese and English.)

4. *Você* _____ *pão todo dia?* (Do you buy bread every day?)

5. *Vocês* _____ *no Brasil?* (Do you (pl.) live in Brazil?)

EXERCISE: MAKE A MATCH

Match the sentence with its missing verb by writing the letter in the blank space.

1. *O concerto* _____ *às cinco horas.*   (a) estudam (study)

2. *Você* _____ *basquetebol?*   (b) pago (pay)

3. *Nós* _____ *em Ipanema.*   (c) joga (play)

4. *Eu* _____ *a conta, sempre!*   (d) moramos (live)

5. *Os alunos* _____ *muitas horas por dia.*   (e) começa (starts)

Verbs with Prepositions

Some verbs that end in *–ar* have prepositions that normally go with them. It is possible that they do not correspond to the same prepositions, or that they even need those prepositions in English. Here are a selected few:

Verbs that Need Prepositions

TRACK 52

Portuguese	English
chamar de	to call [someone or something a name]
entrar em	to enter
gostar de	to like
olhar para	to look at
precisar de	to need

It should be noted that the use of *chamar de* is not as common as the more frequent of *chamar-se*, the reflexive verb used to introduce oneself. In the latter, you don't need a preposition, just the reflexive pronoun as in *Como você se chama?* (What do you call yourself?) and *Eu me chamo José* (I call myself José). Also important is the fact that the prepositions often "contract" with articles to make up some interesting words:

Ele entra **num** *carro.* [*em* + *um* = *num*] (He gets into a car.)
Elas gostam **da** *música.* [*de* + *a* = *da*] (They like the music.)
Eu preciso **dum** *lápis.* [*de* + *um* = *dum*] (I need a pencil.)

EXERCISE: CONJUGATE THE VERB

Try your hand at this exercise for prepositional verbs in Portuguese. Conjugate the verb in parentheses and make any changes needed. Check your answers in Appendix C.

Model: *Você (gostar de) a aula de português?* (Do you like the Portuguese class?) > *Você* **gosta da** *aula de português?*

1. *Ele (precisar de) o dicionário.* (He needs the dictionary.)

   _____

2. *Você (chamar) essa fruta (de) laranja?* (You call this fruit an orange?)

   _____

3. *Eles (gostar de) a comida.* (They like the food.)

   _____

4. *Os alunos (entrar em) a biblioteca.* (The students enter the library.)

   _____

5. *Eu não (entrar em) um banco sem documentos.* (I don't enter a bank without documents.)

   _____

Vocabulary: Going Places

In order to use most of these new verbs, you should learn the names of many places in Portuguese. In this section we will find out the places where you can do things such as *comprar* (to buy), *jogar* (to play), and *estudar* (to study). Let's now match verbs and places!

TRACK 53

Common Places

Portuguese	English
o açougue	the butcher shop
a banca de revista	the newsstand
o banco	the bank
o cabelereiro	the hairdresser
a farmácia/a drogaria	the drugstore
a feira	the street market
o lava a seco	the dry cleaners
a livraria	the bookstore
a loja	the store
a padaria	the bakery
o restaurante	the restaurant
a papelaria	the stationary store
o salão de beleza	the beauty salon
a sapataria	the shoe store
o shopping	the mall
o supermercado	the supermarket

As you can see, many words are cognates; for example, *banco* (bank), *farmácia* (pharmacy), and *restaurante* (restaurant). There are some words that come from the English language such as *shopping*, which means "mall," and the word *cyber café*. The *açougue* is not a common place anymore because most *supermercados* sell fresh meat and poultry in more hygienic conditions. But you can still find some *açougues* in many cities and towns. There are many *bancas de revistas* (newsstands) all over big cities in Brazil where you can by the latest magazines and newspapers. They also sell phone cards, which are needed in order to use the public phones. In drugstores, usually only pharmaceutical products are sold, except for the occasional soap or lotion. There are many *padarias* (bakeries) around, sometimes two on the same street, and there you can buy fresh bread every day. These *padarias* double as *pastelarias* (pastry shops), where you can also buy all kinds of baked goods. Most men still go to the *barbeiro* (barber) instead of the *cabelereiro* (hairdresser) to get a haircut. And most establishments advertise themselves as *unisex*, meaning they can take care of both sexes, just to make sure that the male clientele also patronize them. Nowadays, supermarkets in Brazil sell fresh fruits and vegetables. But you can still find Saturday or mid-week *feiras* (street markets) in most cities, where you can buy anything from edibles to arts and crafts. Finally, the word *loja* applies to any store, so you can say *loja de sapatos* for a shoe store or *loja de roupa* for a clothing store. The following is a list of places and some of the products that are usually associated with these places:

TRACK 54

- *Supermercado: queijo* (cheese), *pão* (bread), *leite* (milk), *ovos* (eggs), *feijão* (beans), *arroz* (rice)
- *Padaria: pão* (bread), *bolos* (cakes), *bolachas* (crackers), *leite* (milk), *queijo* (cheese), *presunto* (ham), *frios* (cold cuts)
- *Livraria: livros* (books), *revistas* (magazines), *CDs*, *jornais* (newspapers)
- *Papelaria: papel* (paper), *canetas* (pens), *lápis* (pencils), *cartões* (cards)
- *Banca: jornais* (newspapers), *revistas* (magazines), *cartões telefônicos* (phone cards)
- *Farmácia: remédios* (medicine), *perfumes* (perfume), *loções* (lotions)

EXERCISE: WHERE CAN I BUY...?

Notice that many foods or products can be bought in a variety of places. Now try to determine where you can buy these products in the following exercise. Write down a couple of places where you can buy these products. Check your answers in Appendix C.

1. *pão* (bread): _____, _____

2. *revistas* (magazines): _____, _____

3. *leite* (milk): _____, _____

4. *frutas* (fruit): _____, _____

5. *bolos* (cakes): _____, _____

Vocabulary: Routine Activities

In a normal day in Brazil, many activities that you perform might be first conjugation verbs. Take a look at some of them below.

Routine Activities

Portuguese	English
acordar(–se)	to wake up
almoçar	to have lunch
brincar com os filhos	to play with the children
escovar os dentes	brush (the) teeth
descansar	to rest
jantar	to have dinner
levantar(–se)	to get up (from bed)
pegar os filhos	to pick up the children
tomar café (da manhã)	to have breakfast (literally to drink coffe in the a.m.)
tomar banho	to take a shower
trabalhar	to work
voltar pra casa	to go back home

Notice that all of these verbs all end in *–ar*, but that does not mean that all routine verbs do so. There are plently of verbs about routine—*assistir televisão* (to watch television), *ir para a cama* (go to bed), *fazer a barba* (to shave)—that end in another way and thus belong to the second or third conjugations. You will see these verbs in later chapters.

EXERCISE: PUT THEM IN ORDER

Try to put these sentences in a logical sequence by writing the numbers in the correct order in the spaces provided. Check your answers in Appendix C.

1. *Anne almoça com os amigos.* _____

2. *Anne brinca com os gatos.* _____

3. *Anne volta para casa.* _____

4. *Anne trabalha na universidade.* _____

5. *Anne se acorda as 8 da manhã.* _____

EXERCISE: WHAT IS YOUR SCHEDULE LIKE?

Use the *eu* form of the verb (first person singular) to write five sentences about your routine in Portuguese.

1. _____

2. _____

3. _____

4. _____

5. _____

CHAPTER 10

Second Conjugation and Beyond

AFTER THE FIRST conjugation comes the second. In this chapter you will learn how to write the verbs that end in *–er*, *–ir*, and even the less common *–or*. We will also practice with very common second conjugation verbs, which are a bit irregular. We will finish up with the vocabulary related to family and family relations so that you can use the just-learned verb ter (to have) with these words. Have fun!

Regular *–ER* and *–IR* Verbs

Verbs that end in *–er* when written in the infinitive are called the "second conjugation." By the same token, verbs that end in *–ir* are named "third conjugation." Beyond that, there are some verbs in Portuguese that end in *–or* in the infinitive. Now that you know how the verbs of the first conjugation are written, here are the verbs from the second and third conjugations.

TRACK 55

Comer (to eat) in the Present Tense

Portuguese	English
eu como	I eat
você come	you eat [one person]
ele/ela come	he/she eats
nós comemos	we eat
vocês comem	you (all) eat [more than one person]
eles/elas comem	they eat

As with the verb *falar* (to speak) of the first conjugation, the *tu* (you [singular]) form is conjugated as *tu comes* (you eat). Again, it is not necessary to learn this form because if you use *você* you will be undertood. But you might hear the form in some parts of Brazil. What about the third conjugation? The good news is that except for the *nós* form, it is exactly the same as the second conjugation. See the following table.

TRACK 56

Abrir (to open) in the Present Tense

Portuguese	English
eu abro	I open
você abre	you open [one person]
ele/ela abre	he/she opens
nós abrimos	we open
vocês abrem	you (all) open [more than one person]
eles/elas abrem	they open

The basic conjugation rule states that in order to say verbs correctly, you have to drop the –*er* of the infinitive and add the endings above, according to the subject. Below is a list of common verbs that end in –*er* and –*ir* and follow this same rule.

Common Verbs Ending in –*ER*

TRACK 57

Portuguese	English
aprender	to learn
atender	to answer the phone, to wait on
beber	to drink
comer	to eat
compreender	to understand, to comprehend
correr	to run
entender	to understand
escolher	to choose
escrever	to write
ler	to read
querer	to want
receber	to receive
responder	to answer
vender	to sell
viver	to live

Common Verbs Ending in –*IR*

TRACK 58

Portuguese	English
aplaudir	to applaud
assistir (a)	to attend, to watch
competir	to compete
conseguir	to achieve, to get

Common Verbs Ending in –*IR*

Portuguese	English
construir	to construct
curtir	to enjoy [slang]
dormir	to sleep
exigir	to demand
impedir	to impede
investir	to invest
partir	to leave
permitir	to allow
reagir	to react
rir	to laugh
transferir	to transfer

Just as you did with the previous chapter, try to put these verbs into separate categories, such as active versus passive verbs or even positive versus negative sounding verbs. Categorizing new vocabulary according to your own world view helps you to truly learn a language.

EXERCISE: FILL IN THE VERB

Try your hand at these exercises to practice your verbs even more. Complete the blanks with the correct form of the verb, depending on the subject. Check your answers in Appendix C.

1. *A criança* _____ *o sanduíche.* (The child eats the sandwich.)

2. *Os jovens* _____ *o filme.* (The youngsters watch the movie.)

3. *Nós* _____ *oito horas por dia.* (We sleep eight hours a day.)

4. *Você* _____ *nos Estados Unidos?* (Do you live in the United States?)

5. *Vocês* _____ *às perguntas?* (Do you [pl.] answer the questions?)

EXERCISE: **THE RIGHT MATCH**

Match the sentence with its missing verb by writing the letter in the blank space.

1. *Minha amiga* _____ *o telefone imediatamente.*

2. *Essa livraria* _____ *livros e revistas?*

3. *Nós sempre* _____ *neste restaurante.*

4. *Eu* _____ *amanhã para o Rio!*

5. *Os amigos* _____ *muito com a comédia.*

   (a) comemos (eat)   *(d) vende* (sell)

   (b) parto (leave)   *(e) atende* (answer)

   (c) riem (laugh)

Special –*IR* Verbs

All the verbs similar to *servir* (to serve) and *dormir* (to sleep), which have these same vowels underline before the last syllable, undergo a special change, aside from the regular conjugation. This change is regular for all of this type of verb in the first person singular or the *eu* (I) form. Below is a model of this conjugation.

TRACK 59

Special Verb: *Servir* (to serve)

Portuguese	English
eu sirvo	I serve
você serve	you serve
ele/ela serve	he/she serves
nós servimos	we serve
vocês servem	you (all) serve
eles/elas servem	they serve

Other verbs that follow the same model are: *mentir*, meaning "to tell a lie" (*eu minto*); *preferir*, meaning "to prefer" (*eu prefiro*); *repetir*, meaning "to repeat" (*eu repito*), and *seguir*, meaning "to follow" (*eu sigo*).

The next table shows the other special *–ir* verb.

TRACK 60

Special Verb: *Dormir* (to sleep)

Portuguese	English
eu durmo	I sleep
você dorme	you sleep
ele/ela dorme	he/she sleeps
nós dormimos	we sleep
vocês dormem	you (all) sleep
eles/elas dormem	they sleep

A few verbs have the vowel *–u–* in the infinitive, and their conjugation is somewhat of the flipside of the previous ones. Instead of only the *eu* form changing, every other person changes, while *eu* and *nós* keep the same regular vowel of the infinitive. Here is a model of this kind of verb.

TRACK 61

Special Verb: *Subir* (to go up)

Portuguese	English
eu subo	I go up
você sobe	you go up
ele/ela sobe	he/she goes up
nós subimos	we go up
vocês sobem	you (all) go up
eles/elas sobem	they go up

EXERCISE: **REGULAR AND SPECIAL VERBS**

Let's see what you have learned. Try to complete the following exercises. Fill in the blanks with the correct conjugations of the verbs in parenthesis. Check your answers in Appendix C.

1. *O garçom* _____ *a cerveja no restaurante,*

   e eu _____ *vinho em casa. (servir)*

2. *Eu* _____ *as escadas e a secretária* _____ *pelo*

   elevador. (subir)

3. *Meus amigos* _____ *oito horas por dia,*

   mas eu só _____ *seis horas. (dormir)*

4. *A aluna* _____ *as frases, e eu* _____

   a tarefa de casa. (repetir)

5. *Eu não* _____ *muito, mas minha irmã* _____

   demais! (mentir)

To Go and To Come: *Ir* and *Vir*

Two very common verbs in Portuguese (as well as in English) are *ir* (to go) and *vir* (to come). They can be used with direction prepositions, *a* or *para*, both meaning "to" or "toward." Here is a sample dialogue:

Q: Márcia: *Oi, Júlio, tudo bem?* (Hi Julio, how is it going?)
A: Júlio: *Tudo bem, Márcia.* (All right, Marcia.)
Q: Márcia: *Para onde você **vai**?* (Where are you going?)
A: Júlio: ***Vou** para o clube, fazer ginástica.* (I'm going to the gym, to do a workout.)
Q: Márcia: *Que legal, você gosta do clube?* (Great, do you like the club?)

A: Júlio: *Eu adoro, mas não **vou** com freqüência.* (I love it, but I don't go often.)
Q: Márcia: *Eu também não.* (Neither do I.)
A: Júlio: *Então **vamos** juntos?* (So let's go together?)
Q: Márcia: *Opa, tá combinado!* (Hey, it's a date!)

Here is the full conjugation for the verb *ir* (to go).

TRACK 62

The Verb *Ir* (to go)

Portuguese	English
eu vou	I go
você vai	you go
ele/ela vai	he/she goes
nós vamos	we go
vocês vão	you (all) go
eles/elas vão	they go

You will use this verb a lot in Portuguese. In addition, much like in English, this verb is used in constructing the future tense.

Future Tense with *Ir*

Ir [conjugated]	+VERB [infinitive]	Translation
eu vou	*falar*	I'm going to speak
você vai	*dormir*	You're going to sleep
nós vamos	*beber*	We're going to drink
elas vão	*jogar*	They're going to play

Use the present tense of the verb *ir* and add the infinitive of the verb, as in English "going to + verb," and you're done! There is another future tense in Portuguese, which is not a combination of verbs, but a "one-word" tense. We will look at that conjugation in upcoming chapters. At this point, just know that the future with *ir* is the most common future structure spoken.

This same kind of future can also be expressed using the above structure and the verb *vir* (to come). Here is the full conjugation of this verb in the present tense.

The Verb *Vir* (to come)

Portuguese	English
eu venho	I come
você vem	you come
ele/ela vem	he/she comes
nós vimos	we come
vocês vêm	you (all) come
eles/elas vêm	they come

In English you could also imply future if you say "I'm *coming* to see," for example, as well as "I'm going to see." In Portuguese the same is true for the verb *vir* (to come). But most of the time you will use this verb by itself to ask where people come from, as in the following dialogue.

Q: Jonas: *De onde você vem?* (Where are you coming from?)
A: Cleuza: *Eu? Venho da feira, e você?* (Me? I'm coming from the market, how about you?)
Q: Jonas: *Venho do banco.* (I'm coming from the bank.)
A: Cleuza: *Ótimo, então você tem mais dinheiro do que eu.* (Great, so you have more money than I do!)

The most important aspect to remember is that the verb *vir* (to come) is usually followed by the preposition *de* (from), which in combination with an article—*o* or *a*—changes, as the dialogue above indicates.

EXERCISE: USING *Ir* AND *Vir*

Now try to see how much you got from this famous pair of verbs. Fill in the blanks with the appropriate verb. Check your answers in Appendix C.

1. *Eu* _____ *do cabelereiro.* (I come from the hairdresser.)

2. *As garotas* _____ *para a casa.* (The girls go/are going home.)

3. *Nós* _____ *do banco.* (We come from the bank.)

4. *Meus amigos* _____ *para a escola todo dia.* (My friends go to school every day.)

5. *Eu* _____ *para o trabalho de carro.* (I go to work by car.)

6. *Os vizinhos* _____ *do parque.* (The neighbors come from the park.)

To Have: *Ter*

TRACK 64

Two verbs that are very common and used in Portuguese are *ter* (to have) and *ver* (to see). *Ter* in particular can be used in many different situations. See the full conjugation in the present tense below:

The Verb *Ter* (to have)

Portuguese	English
eu tenho	I have
você tem	you have
ele/ela tem	he/she has
nós temos	we have
vocês têm	you (all) have
eles/elas têm	they have

Notice that the verb is actually irregular, as compared to the other *–er* verbs. But since it is so frequently used, it is learned very fast. The pronunciation for the third person singular *tem* (has) and plural *têm* (have) are exactly the same, as you might have noticed when listening to the CD. As in English, this verb conveys the notion of possession of or relationship to either a concrete or abstract entity. See the following examples.

A professora tem muitos alunos. (The teacher has a lot of students.)
Eu tenho um livro interessante. (I have an interesting book.)
Meus amigos têm meu número de telefone. (My friends have my phone number.)
A aluna tem uma prova amanhã. (The student has an exam tomorrow.)

Aside from expressing possession of or relationship to, this verb is also used when describing people, in sentences such as *Ele tem olhos verdes* (He has green eyes), and *Ela tem cabelo castanho* (She has brown hair), for example.

There is, also, an impersonal usage of *ter*. By impersonal we mean that there is no clear subject, and the sentence is normally translated as "there is/are." This usage is also referred to as the "existential" use of *ter*. Use this verb when you want to report on what "exists" in some place or situation, as in the following sample sentences:

Tem um livro em cima da mesa. (There is a book on the table.)
Tem muitos alunos na sala de aula. (There are many students in the classroom.)
Tem muita gente no banco. (There are a lot of people in the bank.)
Tem uma padaria aqui perto. (There is a bakery near here.)

Notice that the verb does not change, regardless of the number of the noun that follows; it's always the third person singular form, *tem*.

Finally, the verb *ter* can be used within a structure to mean "obligation." In this case, it is very similar to the structure in English "have to," as in the examples that follow:

Obligation: *Ter que* + Verb

[subject]	Ter [conjugated]	que	verb [infinitive]	
Eu	*tenho*	*que*	*comer*	*verduras.*
I have to eat vegetables.				

Obligation: *Ter que* + Verb

[subject]	Ter [conjugated]	que	verb [infinitive]
Você	*tem*	*que*	*assinar os documentos.*
You have to sign the documents.			
Nós	*temos*	*que*	*dormir oito horas.*
We have to sleep eight hours.			

Notice that the first verb, *ter*, is conjugated according to the person. The second verb is not conjugated—it's in the infinitive. Try to complete the following exercises using the verb *ter* (to have).

Exercise: Using *Ter*

Fill in the blanks with the correct form of the verb *ter* (to have). Check your answers in Appendix C.

1. *Eu* _____ *dois carros.* (I have two cars.)

2. *Minha amiga* _____ *pouca paciência.* (My friend has little patience.)

3. *Nós* _____ *uma casa no Rio.* (We have a house in Rio.)

4. *Eles não* _____ *aula na sexta.* (They don't have class on Friday.)

5. *O menino* _____ *olhos azuis.* (The boy has blue eyes.)

6. _____ *duas janelas na sala.* (There are two windows in the room.)

EXERCISE: I HAVE TO . . .

Write down two obligations, or things that you "have to do," in the upcoming year. Follow the model below. Use some of the verbs and expressions in the box. If you need more words, check the English-Portuguese glossary or your dictionary.

Model: *Eu tenho que estudar muito.* (I have to study a lot.)

> *cozinhar mais* (to cook more) *fazer exercícios* (to exercise)
> *comer bem* (to eat right) *sair menos* (to go out less)
> *ler um livro* (to read a book) *passar numa prova* (to pass a test)
> *arrumar um emprego* (to find a job) *comprar um carro* (to buy a car)

1. _____

2. _____

Vocabulary: Family Relations

One of the most useful batches of vocabulary you will learn in a second language includes the names of family relations. The following are some of the basic words:

TRACK 65

Family Relations

Portuguese	English
pai	father
papai	dad, daddy
mãe	mother
mamãe	mom, mommy
filho	son
filha	daughter
irmão	brother
irmã	sister
primo	cousin (male)
prima	cousin (female)
tio	uncle
tia	aunt
avô	grandfather

Family Relations

Portuguese	English
vovô	grandpa
avó	grandmother
vovó	grandma, granny
neto	grandson
neta	grandaughther
bisavô	great-grandfather
bisavó	great-grandmother
sobrinho	nephew
sobrinha	niece
padrasto	stepfather
madrasta	stepmother
padrinho	godfather
madrinha	godmother
afilhado	godson
afilhada	goddaughter

Remember, as with any other list of words in a second language, try to put them in categories. Perhaps list the relations that you do have and the ones that you do not. Another practice tip is to list the names of all your family members according to their family relation. The following is a list of additional relatives:

More Relations

Portuguese	English
marido, esposo	husband
mulher, esposa	wife
sogro	father-in-law
sogra	mother-in-law
genro	son-in-law

More Relations

Portuguese	English
nora	daughter-in-law
cunhado	brother-in-law
cunhada	sister-in-law
namorado	boyfriend
namorada	girlfriend
noivo	fiancé, groom
noiva	fiancée, bride

Always use the family relations by adding the possessive adjective along: say *meu pai* for "my father" and *minha mãe* for "my mother." The plural of some of these words usually takes the masculine form: *meus pais* means "my parents" (not "my fathers"!), *meus avós* means "my grandparents," and *meus filhos* means "my children," including both males and the females. If only females are included, then use the feminine plural form, as in *minhas filhas* (my daughters), *minhas netas* (my granddaughters), *minhas sobrinhas* (my nieces), and so forth. Careful with a common false cognate that stumps students: *meus parentes* means "my relatives," not my parents.

What about a person's marital status? In Brazil the *estado civil* has to do with a person's civil status before the law. Here are some basic vocabulary words to help convey civil status:

Civil Status

Portuguese	English
solteiro, solteira	single
casado, casada	married
separado, separada	separated
divorciado, divorciada	divorced
viúvo, viúva	widower, widow

One important thing to remember is that in Portuguese we do not use the "apostrophe" to express possession. So, if you want to say, for example, "my brother's wife" you would have to say *a esposa do meu irmão* or "the spouse of my brother," literally. Make sure that when you do so, you make any changes to the preposition *de* (of), as in the example *a irmã da minha mãe* ([the sister of my mother] or [my aunt])! Complete the following exercises to test your knowledge of the family relations in Portuguese.

EXERCISE: WHO IS IT?

Complete the blanks with the correct family name. Check your answers in Appendix C.

1. *O filho do meu filho é o meu* _____ .

2. *A irmã da minha mãe é a minha* _____ .

3. *Os filhos dos meus tios são os meus* _____ .

4. *A mãe da minha mãe é a minha* _____ .

5. *Os pais dos meu pai são os meus* _____ .

6. *O marido da minha irmã é o meu* _____ .

EXERCISE: WRITE A DESCRIPTION

Read the following description and write a similar one, based on your own family.

Oi, meu nome é Júlia. Minha família é pequena. Geraldo é o meu pai, Cristina é a minha mãe, e Orlando é o meu irmão. Eu não tenho irmãs. Meu primo favorito é Cláudio, e a minha tia favorita é Roseane. Eu também adoro minha avó Ritinha.

_____

_____

_____

_____

_____

CHAPTER 11

Important Verbs to Know

THOUGH YOU'VE ALREADY become acquainted with a number of Portuguese verbs, there are some verbs that are important enough to be introduced separately. They are *haver* (to exist/have), *fazer* (to do), *acabar* (to finish), and the duo *saber* and *conhecer* (to know). You'll become a whiz in Portuguese once you master these frequently used verbs.

To Be or To Exist: *Haver*

One of the most common verbs in Portuguese (as well as in English) is the verb "to have." In the previous chapter you learned how to use *ter* in expressing possession, obligation, or simply existence. The verb *haver* used to have the same function of *ter* in many instances, but now it has a more specialized usage. Here is the conjugation of *haver*:

The Verb *Haber*

Conjugated	Verb Tense	English
há	present indicative	there is/there are
havia	imperfect	there was/there were
houve	preterite	there was/there were
haverá	future	there will be
tinha havido	present perfect	there had been
haja	present subjunctive	there is/are
houvesse	imperfect subjunctive	there was/were
houver	future subjunctive	there will be
haveria	conditional	there would be

You will probably only use a couple of the forms above initially. The verb does not have the traditional subject pronoun conjugations, and it basically expresses the idea of "there is/there are," also called the existential use. Third person singular forms are used in both singular and plural contexts, as in the following examples.

TRACK 66

Há muitas pessoas na rua. (There are lots of people in the street.)
Não houve possibilidade de vê-lo. (There was no possibility to see him.)
Haja paciência com aquele menino! ([One should] have patience with that boy!)

The verb is also used as an auxiliary verb in compound verbal phrases, but it is less used nowadays in Brazilian Portuguese. Examples are *eu havia feito* (I had done), which is normally said with the verb *ter* in conversational Brazilian Portuguese, as in *eu tinha feito* (I had done). In some more traditional grammars both verbs are listed as helping verbs in the same compound structures! Here are some more examples with the verb *haver*:

Ela havia feito um bolo. (She had made a cake.)
Eles haviam comprado um carro. (They had bought a car.)

The form of the verb following *haver* is called the past participle. This form also exists in English, such as "done" and "written." Sometimes both the past and the past participle are the same form: "put." This might produce confusion for English speakers). But the past participles in Portuguese are very different and will be explained in a later chapter.

To Make or To Do: *Fazer*

One of the most useful verbs in Portuguese is the verb *fazer*, which is used in many idiomatic expressions. Below is the conjugation for this irregular (but very frequent) verb:

The Verb *Fazer* (to make, to do)

Subject	Present	English	Preterite	English
eu	*faço*	I do	*fiz*	I did
você	*faz*	you do	*fez*	you did
ele/ela	*faz*	he/she does	*fez*	he/she did
nós	*fazemos*	we do	*fizemos*	we did
vocês	*fazem*	you do	*fizeram*	you did
eles /elas	*fazem*	they do	*fizeram*	they did

Here are some sample dialogues used with this verb:

Ele fez o dever de casa? (Did he do the homework?)
Sim, fez. E você? (Yes, he did. And you?)
Eu ainda não fiz. (I didn't do it yet.)
Vamos fazer juntos? (You want to do it together?)
Sim, mas faz tanto sol lá fora! (Yes, but it's so sunny outside!)

Expressions with *Fazer*

You might have noticed that in the last dialogue we expressed the weather with the *fazer* verb. Here are other weather or climate expressions that take this verb:

Expressing Weather with *Fazer*

Portugese	English
Faz (muito) sol.	It's (very) sunny
Faz (muito) frio.	It's (very) cold
Faz (muito) calor.	It's (very) hot

Not all expressions of weather employ the verb *fazer*. Here are other expressions:

Expressing Weather

Portugese	English
Neva (muito).	It snows (a lot).
Chove (muito).	It rains (a lot).
Venta (muito).	It is windy (a lot).

Other expressions with the verb *fazer* probably make very little sense when translated literally to English. Here are some of those expressions, which are very common in Brazilian Portuguese:

Expressions with *Fazer*

Portuguese	English
fazer anos	to celebrate one's birthday; literally, "to make years"
fazer a barba	to shave; literally, "to make the beard"
fazer de conta	to pretend; literally, to make count
fazer compras	to shop; literally, to make purchases
fazer falta	to be missed; to lack
fazer greve	to go on strike; literally, "to make strike"
fazer as pazes	to make peace

EXERCISE: MULTIPLE CHOICE

Choose one of the choices for each question. Check your answers in Appendix C.

1. The workers are getting very low wages, so...
   a. *eles fazem greve.*
   b. *eles fazem a barba.*
   c. *eles fazem anos.*
   d. *eles fazem de conta.*
2. My nephew is having all of his friends over for a party.
   a. *Ele faz de conta.*
   b. *Ele faz greve.*
   c. *Ele faz anos.*
   d. *Ele faz falta.*
3. He has that five o'clock shadow, so...
   a. *ele decide fazer de conta.*
   b. *ele decide fazer greve.*
   a. *ele decide fazer compras.*
   d. *ele decide fazer a barba.*
4. Maria has practically nothing in the fridge, so...
   a. *ela vai fazer de conta.*
   b. *ela vai fazer compras.*
   c. *ela vai fazer anos.*
   d. *ela vai fazer a barba.*

5. They were mad at each other, but not anymore. That means that…
   a. *eles fizeram de conta.*
   b. *eles fizeram as pazes.*
   c. *eles fizeram compras.*
   d. *eles fizeram greve.*

To Know: *Saber* and *Conhecer*

In Portuguese there are two verbs that express the idea of "knowing." The verb *saber* is used when you want to express the notion that you know a piece of information that can be reproduced, such as a set of numbers. For example, *ela sabe o meu número de telefone* (she knows my phone number). Similarly, if you say *eles sabem cantar a canção do Roberto Carlos* (they know how to sing the Roberto Carlos's song), that means that they have the skill to do it. On the other hand, the verb *conhecer* is used with you want to communicate that you are familiar or acquainted with a person, place, or object. For example, if you say *nós conhecemos o nordeste do Brasil* (We know northeast Brazil) this means that you are acquainted with that geographical location, because you perhaps visited there, and so on. The same verb is used when talking about people you know, because you are familiar with them, you are acquainted with them.

Both of these verbs are regular *–er* verbs, except for the first person singular, or the *eu* (I) form: *eu sei* and *eu conheço* (I know). The rest of the subject pronouns follow the same endings for regular verbs, that is *sabe*, *sabemos*, *sabem*, and *conhece*, *conhecemos*, and *conhecem*.

Below is a chart that helps you see the different usages of *saber* and *conhecer*:

When to Use *Saber* and *Conhecer*
Use *Saber*: Before information, such as numbers, dates
Example: *Ela sabe a hora.* (She knows the time.)
Use *Saber*: Before particles que (that), qual (which), quando (when)
Example: *Eu sei que…* (I know that…)

Use *Saber*: Before a verb in the infinitive (–r)

Example: *Ela sabe cozinhar.* (She knows how to cook.)

Use *Conhecer*: before people

Example: *Você conhece Teresa?* (Do you know Teresa?)

Use *Conhecer*: before places

Example: *Eles conhecem o Rio.* (They know Rio.)

Use *Conhecer*: before familiar objects

Example: *Nós conhecemos esse livro.* (We know this book.)

It is important to understand that there are gray areas in the usage of these verbs, and that native speakers might use them interchangeably in some contexts. Also, in some situations, a poem or piece of music, for example, could become more than just familiar (*conhecer*), and be recited or played perfectly, by heart (*saber*). See how well you know these verbs now.

EXERCISE: CHOOSE THE VERB

Circle the verb that should be used in the sentence. Check your answers in Appendix C.

1. *Elas **sabem/conhecem** bem a capital do Brasil.*
   (They know Brazil's capital really well.)
2. *Você **sabe/conhece** andar de bicicleta?*
   (Do you know how to ride a bike?)
3. *Nós **sabemos/conhecemos** os nossos vizinhos.*
   (We know our neighbors.)
4. *Vocês **sabem/conhecem** aquela música do Gil?*
   (Do you guys know that song by Gil?)
5. *Maristela **sabe/conhece** que Magdale é atriz.*
   (Maristela knows that Magdale is an actress.)

EXERCISE: FILL IN THE BLANK

Fill in the blanks with the correct form of either saber or conhecer. Check your answers in Appendix C.

1. *Eu* _____ *Lisboa, a capital de Portugal.*

2. *Vocês* _____ *o Rio Capibaribe?*

3. *Minha esposa e eu* _____ *dirigir muito bem.*

4. *Eu* _____ *que preciso estudar mais.*

5. *Os nossos amigos* _____ *que estamos juntas.*

More Special Verbs

Some second conjugation verbs are indeed very special because, just like *saber* and *conhecer*, they include a modification in the first person singular, *eu* (I) form. Check out these irregular verbs, and try to find some consistency in them.

ouvir (to hear)
- *eu* **ouço**
- *você/ele/ela ouve*
- *nós ouvimos*
- *vocês/eles/elas ouvem*

pedir (to ask for)
- *eu* **peço**
- *você/ele/ela pede*
- *nós pedimos*
- *vocês/eles/elas pedem*

perder (to lose)
- *eu* **perco**
- *você/ele/ela perde*
- *nós perdemos*
- *vocês/eles/elas perdem*

Notice that the forms are very similar, especially the third person singular forms, such as *pede* (he asks for) and *perde* (he loses). This is particularly true if the final syllable /r/ is not clearly pronounced in speech.

The next set of verbs are from the first, second, and third conjugations.

dar (to give)
- *eu* **dou**
- *você/ele/ela dá*
- *nós damos*
- *vocês/eles/elas dão*

sair (to leave)
- *eu* **saio**
- *você/ele/ela sai*
- *nós saímos*
- *vocês/eles/elas saem*

dizer (to say)
- *eu* **digo**
- *você/ele/ela diz*
- *nós dizemos*
- *vocês/eles/elas dizem*

trazer (to bring)
- *eu* **trago**
- *você/ele/ela traz*
- *nós trazemos*
- *vocês/eles/elas trazem*

pôr (to put, place)
- *eu* **ponho**
- *você/ele/ela põe*
- *nós pomos*
- *vocês/eles/elas põem*

In these lists, only the verbs in bold represent some kind of unexpected deviation from the regular conjugation. But notice that even with their irregularities, these verbs have some kind of system, be it the insertion of a –g– (*digo*, *trago*) or the leaving out of a –e– making the form ending in a –z (*diz*, *traz*).

As you learn these verbs, try to use them in real-life situations, such as the ones included in the following exercises.

EXERCISE: **TRANSLATE**

Translate the following sentences to Portuguese. Check your answers in Appendix C.

1. She loses the keys frequently.

_____

2. Mário always asks for *guaraná* at the restaurant.

_____

3. Sabrina never tells the truth.

_____

4. We bring the books to school.

_____

5. Mário and Maria put the cups on the table.

_____

EXERCISE: **MAKE A MATCH**

Match the sentences on the left with the verbs that fit in the blanks. Check your answers in Appendix C.

1. *Eu _____ as chaves do carro.*   (a) *saio*

2. *Eu _____ música muito alto.*   (b) *digo*

3. *Eu _____ os livros para a aula.*   (c) *ponho*

4. *Eu _____ a verdade à mamãe.*   (d) *ouço*

5. *Eu _____ o lápis na mesa.*   (e) *trago*

6. *Eu _____ de casa muito cedo.*   (f) *perco*

CHAPTER 12

Verb Tenses: an Overview

B Y NOW YOU'VE had a pretty solid introduction to the Portuguese language. You've learned a lot of vocabulary, how to handle certain social situations, and when to use some of the more important verbs in the language. Now it's time to focus on the verb tenses. This chapter covers the present tense, the preterite and imperfect past tenses, and the future and conditional tenses. Use this chapter as your verb reference!

Present Tense

The present tense in Portuguese, as in any other language, is necessary to express ideas of habitual activities, state the present situation, and even to explain what is happening at the time of speech. Sometimes we use the present to talk about future actions, if it is allowed by the context. Below is a chart with the present tenses of all the verb conjugations in Portuguese.

TRACK 69

The Present Tense: Regular Endings

Subject	–ar	–er	–ir
eu	falo	como	durmo
você	fala	come	dorme
ele/ela	fala	come	dorme
nós	falamos	comemos	dormimos
vocês	falam	comem	dormem
eles/elas	falam	comem	dormem

To conjugate a verb, simply drop the infinitive endings (–ar, –er, –ir) and add the endings that are in bold, according to the grammatical person. Do this for all verbs, as long as they follow the regular pattern. The above table shows clearly that there is some consistency when it comes to the present tense, if you do not count the irregular first person singular forms from the last chapter—ouço (I hear), peço (I ask for), saio (I leave), dou (I give). For one thing, the você (you) and ele/ela (he/she) forms are the same. Also, vocês (you (pl.)) and eles/elas (they) forms are also written exactly the same. If you look across the table, you will see that all third person singular forms end in a vowel, and that all of the third person plural forms also end in the consonant –m. In addition, all the nós (we) forms end in –mos, which makes it easier to identify the subject by looking at the end of the verb.

Portuguese is a "pro-drop" language, which means that because there is such rich verb morphology (there are so many different verb endings) we do not need to say the subject pronoun in order to be understood, unlike in English, where you need to state the subject explicity all of the time. Learning the endings of the verb is essential to speaking Portuguese fluently.

Preterite Tense

The two past tenses in Portuguese convey ideas of actions and states in the past before the time of utterance, or before what is conceived as the present. They relate not only to actions but also to conditions and situations in the past. The preterite tense is used when speakers try to convey ideas that relate to punctual actions in the past, usually within or in a clearly defined point in time. So, if you say *Eu visitei o Brasil no ano passado* (I visited Brazil last year) you have identified an action that happened in the past, within a certain time frame. Here are the regular endings for verbs in the past, in the three major conjugations:

TRACK 70

The Preterite Tense: Regular Verbs

Subject	*–ar*	*–er*	*–ir*
eu	*falei*	*comi*	*dormi*
você	*falou*	*comeu*	*dormiu*
ele/ela	*falou*	*comeu*	*dormiu*
nós	*falamos*	*comemos*	*dormimos*
vocês	*falaram*	*comeram*	*dormiram*
eles/elas	*falaram*	*comeram*	*dormiram*

Like the present tense, the preterite tense, aside from its seemingly diverse list of endings, has its own internal consistency. The first person has the same ending for the *–er* and *–ir* conjugations, and the second and third persons share the exact same endings. The *nós* form is the same as the present, but should be understood as relating to past actions according to the context of the sentence or situation. Finally, both the second and third person plural are the same.

Be careful! The *–eu* ending for the *você/ele, ela* forms (*ele comeu* [he ate]) is often used by students for the first person, eu. It would be so very nice if it could be done in this way! But unfortunately, the past tense forms for the first person end in either *–ei* or *–i* (*eu falei* [I spoke]; *eu comi* [I ate]) as you may have noticed in the table.

There are several verbs, very common ones in fact, that do not follow this regular system. They are listed below and should each be learned individually.

The Preterite Tense: Irregular Verbs

Changes in the First Person Only

Verb	Conjugation
chegar (to arrive)	*cheguei, chegou, chegamos, chegaram* (arrived)
explicar (to explain)	*expliquei, explicou, explicamos, explicaram* (explained)
dançar (to dance)	*dancei, dançou, dançamos, dançaram* (danced)

TRACK 71

Changes in All Persons

poder (to be able to)	*pude, pôde, pudemos, puderam* (was/were able to)
querer (to want)	*quis, quis, quisemos, quiseram* (wanted)
saber (to know)	*soube, soube, soubemos, souberam* (knew)
trazer (to bring)	*trouxe, trouxe, trouxemos, trouxeram* (brought)
ver (to see)	*vi, viu, vimos, viram* (saw)
vir (to come, arrive)	*vim, veio, viemos, vieram* (came)

The first three verbs above have only one change in the first person singular, *eu* (I). Even so, the change is only there to make sure that the pronunciation does not change in the conjugated forms. If the *–u–* was not inserted in *cheguei*, the –*g*– next to the –*ei* would have sounded like the –*g*– in the English word "gel" and not like the English word "gal." The same principle was followed in the phonetic change to –*qu*– in the *expliquei* form. The other verbs listed have overall changes in all grammatical persons. The last two verbs, *ver* (to see) and *vir* (to come), are very similar in the past tense and must be learned together, especially the first person singular *vim* (I came) versus *vi* (I saw) is the difference of only a nasal and an oral vowel.

Imperfect Tense

In Portuguese, as in other Romance languages, there is a separate past tense to relate to conditions and situations in the past not covered by the Preterite. The imperfect is used to refer to habitual and continuous actions in the past, and there are other usages too. Thus, the verb tense is difficult to translate in English because it could have at least three interpretations. For example, if I say *Eu andava*, that sentence could mean "I walked," "I would walk," "I used to walk," or "I was walking." Many Portuguese grammars are dedicated to the presentation of this verb tense and how it relates to the Preterite. Below is the conjugation for the imperfect verbs:

TRACK 72

The Imperfect Tense: Regular Verbs

Subject	–ar	–er	–ir
eu	falava	comia	dormia
você	falava	comia	dormia
ele/ela	falava	comia	dormia
nós	falávamos	comíamos	dormíamos
vocês	falavam	comiam	dormiam
eles/elas	falavam	comiam	dormiam

As can be seen in the table above, the verb tense is very regular, despite its name being "imperfect." As far as verb tenses go, this one is very student-friendly. For one, the first three grammatical persons are conjugated exactly the same. Second, the first person plural has an accent across the board, in all conjugations. Finally, the *vocês* and *eles* form are also exactly alike, as in all other conjugations. The trick with this verb is to concentrate on its many usages, which can be very distinct. However, there are some irregular imperfect verbs:

The Imperfect Tense: Irregular Verbs

Verb	Conjugation
ser (to be)	*era, éramos, eram* (were, used to be)
ter (to have)	*tinha, tínhamos, tinham* (had, used to have)
vir (to come)	*vinha, vínhamos, vinham* (came, used to come)
pôr (to put)	*punha, púnhamos, punham* (put, used to put)

These are among the few irregular verbs in the imperfect tense, which makes a very "regular" and consistent verb tense. Notice that three out of four verbs have the *–nh–* combination, making it easier to identify this verb. The next section goes into more detail about the difference between the "preterite" and the "imperfect."

The Preterite Versus the Imperfect

So, how do you know when to use one past tense or the other? The following is a handy list of guidelines, along with some examples.

Preterite Versus Imperfect Usage

Preterite	Imperfect
Punctual Actions	Continuous Actions
Time frame is often indicated	Time frame is less important or nonexistent
Action happens often only "once"	Action happens over and over, or is ongoing
Preterite	**Imperfect**
Many times used with actions verbs	Many times used with non-action verbs

Use in narratives, consecutive actions	Used in description, with simultaneous actions or conditions
Not used to tell time	Used to tell time in the past
Not used for age	Used to refer to age in the past

This table will help you to draw a distinction between the two verbs. Other clues to figuring out the correct verb to use are the adverbs (from Latin *ad–* [next to] and *verbum* [verb]). Adverbs are words that are placed close to verbs and modify their meaning, such as "eat fast," where "fast" modifies or "adds to" the meaning of "eat." There are adverbs or adverbial expressions that are more used with each type of past tense. Here is a list:

Adverbs and Adverbial Expressions and Past Tenses

Mostly Used with Preterite	Mostly Used with Imperfect
ontem (yesterday)	*sempre* (always)
na semana passada (last week)	*ao mesmo tempo* (at the same time)
no mês passado (last month)	*enquanto* (while)
no ano passado (last year)	*quando era pequeno* (when I was little)
de repente (all of a sudden)	*quando era adolescente* (when I was a teenager)
naquele dia (that day)	*todos os dias* (every day)
naquele mês (that month)	*todos os meses* (every month)
naquele ano (that year)	*todos os anos* (every year)

Note that these are not mutually exclusive, that is, I could use the imperfect tense with *naquele dia*, as long as I mean that something happened continuously. So, I could say, *Naquele dia chovia muito* (That day it was raining a lot). However, it is true that these expressions are mostly used with the verb tensed under which they are listed. Try your hand at these exercises for the preterite and imperfect use.

EXERCISE A: PRETERITE OR IMPERFECT?

Circle either the preterite or the imperfect form so that they sentence will make sense. Check your answers in Appendix C.

1. *Quando eu era criança,* **comi/comia** *muito chocolate.*
2. *Ontem nós* **vimos/víamos** *um filme interessante.*
3. **Choveu/chovia** *um pouco quando saímos do cinema.*
4. *Meu pai sempre nos* **levou/levava** *para o parque.*
5. *Estava no banho e de repente minha irmã me* **ligou/ligava.**
6. *Em Illinois* **fez/fazia** *um frio horrível.*

EXERCISE B: PRETERITE OR IMPERFECT?

Fill in the blanks with the conjugated form of the verb in parentheses. Check your answers in Appendix C.

1. *No mês passado eu _____ (ir) a Aruba.*
2. *Todos as manhãs, minha irmã e eu _____ (ir) à praia.*
3. *Na adolescência, nós nos _____ (acordar) muito cedo.*
4. *Anteontem nós nos _____ (acordar) tarde.*
5. *Minha esposa _____ (cozinhar) ontem à noite.*
6. *Minha avó _____ (cozinhar) todos os dias.*

Future Tenses

There are at least two straightforward ways to express the future in Portuguese. One way is more colloquial, that is, used more often in everyday speech. The other way to express the future is seen more often in print but can also be heard in more formal interactions. Let's first present the more colloquial version of the future:

Future with Two Verbs

ir (to go)	+ verb [infinitive]
eu vou	*andar* (I'm going to walk)
você vai	*comer* (you are going to eat)
ela vai	*dormir* (she is going to sleep)
nós vamos	*falar* (we are going to speak)
vocês vão	*beber* (you (pl.) are going to drink)
elas vão	*assistir* (they are going to watch)

Make sure that the second verb is always in the infinitive, or in other words, in the /–r/ ending, which could be construed as its "default" form. The first verb is the verb *ir* (to go) and is conjugated for the grammatical person in question. Here is a sample dialogue with the future tense:

Q: Júlia: *Você vai viajar para o Brasil em dezembro?* (Are you going to travel to Brazil in December?)

A: Fernanda: *Não, eu e Jane vamos visitar os pais dela em Washington.* (No, Jane and I will visit her parents in Washington.)

Q: Júlia: *Então quanto tempo você vai ficar lá?* (So, how long will you stay there?)

A: Fernanda: *Acho que vou ficar lá uns dois dias, mas Jane vai voltar somente na outra semana.* (I think I'll stay there a couple of days, but Jane will be back only the following week.)

Q: Júlia: *Que bom, então ela vai ter mais tempo com os pais.* (Great, so she'll have more time with her folks.)

A: Fernanda: *Pois é!* (Right.)

The other way of expressing the future is to use the regular future tense. This is done by keeping the infinitives and adding extra endings, depending on the grammatical person. This is comparable to the English "will" + verb. Here is the regular future tense in Portuguese:

The Future Tense

andar (to walk)	*comer* (to eat)	*dormir* (to sleep)
eu andarei	*eu comerei*	*eu dormirei*
você andará	*você comerá*	*você dormirá*
ele andará	*ele comerá*	*ele dormirá*
nós andaremos	*nós comeremos*	*nós dormiremos*
vocês andarão	*vocês comerão*	*vocês dormirão*
eles andarão	*eles comerão*	*eles dormirão*

Here is a sample dialogue that includes some of the future tense forms:

Q: Professor: *Vocês **entregarão** as tarefas na segunda.* (You will turn in the homework on Monday.)

A: Aluno: *E quando **teremos** a primeira prova?* (And when will we have the first test?)

Q: Professor: *A primeira prova **será** em uma semana.* (The first test will be in one week.)

A: Aluno: *E o exame final? Quantas perguntas **serão** incluídas?* (And the final exam? How many questions will be included?)

Q: Professor: *Haverá cem perguntas de múltipla escolha no exame.* (There will be one hundred multiple choice questions in the exam.)

A: Aluno: *Ah, só? Que bom!* (Oh, that's it? Great!)

Conditional Tense

The conditional is very similar to the future tense, but it denotes the possibility of something happening in the future once a certain condition or stipulation is met. It is comparable to the English "would" + verb. The conditional is used more in colloquial speech than the regular future tense.

The Conditional Tense

andar (to walk)	comer (to eat)	dormir (to sleep)
eu andaria	eu comeria	eu dormiria
você andaria	você comeria	você dormiria
ele andaria	ele comeria	ele dormiria
nós andaríamos	nós comeríamos	nós dormiríamos
vocês andariam	vocês comeriam	vocês dormiriam
eles andariam	eles comeriam	eles dormiriam

There is a lot of regularity in this verb tense, as you can see from the singular forms, which are all the same. Here are some sample sentences with the conditional tense:

Fabiana falou que **mandaria** o cartão postal. (Fabiana said that she would send the postcard.)
Mário e Isabela **chegariam** *a tempo se o trem fosse mais rápido.* (Mário and Isabela would arrive on time if the train was faster.)
Se tivesse mais caipirinha, meus amigos e eu **beberíamos** *mais.* (If there were more Brazilian rum, my friends and I would drink more.)

Practice with the Future and Conditional Tenses

Now let's see if you can remember what you've learned about the future and conditional tenses. Complete the following exercises and check your answers in Appendix C.

EXERCISE A: **FUTURE AND CONDITIONAL VERBS**

Translate the following sentences using the *ir* + verb future.

1. I'm going to call you tomorrow.

_____

2. We are going to visit Brazil in the summer.

_____

3. You are going to write a book?

_____

EXERCISE B: **FUTURE AND CONDITIONAL VERBS**

Fill in the blanks with the verb in parentheses using the future tense.

1. *O advogado _____ (solicitar) uma audiência amanhã.*

2. *A prova _____ (ter) cinco perguntas de ensaio.*

3. *Nós _____ (acompanhar) as crianças até o parque.*

EXERCISE C: **FUTURE AND CONDITIONAL VERBS**

Fill in the blanks using the conditional tense.

1. *Se fosse mais cedo, nós _____ (sair) para dar uma volta.*

2. *Ele disse à Maria que _____ (chegar) tarde.*

3. *As meninas _____ (levantar) mais cedo se pudessem.*

CHAPTER 13

More Verbs

THERE IS MORE to Portuguese than just conjugating regular verbs. Sometimes we have to contend with using two verbs together, past participles, the passive voice, or reflexive verbs. You'll learn how to put all these new verb structures together in this chapter.

Using Two Verbs Together

It is very common to use two verbs together, not only in English, but also in many other languages, Portuguese included. The first situation, which was previously mentioned, is the future tense with *ir* (to go). The important thing to remember is to conjugate the first verb and leave the second verb in the infinitive. Here are some examples:

*Nós **vamos visitar** o Brasil no ano que vem.* (We're going to visit Brazil next year.)
*Eu **vou fazer** exercícios amanhã!* (I'm going to exercise tomorrow!)
*Você **vai sair** hoje à noite?* (Are you going to go out tonight?)
*Eles **vão pôr** a mesa para as visitas.* (They will set the table for the guests.)

Here are other expressions that require two verbs in Portuguese. In all of these, you conjugate the first verb and add another verb in (you guessed it) the infinitive. The formula looks like this: *querer* + infinitive (Portuguese) = "want" + infinitive (English). The following table shows this pattern clearly:

TRACK 74

Portuguese	English
Queremos desejar um Feliz Natal a todos.	We want to wish a Merry Christmas to all.
Quero ver esse filme neste fim de semana.	I want to see this movie this weekend.
Vocês querem ir ao barzinho?	Do you guys want to go to the club?
Ele quis impor sua vontade.	He wanted to impose his will.

Use this pattern to express wishes and desires. As long as the first verb *querer* is conjugated, and the next verb is in the infinitive, you are in good shape. This pattern can be used in the present to express future meaning (for example, *Quero sair amanhã* [I want to go out tomorrow]), but it could also be used in the past tense (for example, *Eu quis visitá-lo* [I wanted to visit him]) to express a wish that was not completed or realized. Here's the formula: *ter* + *vontade de* + infinitive = "feel like -ing."

Portuguese	English
Eu tive vontade de sentar-me.	I felt like sitting.
Nós temos vontade de sair.	We feel like going out.
Vocês têm vontade de fazer exercícios?	Do you (pl.) feel like exercising?
Ela tem vontade de compor.	She feels like composing.

This pattern is used when you want to relate to things that you want to do or feel like doing. The word *vontade* means "will" or "desire." An alternative construction is to say *estou com vontade de* (I feel like…), which is also a bit difficult to translate in a literal sense.

EXERCISE A: USING TWO VERBS TOGETHER

Fill in the blanks with conjugated forms of the verb querer or ter depending on the structure of the sentence. Check your answers in Appendix C.

1. *A minha irmã _____ ir para a Inglaterra no ano que vem.*
   (My sister wants to go to England next year.)

2. *Eu _____ vontade de comer doce depois das quatro da tarde.*
   (I feel like eating sweets after four in the afternoon.)

3. *Os meus primos _____ visitar o Museu de Arte Moderna de São Paulo.*
   (My cousins wanted to visit the Modern Art Museum in São Paulo.)

4. *A minha amiga Júlia e o marido _____ sair para jantar na sexta-feira à noite.* (My friend Julia wants to go out to eat on Friday night.)

5. *Nós os brasileiros sempre _____ vontade de ir à Disneylândia de férias.*
   (We Brazilians always feel like going to Disneyland for vacation.)

EXERCISE B: **USING TWO VERBS TOGETHER**

Now it's your turn! Write two sentences in Portuguese that refer to what you "want to do" or "feel like doing."

1.

_____

2.

_____

Here are more "two-verb" structures common in Portuguese:

acabar de (past) + infinitive *"have just _____"*

Portuguese	English
Ele acabou de chegar.	He has just arrived.
Vocês acabaram de ligar?	Have you guys just called?
Nós acabamos de ver o filme.	We have just seen the movie.

The literal translation for this expression in English is "finished doing," from the verb *acabar* "to finish," but the best way to say would be "have just [done something]." Again, the first verb is conjugated and the second verb stays the same, in the infinitive form. This next structure also uses the infinitive.

***ter* + *que* + infinitive**   **"have to" + verb**

Portuguese	English
Eu tenho que terminar o livro.	I have to finish the book
Ela tem que fazer compras.	She has to go shopping.
Nós temos que ir ao banco.	We have to go to the bank.

This pattern is used to convey the idea of obligation, as you have seen in Chapter 10. It might be useful to avoid translating *ter que* literally, since you would end up with "I have to that"! Simply remember that this pattern is used to relate to things you must or have to do. This next structure relates to "abilities" and "skills."

poder + infinitive "can/is able to" + verb

Portuguese	English
Pode sentar!	You can sit down!
Eu posso fazer exercícios fáceis.	I can do easy exercises.
Nós podemos sair hoje à noite.	We can go out tonight.

The verb *poder* is conjugated and the following verb, which describes the ability, is in the infinitive. At the same time, this structure can also refer to "permission," more commonly translated in English with the modal verb "may," as in *Eu posso entrar?* (May I come in?). The following exercises give you more practice with these verbs.

EXERCISE C: USING TWO VERBS TOGETHER

Translate the following sentences, using the information you learned in the previous pages. Check your answers in Appendix C.

1. Elvis has just left the building.
2. May I go now?
3. Maria can run for a long time.
4. The teacher has to correct the tests.
5. We have just finished reading the paper.
6. Can you go out tonight?
7. They can come in.

EXERCISE D: USING TWO VERBS TOGETHER

Now it's your turn! Write two sentences expressing what you "have to do" in the next few days or months.

1.

_____

2.

_____

Past Participles

Past participles are verbal forms that are used in combination with the verb *estar* (to be) to denote the resulting effect of an action or condition. The comparable sentence in English would be "is/are [done]." Of course, the other tenses are also used; for example, "was/ were done" or "will be done," and so forth.

> Past participles in English usually end in "–ed" and are similar to the past tense form: "talked" and "have talked." However, there are some that end in "–en," such as "written" and "given"; use of these forms is decreasing, especially in colloquial speech. On the other hand, past participles are very frequently used in Portuguese.

The following table shows how to arrive at the past participle form of the verb.

Past Participle Endings According to Verb Conjugation

–ar verbs > drop the *–ar* ending and add *–ado* (*–ados*, *–ada*, *–adas*)
–er verbs > drop the *–er* ending and add *–ido* (*–idos*, *–ida*, *–idas*)
–ir verbs > drop the *–ir* ending and add *–ido* (*–idos*, *–ida* *–idas*)

However, there are some irregular past participles in Portuguese.

Irregular Past Participles

abrir (to open)	*aberto* (opened)
cobrir (to cover)	*coberto* (covered)
dizer (to say)	*dito* (said)
escrever (to write)	*escrito* (written)
entregar (to hand, to give)	*entregue* (handed, given)
fazer (to make, to do)	*feito* (made, done)
ganhar (to win)	*ganho* (won)
gastar (to spend)	*gasto* (spent)
morrer (to die)	*morto* (died)

pagar (to pay)	*pago* (paid)
pôr (to put, to set)	*posto* (put, set)
ver (to see)	*visto* (seen)
vir (to come, to arrive)	*vindo* (come, arrived)

The following are sample sentences with the *estar* + past participle construction.

TRACK 75

estar + past participle	English
O restaurante está aberto.	The restaurant is open.
A porta está fechada.	The door is closed.
Os cheques estão assinados.	The checks are signed.
As mesas estão postas.	The tables are set.

Notice that with the past participle after the verb *estar* (to be) there needs to be agreement with the subject. For example, *mesas* (tables) is a feminine and plural word, so the past participle needs to match these two categories and end in *–as*, which is the feminine plural form. There are four different forms for the past participle, unless it ends in *–e*, in which the masculine and feminine forms are the same and the word varies only in number (i.e., *entregues* "given").

EXERCISE: PAST PARTICIPLES

Fill in the blanks with the correct form of the past participle of the verb in parentheses. Check your answers in Appendix C.

1. *As portas estavam* _____ *(abrir).* (The doors were open.)

2. *O mecânico está muito* _____ *(ocupar).* (The mechanic is very busy.)

3. *O que está* _____ *(escrever) ali?* (What is written there?)

4. *A mesa está* _____ *(pôr) para o jantar.* (The table is set for the dinner.)

5. *Os bancos estão* _____ *(cobrir) de neve.* (The benches are covered with snow.)

Passive Voice

Past participles are also used with the verb *ser* (to be) to denote the passive voice. To understand the passive voice, first you need to understand the active voice. In a sentence in the active voice, the subject and the agent are the same, as in the sentence "The boy closed the door." In this case, "the boy" is both the subject of the sentence and the agent, in other words, the entity that completes the verbal action. On the other hand, the passive voice sentence would express the same idea, but said in a different way: "The door was closed by the boy." In this sentence, "the door" is the subject of the sentence, not "the boy." In fact, in this sentence, the subject is the "recipient" of the verbal action. To summarize, an active sentence is one in which the subject is also the agent of the action, while a passive sentence is one in which the subject is the recipient of the verbal action. Speakers use the passive voice in order to focus attention away from the agent of the action. You might not want to call attention to the fact that "the boy" was the agent of the action, but you want to emphasize the fact that the action actually occurred. Using the passive voice allows you to shift focus away from the agent, which can be mentioned or not (i.e., you can simply day "the door was closed" and not mention "by the boy").

Here are some passive voice sentences in Portuguese:

Passive Voice Examples

Portuguese	English
A mesa foi posta pelas empregadas.	The table was set by the maids.
Os livros foram escritos pelas poetas.	The books were written by the poets.
As portas foram fechadas.	The doors were closed.
O ladrão foi pego.	The thief was caught.

Most, but not all, passive voice sentences are written in the past tense. There can be passive sentences written in the present or future. For example: *Como pessoa famosa, ele **é reconhecido** todos os dias* (As a celebrity, he **is recognized** every day). Or even: *O aniversário dele vai ser comemorado no restaurante* (His birthday will be celebrated in the restaurant).

EXERCISE: **PASSIVE VOICE**

Translate the following sentences. Check your answers in Appendix C.

1. The two men were seen near here.

   _____

2. The money was spent very fast.

   _____

3. What was said yesterday?

   _____

4. The food was consumed by the birds.

   _____

Reflexive and Reciprocal Verbs

Some verbs in Portuguese are labeled "reflexive" and/or "reciprocal." Reflexive verbs reflect an action that is done to the agent to itself. They can be translated to English by using the reflexiv e pronouns "–self" and "–selves," as in *eu me chamo* (I call myself). By the same token, reciprocal verbs can be translated to English by using the construction "each other." In this case, the action is done to an entity, which in turn does the same action to the other entity, as in the expression *se beijam* (they kiss each other). In Portuguese, reflexive and reciprocal verbs are conjugated by using reflexive pronouns, as listed below.

Reflexive and Reciprocal Pronouns

Pronoun + Verb	English
eu me chamo	I call myself
você se chama	you call yourself
ele/ela se chama	he/she calls him/herself
nós nos chamamos	we call ourselves
vocês se chamam	you (pl.) call yourselves
eles/elas se chamam	they call themselves

Notice that the pronoun is placed before the verb and that the pronouns serve for both reflexive and reciprocal ideas.

> Not all reflexive verbs in Portuguese have a corresponding English reflexive verb. In the case of *chamar-se* (to call oneself) this works out fine, but there are reflexive verbs in Portuguese that are not reflexive in English, such as *levantar-se* (to get up), which is not considered reflexive in English.

Here is a list of common reflexive verbs in Portuguese:

TRACK 76

Common Reflexive Verbs

Verb	English
lavar-se	to wash oneself
vestir-se	to put on clothes, to dress oneself
olhar-se	to look at oneself
pentear-se	to brush/comb oneself
sentar-se	to seat oneself
divertir-se	to entertain oneself, to have fun
deitar-se	to go to bed, to retire
machucar-se	to hurt oneself
reunir-se	to get together

In order to conjugate the verb, you must drop the *-se* and add one of the reflexive pronouns according to the grammatical person. So *deitar-se* would be conjugated as *eu me deito* (I go to bed) for the first person singular.

Reflexive Verbs with Prepositions

Some reflexive verbs have prepositions that are used with prepositions in the sentence. Here's a list of these verbs:

TRACK 77

Reflexive Verbs with Prepositions

Verb	English
aproveitar-se de	to take advantage of
convencer-se de	to convince oneself of
esquecer-se de	to forget + infinitive
lembrar-se de	to remember + infinitive
queixar-se de	to complain about
rir-se de	to laugh at
decidir-se a	to decide + infinitive
dedicar-se a	to dedicate oneself to
acostumar-se com	to get used to
parecer-se com	to look like
casar-se com	to marry
preocupar-se com	to worry about
surpreender-se com	to be surprised

Notice that not all verbs are translated with the same proposition (some can be translated as "at," "about," or "with"). In addition, some verbs such as "to marry" and "to be surprised" do not require a preposition at all in English.

Practice with Reflexive and Reciprocal Verbs

Now let's see what you can remember about using reflexive and reciprocal verbs. Try out the following two exercises and then check your answers in Appendix C.

EXERCISE A: REFLEXIVE AND RECIPROCAL VERBS

Match Column A (expressions) with Column B (verbs).

1. *Eles* _____ *na igreja.*   (a) *me deito*

2. *Nós* _____ *muito na festa.*   (b) *se preocupa*

3. *Minha amiga* _____ *com a família.*   (c) *nos divertimos*

4. *Meu irmão* _____ *com meu pai.*   (d) *se queixam*

5. *Os alunos* _____ *do livro sempre.*   (e) *se parece*

6. *Eu* _____ *às 11 da noite.*   (f) *se casaram*

EXERCISE B: REFLEXIVE AND RECIPROCAL VERBS

Translate the following sentences to Portuguese.

1. The professor dedicates herself to teaching.
2. Our neighbor was surprised with the visit.
3. The man laughed at the situation.
4. I look like my father.

1.

_____

2.

_____

3.

_____

4.

_____

CHAPTER 14

Negative Words and Constructions

T HERE ARE MANY times when you want or need to negate, refuse, or just plain say no to something. When the waiter asks you if you'd like to order more food, you might be too full. If a friend invites you out on a night when you already have plans, you'll need to kindly refuse and possibly suggest an alternate plan. Those types of situations are covered in this chapter; you'll learn how to make negative sentences, become familiar with common negative expressions, and discover how to distinguish between the negative and the positive.

How to Say No

The word for "no" in Portuguese is *não*, a one-syllable word with a nasal diphthong that sometimes takes practice to pronounce. In order to say a sentence in the negative, simply put the word *não* before the verb. This is very different from English, where negative sentences are constructed with a system of auxiliary verbs (don't, etc.). See the table below to understand the simplicity of Portuguese.

In order to pronounce the word correctly try saying the word "now" in English but try to make it nasal, as you would if you said "huh?"

Sentences in the Negative

Portuguese	English [many possibilities]
Eu não tenho um cachorro.	I don't have a dog.
Ela não quer conversar.	She doesn't want to talk.
Nós não podemos acreditar.	We can't believe this.
Vocês não souberam da verdade?	You guys didn't find out the truth?
Você não deve fazer isso.	You shouldn't do that.

As you can see, the Portuguese system is pretty straightforward. The negative is simply made by placing the negative word *não* before the verb. No alterations or auxiliary verbs are needed. What if you want to say "never" or "nobody"? Read more to find out.

TRACK 78

More Negative Words in Portuguese

Word	Example	English
Nunca	Eu nunca estive em Manaus.	I've never been to Manaus.
Nada	Nada a declarar.	Nothing to declare.
Ninguém	Ninguém chegou na hora.	Nobody arrived on time.
Nem... nem	Nem um nem outro.	Neither one nor the other.
Nenhum	Nenhum artigo foi perdido.	Not one article was lost.
Nenhuma	Nenhuma pessoa ficou lá.	Not one person stayed there.

What if this is still not enough? Read on to find out how to out sentences together in the negative.

Two Negatives Make a Negative

In English the rule is to say only one negative word per sentence ("I saw no one" or I didn't see anyone"). Double negatives are a big no-no, unless you speak a dialect of English in which they are accepted in conversation ("I didn't see nobody"). Portuguese is similar to these nonstandard English dialects, because two negatives are not only allowed, they are the rule! Here is a list of negative words used together:

TRACK 79

Double Negatives in Portuguese

Portuguese	English
Eu não faço exercício nunca.	I don't exercise ever.
Eu não digo nada.	I don't say anything.
Eu não vejo ninguém.	I don't see anyone.
Eu não tenho nenhum (or nenhuma)...	I don't have any...

Use *nenhum* before masculine words, such as *nenhum problema* (any problem) and *nenhuma* before feminine words, such as *nenhuma sugestão* (any suggestion). How do you answer in the negative when asked a "yes-no" question? Here are several possibilities:

Você vai para o cinema amanhã? (Are you going to the movies tomorrow?)
ANSWER 1: *Não, não vou.*   No, I'm not (going).
ANSWER 2: *Não, não vou não.*   No, I'm not (going).
ANSWER 3: *Não, vou não.*   No, I'm not (going).

There are subtleties to the answers, but they all mean the same thing. Answers 1 and 2 are spoken by more educated speakers, mostly in formal contexts. Answer 3 is considered more colloquial, informal speech, if not ungrammatical by some. Be prepared to hear all these possibilities in Brazilian Portuguese.

Common Negative Expressions

There are many expressions that are negative but that might not seem so at first glance from an English-language perspective. Here are some of them:

Negative Expressions

Portuguese	English	Situation
Pois não?	Yes? May I help you?	When answering the phone, door, or asking if you need help.
Pois não.	Sure.	When agreeing (!) to do something.
Absolutamente!	Absolutely not! No way!	When refusing or disagreeing.
Sei lá!	Who knows? I don't know.	When denying that you know something.
Não tem importância.	No problem.	When reassuring someone that it was nothing.
De jeito nenhum.	No way.	When refusing or rejecting something.

Make sure you train your ears and tongue to understand as well as use these expressions. Pay attention to interactions among Brazilians when they use these expressions, especially in restaurants and supermarkets.

Here are some examples of the usage of negative words in typical conversation in Brazilian Portuguese:

Q: *Oi, tudo bem?* (Hi, is everything alright?)

A: *Não, tudo mal!* (No, everything's bad!)

Q: *Por que? O que aconteceu?* (Why, what happened?)

A: *Não recebi dinheiro ontem.* (I didn't get any money yesterday.)

Q: *Ontem foi dia de pagamento?* (Yesterday was payday?)

A: *Não era anteontem, mas eles não me nem um tostão!* (No, it was the day before, but they didn't give me one cent!)

Q: *Nada?* (Nothing?)

A: *Nadinha mesmo.* (Nothing at all.)

Q: *Nossa, que coisa. E agora?* (Wow, that's amazing. And now?)

A: *Não sei o que fazer. Você tem algum dinheiro para me emprestar?* (I don't know what to do. Do you have any money to lend me?)

Q: *Não, de jeito nenhum. Não tenho nada mesmo.* (No, not at all. I don't have anything, really.)

A: *Não faz mal.* (It's alright.)

Practice with Negatives

Fill in the blanks with the best negative word in Portuguese. Check your answers in Appendix C.

1. *Eu _____ me lembro de _____ da escola primária.* (I don't remember anyone from elementary school.)

2. *A minha amiga Júlia _____ se acorda antes das dez da manhã.* (My friend Julia never gets up before ten in the morning.)

3. *Sofia _____ tem _____ contra seus colegas de trabalho.* (Sofia has nothing/doesn't have anything against her coworkers.)

4. *Nós _____ fizemos _____ exercício hoje.* (We did not do any exercises (or: not one exercise) today.)

5. *Os escritores _____ completaram _____ página nesta semana.* (The writers did not complete any pages (or: not one page) this week.)

Positive Versus Negative

Comparing the positive versus the negative words is a good way to understand the differences in Portuguese and English. Here is a list of these expressions:

Positive Versus Negative Words

Positive	Negative
alguma coisa, algo (something)	*nada* (nothing)
alguém (somebody)	*ninguém* (nobody)
em algum lugar (somewhere)	*em lugar nenhum* (nowhere)
sempre (always)	*nunca, jamais, em tempo algum* (never)
também (also)	*também não* ([not] either neither)
já (already)	*ainda não* (not yet)
ainda (still yet)	*não... mais* (not anymore)

EXERCISE: POSITIVE TO NEGATIVE

Change all the positive sentences into negative ones. Use the words that you just learned above. Check your answers in Appendix C.
Model: *Eu **já** vi o filme.* (I already saw the movie.)
    *Eu **ainda não** vi o filme.* (I did not see the movie yet.)

1. *Eu já fui no banco.* (I already went to the bank.)

_____

2. *Você ainda tem medo de avião.* (You are still afraid of planes.)

_____

3. *Tem alguém na sala.* (There is someone in the room.)

_____

4. *Eles estão fazendo alguma coisa.* (They are doing something.)

_____

5. *Elas sempre vão ao supermercado.* (They always go to the supermarket.)

_____

EXERCISE: NEGATIVE TO POSITIVE

Change all the negative sentences into positive ones.

1. *Eles não encontraram nada em casa.* (They did not find anything at home.)

   _____

2. *Eu não vi ninguém na festa.* (I didn't see anybody at the party.)

   _____

3. *Nós não o vimos em lugar nenhum.* (We did not see him anywhere.)

   _____

4. *Você jamais telefona à noite.* (You never call at night.)

   _____

5. *Eu ainda não terminei o capítulo.* (I did not finish the chapter yet.)

   _____

CHAPTER 15

Questions and Exclamations

How do you ask questions in Portuguese? In this chapter, you'll learn the answer to this question and more. This chapter covers the most useful interrogative words and questions tags and ends with interjections. You will also learn how to show surprise in Portuguese. Read on!

How to Ask Questions

In Portuguese, asking questions does not require complicated inversion rules as French does or the use of auxiliaries and inversion as English does. For the most part, questions are asked by using a rising intonation at the end of the utterance. Below are some examples of "yes-no" questions:

TRACK 82

Questions in Portuguese

Portuguese	Literal English Translation	English Equivalent
Você vai para o cinema?	You going to the movies?	Are you going to the movies?
As meninas já chegaram?	The girls already come?	Have the girls come already?
A conversa foi boa?	The talk was good?	Was the talk good?
Eu ligo pra você?	I call you?	Should I call you?

In order to ask a question in Portuguese, simply raise the tone of the last word in the utterance. In very colloquial speech in English this is also done. Have you ever heard people say "You're going?" instead of "Are you going?" These two sentences have similar meanings, at least superficially. The first example, "You're going?", implies that the speaker is surprised about the fact that listener is leaving, as suggested by contextual evidence. The second sentence, "Are you going?", is simply a yes-no question that shows that the speaker really wants information that is not contextually available. In any case, Portuguese speakers use the first type of sentence to ask a yes-no question.

EXERCISE: IS IT A QUESTION?

TRACK 83

Listen to the utterance and decide if it is uma pergunta (a question) or uma afirmação (a statement). Check the script and answers in Appendix C.

1. *uma pergunta*   *uma afirmação*
2. *uma pergunta*   *uma afirmação*
3. *uma pergunta*   *uma afirmação*
4. *uma pergunta*   *uma afirmação*
5. *uma pergunta*   *uma afirmação*

Interrogative Words

Not all questions are yes-no questions. Some questions begin with a "question word" or interrogative word (also called a "wh-question" because in English the interrogative word begins with those letters). If you use an interrogative word, you don't need to use the rising intonation at the end of the utterance. The presence of the word itself will suffice. These are the most common interrogative words in Portuguese:

Interrogative Words Followed by Nouns

TRACK 84

Portuguese	Example	English
que?	Que filme você quer ver?	Which film do you want to see?
qual?	Qual blusa você vai comprar?	Which blouse will you buy?
quantos?	Quantos irmãos você tem?	How many siblings do you have?
quantas?	Quantas irmãs você tem?	How many sisters do you have?

Sometimes the interrogative *o que?* (what?) is said in a longer form—*o que é que... ?* or more literally, "What is it that...?"—but it means the same thing. There is not much difference between *que* and *qual* (which), except that when using *qual* (or *quais*, the plural form) there is an implicit choice between two or more possibilities. And make sure to pay attention to the gender of the noun that follows either *quantos* [masc.] or *quanta* [fem.].

Other interrogative words are followed by verbs, not nouns. These are listed below.

Interrogative Words Followed by Verbs

Portuguese	Example	English
o que?	O que você estuda?	What do you study?
como?	Como vai?	How are you?

Interrogative Words Followed by Verbs

Portuguese	Example	English
quanto?	Quanto custa isso?	How much does this cost?
quando?	Quando é a festa?	When is the party?
onde?	Onde você pôs as chaves?	Where did you put the keys?
aonde?	Aonde ela está indo?	Where is she going to?
por quê?	Por quê você foi embora?	Why did you leave?

In this group, notice that these interrogatives are followed by either a verb (*vai*, *custa*) or a subject and a verb (*você pôs*, *ela está*). Sometimes inversion is allowed in the first case, when the interrogative is followed only by the verb. So, for some interrogative-word questions you can say *Quando seu avô morreu?* or *Quando morreu seu avô?* (When did your grandfather die?), and they mean the same thing. Try to complete the exercises below on the ways to form a question in Portuguese.

Here is a typical conversation between a reporter and a famous person in Brazil.

Q: Olá, como vai? (Hi, how are you?)

A: Bem, obrigada, e você? (Well, thanks, and you?)

Q: Muito bem, agora que você está aqui conversando conosco. Quanto tempo você vai ficar em São Paulo? (Very well, now that you are here talking to us. How long will you stay in São Paulo?)

A: Uns dois dias, promovendo o filme. (A couple of days, promoting the movie.)

Q: Quando é a estréia do filme? (When is the release of the movie?)

A: Já nessa semana que vem! (Already this next week!)

Q: Você gostou de trabalhar com o diretor? (Did you like working with the director?)

A: A melhor parte é que ele é um profissional. (The best part is that he is such a professional.)

Q: Você acha que o filme terá sucesso internacional? (Do you think the movie will have international success?)

A: Acho que sim, tem um apelo para a gente jovem. (I think so, it has an appeal to younger people.)

Q: Qual foi a parte mais difícil de interpretar para você? (What was the most difficult part about acting for you?)

A: Acho que a parte dramática é mais fácil que a comédia. (I think the dramatic roles are easier than the comedic roles.)

Q: Como anda a família, tudo bem? (How's the family doing, all right?)

A: Tudo em ordem. (Everything is fine.)

Q: Aonde vocês vão passar as férias? (Where will you guys go for vacation?)

A: Não posso dizer, é segredo de estado! (I can't tell, it's a state secret!)

Q: Você promete voltar ao nosso programa antes do final do ano? (Do you promise to come back to our show before the end of the year?)

A: Claro que sim, com o maior prazer! (Of course, it will be my pleasure!)

Q: Um grande abraço e obrigada! (A big hug to you, and thanks!)

EXERCISE: INTERROGATIVE WORDS

Fill in the blanks with the most appropriate question word. Check your answers in Appendix C.

1. _____ *é seu aniversário?* (... is your birthday?)

2. _____ *custa essa blusa?* (... is this blouse?)

3. _____ *você quer ir hoje?* (... do you want to go today?)

4. _____ *ele foi tão cedo?* (... he left so early?)

5. _____ *você mora?* (... you live?)

6. _____ *se diz em português?* (... you say it in Portuguese?)

7. _____ *você acha disso?* (... do you think of that?)

EXERCISE: ASKING QUESTIONS

Write a question for the following answers in Portuguese.

1. _____ . *Eu me chamo Daniel.*

2. _____ . *Eu moro no Rio de Janeiro.*

3. _____ . *Eu tenho três irmãos.*

Question Tags

Question tags are words that are said at the end of utterances in order to make a question. English has a very complex set of so-called "tag-questions" because of all the many auxiliary and modal verbs in the language (do, should, can, etc.). It is possible to also use the original verb in Portuguese to make a tag question, as in *Você visitou os Estados Unidos, **não visitou?*** (You visited the United States, didn't you?). However, it is far more simple (and more common) to simply use the expression *não é?* at the end of any declarative sentence to make a question. So, for example, you could say *Ele não comeu nada, **não é?*** (He did not eat anything, did he?).

> In Brazilian Portuguese, speakers will very often reduce the expression *não é?* to the one-syllable *né?* Common sentences would be *Ela vai ligar depois, né?* (She will call later, won't she?), and so forth. Pay attention to this frequent abbreviation and use it yourself sometimes!

Exclamations

Exclamations are very common in any language, but in Portuguese the actual grammar constructions are a little different from exclamations in English. In English we say "what a... " followed by a comment. However, in Portuguese we only say *que...* followed by a comment, as in the following examples:

Que capítulo fácil! (What an easy chapter!)
Que país lindo! (What a beautiful country!)

The word *que* is also used in shorter expressions that simply include the adjective, such as

Que lindo! (How beautiful!)

The other type of construction has to do with the one that can be translated to English as "how." In Portuguese we would use *que*, as in the following examples:

Que simpática (que) ela é! (How nice she is!)
Que bem (que) ele toca! (How well he plays!)

It should be noted here that the second *que* is optional, but very frequently heard in popular Brazilian Portuguese. In addition, we could also use the word *como* in order to convey the same meaning, as in these examples:

Como ela é simpática! (How nice she is!)
Como ele toca bem! (How well he plays!)

Another exclamatory word is *mas* (but), used as a type of reinforcement along with *que* and *como*:

Mas que chato! (What a bore!)
Mas como ele é persistente! (How persistent he is!)

Finally, there is also the use of *cada* (each, every), which can be exclamatory and translated in English as the word "such." Here is an example:

Ele me deu cada olhada! (He gave me such looks!)

EXERCISE: TRANSLATE EXCLAMATIONS

Translate the following sentences to Portuguese. Check your answers in Appendix C.

1. What a pretty girl she is! _____

2. What an excellent hotel! _____

3. How badly he drives! _____

4. What horrible cold weather! _____

5. How interesting! _____

CHAPTER 16

The Future and Other Tenses

THIS CHAPTER REVIEWS the uses of the future and other tenses in Portuguese. One unique aspect of Portuguese is the personal infinitive, a rare flower indeed in the grammatical world. In addition, you will learn about impersonal assertions and finish off by discussing the weather and clothing using some of these grammar points!

The Present Versus the Future or the Preterite

You can use the present tense in Portuguese to denote a future event. For example, we might say *Eu vou ao banco* (I go to the bank) when you mean that you will in the near future, say the next day or in a couple of hours. It does not mean that "you always go to the bank," as the present tense usually means; that is, the present tense is not used to describe habitual actions. Here is a dialogue where speakers use the present tense to denote the future:

> **Q:** *Você **vai** amanhã para Brasília?* (You go tomorrow to Brasília?)
> **A:** *Sim, a gente **sai** às duas da tarde.* (Yes, we leave at two in the afternoon.)
> **Q:** *E quando vocês **voltam**?* (And when do you (pl.) come back?)
> **A:** *Nós **voltamos** na semana que vem.* (We come back next week.)
> **Q:** *Que legal, aproveitem!* (Great, enjoy!)
> **A:** *Nós **vamos** sim!* (Yes, we will!)

Notice that this is also the same in English, in other words, the present tense can also be used with future meaning. The big difference between English and Portuguese has to do with the present progressive.

In English you can say "I'm leaving" to express an action in the future, as in "I'm leaving to Rio next month." But in Portuguese we could not use the *presente contínuo* to mean something in the future. We would have to use the future tense, and say either *Eu vou viajar para o Rio no mês que vem* (I'm going to travel to Rio next month) or *Eu viajarei para o Rio no mês que vem* (I will travel to Rio next month). But if you say *Eu estou viajando para o Rio* (I'm traveling to Rio) that means you are actually sitting on the plane talking to someone about what you are doing at that very moment!

What are the other uses of the present? One is common in historical texts. It is possible to read a sentence such as *Naquele momento D. Pedro grita: 'Independência ou Morte!'* (At that moment, D. Pedro cries out "Independence or Death!"). This sentence reveals a historical fact that happened in the early history of Brazil, when the son of the King of Portugal took sides and decided to fight for Brazilian independence. That is called the "historical present," and you might encounter it instead of the regular past tense—another similarity to English!

The Personal Infinitive

The similarities might just end there, as far as regular verb tenses go. The personal infinitive is a peculiarity of Portuguese that is not common in other languages. It deals with the use of an infinitive that has been modified to give more information about the agent of the action. An infinitive normally is not supposed to have any such information. Usually, we use a conjugated verb (with personal information) followed by an infinitive (bare of any personal data). Some examples are *Eu quero **comer** pão* (I want to eat bread), or *Você sabe **jogar** xadrez?* (Do you know how to play chess?), or even *Eles vão **dirigir** até a festa* (They will drive to the party). Notice that the verbs in bold are infinitives, which means that they end in –*r*. The previous verb is conjugated according to the person or the subject. So, why add more information? This verb tense is used with impersonal expression when there might be some ambiguity of who is carrying out the action, as in the examples below:

A: *É importante estudar a gramática.* (It's important to study the grammar.)
B: *É importante estudar**mos** a gramática.* (It's important (**for us**) to study the grammar.)

Notice that in Example A there is no personal information of who might be doing "the studying." The sentence would generally be understood as an impersonal sentence that might apply to any subject. On the other hand, if I use Example B, I am being more specific as to who is going to be doing "the studying": it is "us"! Both sentences are grammatically correct, one just gives a little more information. How do you go about conjugating the personal infinitive? Here is a chart:

Personal Infinitive

–ar verbs *(lembrar)*	–er verbs *(trazer)*	–ir verbs *(dormir)*	–or verbs *(pôr)*
eu lembrar	*eu trazer*	*eu dormir*	*eu pôr*
remember (me)	bring (me)	sleep (me)	put (me)
você lembrar	*você trazer*	*você dormir*	*você pôr*
remember (you)	bring (you)	sleep (you)	put (you)
ele lembrar	*ele trazer*	*ele dormir*	*ele pôr*
remember (he/she)	bring (he/she)	sleep (he/she)	put (he/she)
nós lembrarmos	*nós trazermos*	*nós dormirmos*	*nós pormos*
remember (us)	bring (us)	sleep (us)	put (us)
vocês lembrarem	*vocês trazerem*	*vocês dormirem*	*vocês porem*
remember (you [pl.])	bring (you [pl.])	sleep (you [pl.])	put (you [pl.])
eles lembrarem	*eles trazerem*	*eles dormirem*	*eles porem*
remember (they)	bring (they)	sleep (they)	put (they)

Notice that for the first three persons (the singular ones) there is no change in the infinitive. You can maybe say that the conjugation means adding nothing, or "zero." You will only know it is not a regularly conjugated verb because it will come right after the pronoun and it will be in the infinitive. Compare *Eu falo baixo* (I speak softly) with *É possível eu falar baixo* (It's possible for me to speak softly). The first sentence has a conjugated verb in the present and the second has a personal infinitive in it!

The personal infinitive is also used after certain prepositions, when they connect complex sentences, as in the following examples:

***A fim de** eu terminar o livro, escrevi toda a noite.* (**So that** I would finish the book, I wrote the whole night.)

***Antes de** eu jogar o papel fora, copiei a informação.* (**Before** throwing (I) away the paper, I copied the information.)

***Até** eles compreenderem a lição, eles estudam.* (**Until** comprehending (they) the lesson, they study.)

Ao abrirem o livro, vocês podem começar a ler. (**Upon** opening (you [pl.]) the book, you may start to read.)

Depois de eu entrar na casa, falo com os gatos. (**After** entering (I) the house, I greet the cats.)

Para ela terminar o trabalho, lhe deram mais tempo. (**In order to** finish (she) the work, they gave her more time.)

Sem eles verem, abri a janela. (Without seeing (they), I opened the window.)

The personal infinitive is a rather cumbersome structure in English, as you can tell from the translations. However, it is very common in everyday language of Brazilians. Make sure to master this verb form, because you will garner immense rewards if you do. For one thing, using it will help you to avoid using the dreaded subjunctive!

Now try your hand at the following exercises in the personal infinitive.

EXERCISE A: THE PERSONAL INFINITIVE

Rewrite the following sentences using the personal infinitive. Start with the impersonal expression—É importante (It's important), É essencial (It's essential)—and follow with the rest of the sentence, as in the model below. Check your answers in Appendix C.

Model: *Eu estudo todos os dias. > É importante eu estudar todos os dias.*
(I study every day.) > (It's important I study every day.)

1. *Eu lembro dos nomes dos alunos.* (I remember the names of the students.)

   É importante _____.

2. *Vocês dizem a verdade.* (You [pl.] tell the truth.)

   É essencial _____.

3. *Elas trazem os livros para a escola.* (They bring the books to school.)

   É imprescindível _____.

4. *Nós visitamos nossos avós.* (We visit our grandparents.)

   É necessário _____.

5. *Você e o Roberto põem a mesa.* (You and Robert set the table.)

   É bom _____.

6. *As meninas dormen cedo.* (The young girls sleep early.)

   É importante _____.

EXERCISE B: **THE PERSONAL INFINITIVE**

Complete the sentence with a verb in the personal infinitive. Check your answers in Appendix C.

1. *Antes de eu* _____ *(ligar), eu procurei o número.* (Before calling, I looked for the number.)

2. *Até eles* _____ *(chegar), nós esperamos.* (Until arriving [they], we waited.)

3. *Depois de vocês* _____ *(comer), podem lavar os pratos.* (After eating [you (pl.)], you can wash the dishes.)

4. *Para você* _____ *(receber) os presentes, é preciso ser um bom menino.* (In order for you to receive the presents, you must be a good boy.)

Impersonal Assertions

As you saw in the previous section, impersonal expressions are part and parcel of more complex sentences in Portuguese. They are essential in constructing sentences with the personal infinitive and the subjunctive, a verb mood that you will see in subsequent chapters. Here are a few common impersonal expressions:

Portuguese	English
É bom.	It's good.
É essencial.	It's essential.
É importante.	It's important.
É necessário.	It's necessary.
É preciso.	It's necessary.
É triste.	It's sad.
É legal.	It's great.

Some expressions that are considered "impersonal" have to do with the use of the particle *se* in Portuguese. When used before a verb it means that there is no specific subject, but rather that something "is done." Take a look at these examples:

Vende-se carro. (Car(s) is (are) sold [here].)
Conserta-se roupa. (Clothes are fixed [here].)
Fala-se português. (Portuguese is spoken [here].)

Additional impersonal forms might be associated with the weather, since there is no obvious subject in those expressions. Read on and find out how to say those in Brazilian Portuguese.

Discussing the Weather

How do you say "It's raining" in Portuguese? What about "It snows a lot here"? In this section you will learn how to discuss the weather in Portuguese.

Here is a list of common expressions that relate to the climate:

Weather Expressions

Portuguese	English
Faz (muito) frio.	It's (very) cold.
Faz frio no Sul do Brasil.	It's cold in the south of Brazil.

Weather Expressions

Portuguese	English
Faz (muito) calor.	It's (very) hot.
Faz calor no nordeste.	It's hot in northeast Brazil.
Venta (muito).	It's (very) windy.
Venta muito em Fortaleza.	It's very windy in Fortaleza.
Neva (muito).	It snows (a lot).
Neva um pouco no Chile.	It snows a little in Chile.
Chove (muito).	It rains (a lot).
Chove muito em Belém.	It rains a lot in Belém.

Sometimes it is common to state how the weather is at the moment of speech. In this case you should use the verb *estar* (to be) plus the weather expression, as in the following examples:

Current Weather

Portuguese	English
Está fazendo frio hoje.	It's cold today.
Está fazendo calor hoje.	It's hot today.
Está ventando muito.	It's very windy.
Está nublado.	It's cloudy.
Está húmido!	It's humid!
Tem neblina na estrada.	There is fog on the road.
Tem relâmpago e trovoada.	There is lightening and thunder.
O tempo está feio!	The weather is ugly./It will rain.
O tempo está bonito!	The weather is nice.

Even though you will not encounter a lot of bad weather in Brazil, remember that it is a tropical country, and it will probably rain unexpectedly. Also, be sure to understand the temperature readings, which are not in Fahrenheit, but rather in Celsius (i.e., freezing point is 0°C same as 32°F). Hot weather is probably 40°C, or about 99°F. Fair weather is about 25°C or 75°F. Brazilians will feel cold at 15°C or about 60°F!

EXERCISE: WHAT'S THE WEATHER LIKE?

Now put your new knowledge to use! Translate the following sentences about the weather. Check your answers in Appendix C.

1. It's really hot in the Amazon. _____.

2. It does not snow in Brazil. _____.

3. It's hot in the North of Brazil. _____.

4. There is some fog on the road. _____.

5. The weather is nice today. _____.

The Vocabulary of Clothes

Since you just learned expression for the weather, it is good to make connections with another important set of vocabulary, namely clothes! What kinds of clothes do you wear during the different seasons? What accessories do you have with you depending on the weather? In this section you will learn these vocabulary items and much more.

Roupa de Verão/Praia (Summer Clothes/Beach Wear)

Portuguese	English
calção de banho	men's swim trunks
maiô	women's swimsuit
biquíni	bikini

Roupa de Verão/Praia **(Summer Clothes/Beach Wear)**

Portuguese	English
shortes	shorts, short pants
saída de praia	cloth you wear around your waist as you leave the pool/beach
camiseta	t-shirt
camiseta sem manga	sleeveless shirt, tank top
sandálias	sandals
sandália japonesa	flip-flops

Here's a short list of accessories or products that you would wear or take with you to the beach:

Acessórios e Produtos de Praia **(Beach Accessories and Products)**

Portuguese	English
óculos de sol, óculos escuros	sunglasses
bolsa de praia	beach bag
cadeira de praia	beach chair
sobrinha de praia	beach umbrella
bronzeador	tanning lotion
protetor solar	sunscreen

Brazilians don't usually read magazines or books when they go to the beach. The beach is a place to see and to be seen, and a place to flirt. It is the quintessential social hangout, where friends and acquaintances meet. When visiting a beach in Brazil, try to start up a conversation with a local beach-goer!

What about the clothes one might wear during the winter months? First of all, in Brazil the seasons are not as clearly delineated as in the United States. And because Brazil is a continental country, the north and northeast can have a array of tropical and subtropical climates while the south and southeast is more temperate. In any case, if you are visiting southern cities such as Rio de Janeiro and São Paulo in the winter months (June, July, and August for countries located below the Equator!), you should know the following vocabulary items:

Roupa de Inverno (Winter Clothes)

Portuguese	English
botas	boots
luvas	gloves, mittens
chapéu, touca	hat
malha	sweater, sweatshirt
xale	scarf
casaco de frio	winter coat
casaco de couro	leather coat
impermeável	rain coat
jaqueta	jacket
pulôver	pullover, vest

Here is a typical conversation at a store where someone is trying to purchase clothes for the winter/autumn season:

Q: *Bom dia, senhora, em que posso servi-la?* (Good morning, ma'am, how can I help you?)

A: *Bom dia, estou procurando um pulôver.* (Good morning, I'm looking for a pullover.)

Q: *Pois não, nós temos aqui uma variedade para a senhora.* (Of course, here we have a great variety for you ma'am.)

A: *Ah, sim, vocês têm algum sem manga?* (Oh, yes, do you have a vest?)

Q: *Sim, temos. São inclusive mais baratos.* (Yes, we sure do. In fact they are less expensive.)

A: *Ah, são lindos.* (Oh, they are beautiful.)

Q: Quer experimentar esses? (Do you want to try these on?)

A: Quero, sim. (I sure do.)

Q: Então o lugar de experimentar fica logo ali. Qualquer coisa, pode falar comigo.
(The fitting rooms are right over there. If you need anything, just call me.)

A: Muito obrigada. (Thank you very much.)

Q: Pois não, senhora. (Sure, ma'am.)

EXERCISE: WHAT WOULD YOU WEAR?

Make a list of all the clothes and accessories you would wear according to the weather conditions. You can see some possible answers in Appendix C.

1. *Faz muito sol, a temperatura é de 38 graus Celsius.*

   _____

   _____

2. *Chove muito!*

   _____

   _____

3. *Está nevando.*

   _____

   _____

4. *Está um pouco frio, a temperatura é de 15 graus Celsius.*

   _____

   _____

5. *Você está em Copacabana!*

   _____

   _____

CHAPTER 17

Imperative and Subjunctive Constructions

THE IMPERATIVE AND the subjunctive forms in Portuguese are intricate, but don't be intimidated by them! The imperative forms are the basis for the subjunctive constructions, which you will see later in this chapter. You will also learn the past subjunctive, as well as when to use the indicative and when to use the subjunctive. Have fun!

Imperative Constructions

When you want to have something done, you need a quick and easy way to express yourself. The English equivalent would be a verbal "command" or forceful request. In Portuguese, we use the imperative mode. Here are some examples of imperative constructions:

> ***Ligue*** *para mim mais tarde.* [you] (Call me later.)
> ***Comam*** *tudo!* [you (pl.)] (Eat everything!)
> ***Abra*** *a janela, por favor!* [you] (Open the window, please!)
> ***Trabalhem*** *mais rápido!* [you (pl.)] (Work faster!)

Notice that you usually give commands to either one person (you) or a group of people (you (pl.)). Normally we don't tell ourselves what to do, or even just ourselves and a group of people (i.e., we could say "let us [verb]" or "let me [see]," but that's not strictly a command or imperative construction). So the imperative is relatively easy to learn because you only have to know two basic forms, singular and plural.

The table that follows shows how to write the imperative in Portuguese.

Imperative of –*AR* Verbs

TRACK 85

Verb	First Person Form	Imperative	English
estudar (to study)	*estudo*	*Estude! Estudem!*	Study!
começar (to start)	*começo*	*Comece! Comecem!*	Start!
chegar (to arrive)	*chego*	*Chegue! Cheguem!*	Arrive!

In writing this verb, start with the first person singular, present indicative form of the verb. If the verb is *estudar* (to study) then the first person form is *estudo* (I study). Next, drop the last vowel and add the endings –*e* for singular forms and –*em* for plural forms. You are done! Now remember the rules in Portuguese about the phonetic adjustments. That means that depending on the end vowels, you might have to add other letters to make the verbs sound alike, across conjugations. This is what happens to the verb *começar* (to start). This verb ends in –*a* and is preceded by the consonant –*ç*–. This makes the sound soft, like a /s/, as in "sat" or "sought." When the –o is dropped, and the –e is added, there is no need to include the soft –ç– sound, because the next vowel is –e, and it's already soft, so just include –c–. A somewhat similar situation occurs with the verb *chegar* (to arrive). In this case, it is necessary to include change to the combination –gu–; otherwise a –ge– would sound like *gente* (people), with a soft consonantal sound.

> Here we use the words "soft" and "hard" to describe consonants and vowels in Portuguese, but we need to make sure that everyone understands what we mean. By "soft" we mean sounds that are made with some friction of the air leaving the mouth, like the "j" in "jewel" or the "g" in "gist." By "hard" we mean sounds that are made with the sudden release of air, as in the "g" of "ghost."

Next, look at the imperative forms of verbs that end in –*er* and –*ir*.

TRACK 86

Imperative of –er and –ir Verbs

Verb	First Person Form	Imperative
beber (to drink)	*bebo*	*Beba! Bebam!* (Drink!)
fazer (to do)	*faço*	*Faça! Façam!* (Do!)
trazer (to bring)	*trago*	*Traga! Tragam!* (Bring!)
dormir (to sleep)	*durmo*	*Durma! Durmam!* (Start!)
partir (to leave)	*parto*	*Parta! Partam!* (Leave!)
pedir (to ask for)	*peço*	*Peça! Peçam!* (Ask for [it]!)
vir (to come)	*venho*	*Venha! Venham!* (Come!)

So, in this case, we drop the –*o* and adding either –*a* or –*am* according to the number of listeners. Although they might look irregular, because they are based on the irregular first person form, these imperative verbs are actually very regular. Now, here's a list of the truly irregular imperative/command forms:

Irregular Imperatives

Verb	Imperative	Example
dar (to give)	*Dê ! Dêem!*	*Me dê isso!* (Give me that!)
ser (to be)	*Seja! Sejam!*	*Sejam bonzinhos!* (Be nice [you (pl.)].)
estar (to be)	*Esteja! Estejam!*	*Esteja aqui às nove!* (Be here at nine!)
ir (to go)	*Vá! Vão!*	*Vá embora!* (Go away!)
saber (to know)	*Saiba! Saibam!*	*Saiba que eu sou forte!* (Know [be aware] that I am strong!)

As you can see, there is no need to indicate the first person singular form of the present tense, since it does not matter for the purposes of cre-ating the imperative verbs. They are all irregular from the start. These verbs are very handy when you want to communicate something immediate without a lot of subtlety.

If you would like to be a little more polite, you have to use what we call a present subjunctive. Read on.

Introducing the Subjunctive

The subjunctive scares a lot of language learners, especially those whose native language is not Italian, Spanish, or French. This of course includes English speakers, to whom the subjunctive seems unfamiliar and formal. The use of the subjunctive that is easiest for students to understand is the one that relates to "suggestion" or "want." You have just learned how to give a "command" for something you want done. Now you are going to achieve the same result, but you will do it in a more educated, polite way.

The other good news is that the forms of the subjunctive are the same as the commands you just learned! Look at the following comparative list of examples.

Limpe a mesa! (Clean the table!) [direct command]
*Quero **que** você **limpe** a mesa.* (I want you to clean the table.) [subjunctive]

Façam *o trabalho de casa!* (Do (you all) the homework!) [direct command]

Eu quero **que** *vocês* **façam** *o trabalho de casa.* (I want you all to do the homework.) [subjunctive]

Notice that the subjunctive forms happen when followed by the word *que* (that). So you use the subjunctive form after the introduction of another subordinate clause introduced by the relative pronoun *que.* See the chart below to get a clear picture of this subjunctive "map."

Subjunctive Construction

TRACK 88

Expression of "Want"	QUE	[another subject]	Subjunctive Verb
Eu quero	*que*	*vocês*	*aprendam.*
Literal Translation: I want that you (pl.) learn.			
Eu preciso	*que*	*ela*	*me chame.*
Literal Translation: I need that she call me.			
Eu sugiro	*que*	*você*	*estude mais.*
Literal Translation: I suggest that you study more.			
Eu desejo	*que*	*eles*	*saibam de tudo.*
Literal Translation: I desire that they know everything.			

Translating sentences from the Portuguese subjunctive to English is hard because English speakers don't usually say "We want that she learn." In fact, this sentence is a bit awkward. English speakers today are far more likely to say "We want her to learn." So, given the choice, English speakers would generally much rather use the infinitive rather than the subjunctive form.

Now, the complex sentences above are written in the present tense. This means that both the first part of the sentence (the main clause, *quero* [I want]) and the second part (the *que,* or subordinate clause) are all in the present tense. But what if I wanted to say not "I long" but rather "I longed"? What would happen to the second part of the sentence? Read on to find out.

Past Subjunctive

The past subjunctive is used when the main clause is also in the past and also requires you to play the "agreement game" again. Look at the following chart to get a better understanding:

Past Subjunctive Construction

Expression of "Want"	que	[another subject]	Subjunctive Verb
Eu gostaria	que	*vocês*	*aprendessem.*
Translation: I wanted you (pl.) to learn.			
Eu precisava	que	*ela*	*me chamasse.*
Translation: I needed for her to call me.			
Eu sugeri	que	*você*	*estudasse mais.*
Translation: I suggested that you study more.			
Eu desejava	que	*eles*	*soubessem de tudo.*
Translation: I longed for them to know.			

Notice that the first verb is in either the preterite (*sugeri* [I suggested]) or in the imperfect (*precisava* [I needed]), or even in the conditional (*gostaria* [I wanted] or [would have liked]). All of these verb tenses imply that the desire existed before, and the next verb is a longing or unrealized event or action on the part of another agent.

You may also use the past subjunctive when you express doubt in the first clause. The verb that comes in the subordinate clause is in the past subjunctive, as in the following examples:

Duvidávamos que eles viessem. (We doubted that they would come.)
Não era certo que ela estivesse ali. (It was not certain that she was there.)

Finally, if there is a verb of emotion or surprise in the main clause, the next one in the subordinate is also in the past subjunctive:

*Era surpreendente que ele **tivesse** medo.* (It was suprising that he would be afraid.)
*Fiquei triste que eles não **telefonassem**.* (I was sad that they did not call.)

Future Subjunctive

Portuguese also has a verb mood called the future subjunctive. This construction works much the same way as other subjunctive forms. Use this verb with the words *se* (if), *quando* (when), and *enquanto* (while) in order to describe something that has not happened yet, as in the the following examples:

> *Podemos ir ao cinema, **se** você **quiser**.* (We can go to the movies, if you want.)
> ***Se fizer** frio, pomos o casaco.* (If it becomes cold, we'll put on the coat.)
> *Limpo a casa **quando** ela **vier**.* (I'll clean the house when she comes.)
> ***Quando** eu **puder**, ligo para você.* (When I can, I'll call you.)
> ***Enquanto** eu **dormir**, não faça barulho.* (While I sleep, don't make any noise.)
> *Fique em casa **enquanto** eu **estiver** fora.* (Stay home while I am out.)

Here is how you come up with the future subjunctive forms: first, start with the preterite tense form of *eles* (they) of any verb. For example, *falaram* (they spoke). Then remove the *—am* ending and add the following endings for the other persons.

Conjugating the Future Subjunctive

if-clause	—*ar* verb	—*er* verb	—*ir* verb
	falaram	*comeram*	*dormiram*
Se eu	*falar*	*comer*	*dormir*
Se você	*falar*	*comer*	*dormir*
Se ele/ela	*falar*	*comer*	*dormir*
Se nós	*falarmos*	*comermos*	*dormirmos*
Se vocês	*falarem*	*comerem*	*dormirem*
Se eles/elas	*falarem*	*comerem*	*dormirem*

Notice that the first three persons (I, you, she/he) are conjugated by simply dropping the original ending and adding nothing. The next three persons are conjugated by adding some endings. Again, the same endings apply to all *—ar*, *—er*, and *—ir* verbs, respectively. Other subjunctive forms are *for* (be), *estiver* (be [located]), and *souber* (know).

Indicative or Subjunctive?

Sometimes it is difficult to decide whether to use one of the indicative tenses or the subjunctive tenses. In order to figure this out, ask yourself these questions: first, is the form in the main or the subordinate clause? If it's in the main clause, chances are you will need the indicative. Remember that most of the time the subordinate clause comes after the relative pronoun *que* (that). Second, ask yourself whether the action is a hypothetical or an action based on a condition. Chances are that that action will be expressed in the subjunctive. If you are dealing with statements of fact, use the indicative. Here are some examples that help you clarify these ground rules:

Indicative Versus Subjunctive Examples

Indicative [fact]	Subjunctive [desire, doubt, request]
Você estuda muito.	*Eu quero que você estude muito.*
You study a lot.	I want to study a lot.
Ele tem um carro azul.	*Ele quer um carro que seja azul.*
He has a blue car.	He wants a car that is blue.
Elas foram ao banco.	*Eu queria que elas fossem ao banco.*
They went to the bank.	I wanted them to go to the bank.

Practice with the Subjunctive Forms

Now that you've had some experience with the subjunctive forms, let's see what you remember? The following exercises will test your knowledge and push you to determine which form should be used where. Check your answers in Appendix C when you're finished.

EXERCISE A: SUBJUNCTIVE FORMS

Write the verbs in parentheses in the subjunctive, depending if it is present, past, or future.

1. *Eu preciso que vocês me* _____ (respond). (I need you to answer me.)

2. *Ela deseja que você lhe* _____ (give) *o livro.* (She wants you to give her the book.)

3. *Nós gostaríamos que ele* _____ (come) *mais cedo.* (We wanted him to come earlier.)

4. *Eles se surpreenderam que ela* _____ (was) *tão magra.* (They were surprised that she was so skinny.)

5. *Se não* _____ (be) *muito tarde, vou pegar o ônibus.* (If it is not too late, I will take the bus.)

6. *Enquanto ele* _____ (need) *de mim, eu vou ajudá-lo.* (While he needs me, I will help him.)

EXERCISE B: SUBJUNCTIVE FORMS

Indicative or Subjunctive? Circle the correct verb.

1. *Se eu me* **lembro/lembrasse** *de tudo, seria mais fácil.* (If I remembered everything, it would be much easier.)
2. *Elas não se* **esquecem/esqueçam** *de nada.* (They do not forget anything.)
3. *Nós gostaríamos que eles* **trouxeram/trousessem** *a cerveja.* (We would like them to bring the beer.)
4. *É bom que eles* **comem/comam** *tudo.* (It's nice that they eat everything.)

Expression with the Verb *Dar*

At this point in your language learning, it is important to add some idiomatic expressions that will help you sound more "native." These expressions do not necessarily follow subjunctive clauses, but they may. The important thing to learn is that this particular verb *dar* (to give) is very versatile in the Portuguese language.

Dar (to give) Expressions

Expression: *dar* (to be sufficient)

Example: *O dinheiro não dá para sair de ferias.* (The money is not enough for vacation.)

Expression: *Assim não dá!* (That's unacceptable!)

Dar (to give) Expressions

Example: *Mais que vinte dólares? Assim não dá!* (More than 20 bucks? That's not right!)

Expression: *dar certo* (to work out [well])

Example: *Faça assim que dá certo.* (Do it this way and it will work out.)

Expression: *dar em nada* (to fall through)

Example: *Tentei, mas não deu em nada.* (I tried, but it fell through.)

Expression: *dar um jeito/jeitinho* (to find a way)

Example: *Dá um jeitinho pra mim?* (Can you help me out/find a way for me?)

Expression: *dar em* [person] (to hit someone)

Example: *Ela deu no irmão dela.* (She hit her brother.)

Expression: *dar um passeio* (to go for a stroll/on an outing)

Example: *Vamos dar um passeio?* (Do you want to go out for a stroll?)

Expression: *dar um pulo* (to stop by)

Example: *Vou dar um pulo na casa dela.* (I'll make a quick stop my her house.)

Expression: *dá para/pra* [verb] (It's possible to/can [verb])

Example: *Dá pra entender isso?* (Can you understand that?)

Using the Verb *Dar*

Now see if you can finish the next set of activities that test your comprehension on these new expressions. Determine the best translation for the following sentences in English. Check your answers in Appendix C.

1. I made breakfast, but it didn't turn out well.

    _____

2. This is just not right!

    _____

3. I'll call a friend, and we'll find a solution.

    _____

4. The new venture fell through.

    _____

CHAPTER 18

Carnaval, Samba, Feijoada, and *Futebol*

THIS CHAPTER COVERS the Brazilian feast of *Carnaval* and the love for food, music, and soccer shared by many Brazilians. You will learn about the origins of unique musical expressions, an incredible feast for the senses, the national dish of Brazil, and the Brazilians' uncanny ability to win world soccer championships. Pay attention to new vocabulary so you can talk about these exciting aspects of Brazilian culture in Portuguese!

Brazilian *Carnaval*

This "feast" of music and dance traditionally lasts several days in mid-February. The name comes from the Latin words *carne* meaning "meat" or "flesh," and *vale*, meaning "ball" or "feast." This was the time when Catholics would enjoy eating and drinking excessively just before the Lent period. *Carnaval* continues to be a "feast of excesses," but its original religious nature has been lost to many Brazilians and Latin Americans.

The tradition of *Carnaval* celebration started with the seventeenth century Portuguese folkloric practice called *entrudo* when, during the weeks before Lent, people would throw eggs, water, or flour at passersby in the streets. The custom was based in mischief and fun, much like many other European traditions where tomatoes or oranges are thrown at people at the end of the harvest.

As a colonial country, Brazil was very much affected and influenced by other traditions originating in France and Italy, where *Carnaval* signified urban parades, with typical characters such as the *Pierrot*, the *Colombine*, and the *Rei Momo*, the King of Carnaval. During the nineteenth century, the first *corsos* or decorated car parades would appear. Groups of people who would decorate their cars and parade in the streets singing and dancing. These became more popular in the beginning of the twentieth century, and in Brazil the *escolas de samba* or "samba schools" were organized.

One of the first *escolas de samba* in Brazil was called *Deixa Falar* (literally meaning "Let Speak"), which later became known as *Estácio de Sá*, after a locality in Rio. Schools were later organized into a *Liga de Escolas de Samba* or a "League of Samba Schools," which regulated the *Carnaval* parade in Rio. People wanted to know which school had the best performance, the most animated group of people, the best musical emsemble, the best costumes, and so on. Nowadays the *Desfile de Carnaval* or "*Carnaval* parade" in Rio de Janeiro lasts two days and follows a complicated set of rules. "*Carnaval* judges" rate the schools based on several artistic and musical categories. Each year the winner has bragging rights until the next *Carnaval* season!

Along with *samba schools, cordões* and *blocos carnavalescos* developed in which groups of people that would dress alike and march along singing, drinking, and dancing. These became increasingly popular with the addition of music that was being composed and played called the *marchinhas carnavalescas* or "little Carnaval songs."

Carnaval Beyond Rio and São Paulo

In northeastern cities of Recife and Olinda, the *Carnaval* tradition is not based on *samba* but rather on more local musical styles, namely the *frevo,* which is a frenetic, rhythmic sound, and the *maracatu,* an African-based musical and dance tradition that includes elaborate costumes and a distinctive staccato beat.

In the city of Salvador, in the state of Bahia, the *trios elétricos* are basically large trucks that have been adapted to include a top platform with musicians that play a more electric *samba* sound, amplified by huge speakers that make most of the sides of the truck. People dance around these trucks and sing along with famous Brazilian musical performers. The *trios elétricos* are a show in and of themselves.

Salvador is known for its strong African connection, and many black musical groups, such as the *Olodum, Ileyaê,* and the *Afoxé Filhos de Ghandi* have put Brazil on the map as far as world music is concerned. If you want to hear a disctintive "black" sound in Brazil, check out these musical groups.

In Rio de Janeiro, the biggest parade of *samba* schools happens in the *Sambódromo* a place especially built for people to admire the parade. During *Carnaval* this is primetime entertainment on TV, since the schools are judged on a series of factors, such as overall originality, songs, costumes, dancing, and performance quality.

The Music of Brazil

Brazil is the birthplace of *samba*, a highly rhythmic, melodious, and lively musical expression. It is also a dance, often performed during *Carnaval*. The samba sound has its origins or roots in the African tradition in Brazil. The slaves brought not only the instruments (*agogô*, *cuíca*) but also the syncopated rhythms and gyrating dance moves.

Instruments

The unique samba sound is achieved through an array of interesting instruments. Possibly the best well-known musical elements in *samba* are the *pandeiro*, a larger version of the tambourine, and the *cuíca*, a drum-like instrument that produces a squeaky sound, very typical of *samba* songs. Here is a list of some other *samba* instruments and their descriptions:

TRACK 89

- *agogô:* two bells together, which are struck with a stick or squeezed together
- *caixa:* a smaller drum with strings in the bottom that creates a sound like a "snare-drum"
- *cavaquinho:* a small, four string guitar-like instrument created in Portugal that later inspired the ukulele
- *chucalho:* a shaker instrument made by putting metal cans together and filling them with rocks, sand, or beans
- *cuíca:* a drum-like instrument with a stiff string inside, upon which the player slides his fingers up and down to produce a squeaky sound; the quality of the sound can change depending on how fast you slide and pressure put on the skin of the drum.
- *pandeiro:* larger version of the tambourine, which is played fast, and sometimes spun on one finger for show
- *repenique:* a medium-size drum, larger than a snare drum, that is played with a stick and one hand
- *surdo:* a very big drum that has a low but loud sound (surdo means "deaf" in Portuguese)
- *tamborim:* a very small, short drum, without bells or metal parts, that is played very fast with a stick

Types of Samba

Like many other musical genres, the samba has many subcategories. Aside from the *samba enredo*, the kind of fast, highly rhythmic samba performed during *Carnaval*, there are other slower versions of *samba*. One of the most famous one is the *samba canção* or "samba song." These are slower *samba* pieces with romantic lyrics that are put to music and performed by traditional crooners. The *pagode*, which came into being in Rio and has been reproduced in other parts of Brazil, is the kind of *samba* sound that originated in the Brazilian backyards from people getting together and playing the various *samba* instruments for hours on end. All of these *samba* parties had the obligatory *cerveja* (beer) or *cachaça* (sugarcane rum) that came with it a traditional party. There is a good amount of humor in the lyrics, which makes them extremely popular.

For more information about *samba*, check out *www.worldsamba.org*.

Bossa Nova

Brazil is not famous just for *samba*. There are several musical expressions that can trace its roots back to the country of Carmen Miranda. One of the most popular is *bossa nova*. This musical expression was started in the late "fifties by upper middle class composers. It is a jazzy musical style that emphasizes the carefree living so typical of the Rio de Janeiro beach scene. For that very reason *bossa nova* was criticized, because it bore very little resemblance to the life of working class Brazilians, as many of the *samba* lyrics would have. One of the most famous *bossa nova* songs is *A Garota de Ipanema* ("The Girl from Ipanema") by Antonio Carlos Jobim. This song is nothing more than a description of a beautiful woman walking to the beach. It's about the sweet way she moves and the sentiment of the composer, who confesses that she is the most beautiful thing that he has ever seen go by. The song became known to American audiences when Frank Sinatra recorded its English version and is known all over the world as one of the most recognized Brazilian tunes.

Música Popular Brasileira or "Brazilian Popular Music"

Also called "*MPB*" for short, this type of song grew out of the Brazilian protest songs of the sixties. This musical style can be traced to a strong reaction against the carefree lyrics of *bossa nova*. After the military coup of 1964, *MPB* artists strived to put the harsh reality of Brazilian life front and center. One of the songs that clearly depict working class Brazilians is *Pedro Pedreiro* by Chico Buarque de Hollanda. The song is a wonderfully written narration of the monotonous life of a bricklayer. Other famous *MPB* singers and composers include Milton Nascimento, Caetano Veloso, and Gilberto Gil. Veloso and others created the psychedelic music style of the seventies called *Tropicália*, which added to the richness of musical styles of the time. *MPB* is part of the Brazilian music scene to this day, with an incredible array of female interpreters, such as Maria Bethânia, Marisa Monte, Ana Carolina, and many others. Do not be surprised if you are invited to a party and one of the guests pulls out a guitar, starts a tune, and is joined by several others guests in singing well-known *MPB* lyrics.

Música Sertaneja: Brazil's Answer to Country Music

In contrast to *samba* and *bossa nova*, which are truly urban styles of music, *música sertaneja* has its origin in the interior or back country of Brazil. It has similarities to American country music, in that the lyrics reflect romantic themes and the plight of cowboys. It can be associated with the uneducated class, but the record sales of *sertaneja* songsters are a testament to its popularity.

Brazilian Classical Music

Perhaps people do not normally associate Brazil with classical music, but classical musicians are very familiar with the music of famous Brazilian classical composers. Two of the most famous ones are Carlos Gomes and Heitor Villa-Lobos. Gomes (1836-1896) was a distinguished nineteenth-century romantic composer born in Campinas, Brazil. He was one of the first New World composers to be accepted by the musical establishment in Europe. He became the protégé of D. Pedro II, Emperor of Brazil. He wrote piano pieces and operas, the most famous of which is *Il Guarany*, based on a romantic novel by the nineteenth-century Brazilian writer José de Alencar.

Villa-Lobos (1887–1959) is perhaps the best well-known South American classical composer. He was largely self-taught and wrote *Bachianas Brasileiras*, inspired by the art of Johann Sebastian Bach and the Brazilian musical tradition. He traveled extensively in Brazil collecting samples of folk songs, even going to the Amazon to familiarize himself with the music of the indigenous peoples. He wrote many piano pieces that incorporated both Brazilian folk music and stylistic elements of European tradition.

Futebol (Soccer) in Brazil: Five-Time World Champions

Brazilians have enjoyed international reputation as one of the world's soccer powerhouses. Children play soccer in the streets from an early age in much the same way that American kids play baseball or football. There are no official "little leagues," and it is still a very male-dominated sport. In schools and colleges there are some leagues that play *futebol de salão*, an indoor version of the sport played with a smaller ball and smaller nets.

There are numerous independent *futebol* teams in Brazil, sometimes two or three in one city. In the past, teams survived with donations from the club members and ticket sales, but nowadays corporate advertisement is part of the sport reality, changing the team's uniforms and the ability for teams to get players of international fame.

Following is a table with Brazil *futebol* World Cup championships:

Brazil's Five *Futebol* Championships

Year	Host Country	Final Score
1958	Sweden	Brazil 5, Sweden 2
1962	Chile	Brazil 3, Czechoslovakia 1
1970	Mexico	Brazil 4, Italy 1
1994	United States	Brazil 3, Italy 2 (in penalty shootout)
2002	Korea/Japan	Brazil 2, Germany 0

There was a dry spell after the 1970 championship, where all Brazilians talked about was how and when they would get the "Tetra," meaning the "fourth" championship. But the Brazilian team came close a couple of times, such as in 1998, when they lost to France in the final. A common phrase that is heard about soccer is "The English invented it, the Brazilians perfected it."

Culinary Expressions

There are many interesting culinary traditions in Brazil due to the diversity of immigrant populations. There are Italian, Japanese, Chinese, German, and many other immigrant groups that have contributed to the tastes and aromas of the Brazilian kitchen. But the national dish of Brazil comes from an unlikely source: concocted by African slaves, *feijoada* is based on pork leftovers and black beans. The white slavemasters would throw away the pig's snout, feet, and ears. Slaves would assemble a heavy stew with pork pieces and fat in order to feed themselves. The wonderful smells coming from the kitchen would eventually entice a whole nation, and *feijoada* became a national standard. Nowadays you can be served *feijoada* in fancy, five-star hotels. Today, the snout and feet are usually replaced by generous pieces of pork sausage, but traditionalists still keep tasty pigs' ears in the mix.

If you're interested in trying to make this and other Brazilian dishes at home, go to your local bookstore and invest in a couple of Brazilian cookbooks. You can also find lots of great recipes online. One Web site that offers a recipe for *feijoada* is *www.brazilbrazil.com*.

What's on Brazilian TV?

Brazil is world famous for its *novelas* or television soap operas. Unlike American TV soaps, which can go on for decades, *novelas* normally last six to eight months at the most. Because the novelas are so popular, they have been exported to Portugal, where the Portuguese people have learned how to pronounce some typically Brazilian idioms. One of the most famous Brazilian soaps was *Roque Santeiro*, which had been banned during the military dictatorship for its irreverent humor and distinctly anti-government bias. It was later remade in the early nineties to great success. Because of its popularity, the writers even extended the *capítulos* or "daily episodes" to make the novela last longer. If you have extended cable or satellite TV service, you can watch current *novelas* in Brazilian channels, especially the *Globo* network, one of the biggest and most-watched channels in Brazil.

Brazilian Cinema

Brazil has made a significant contribution to international cinema, starting from the sixties revolution of modernist *cinema novo* with directors Glauber Rocha and Nelson Pereira dos Santos to the more recent work of Carlos Diegues, Hector Babenco, and Walter Salles. Here is a list of the titles, dates, and corresponding Brazilian directors.

Award-Winning Brazilian Movies

Title	Year	Director
Vidas Secas (Barren Lives)	1963	Glauber Rocha
Terra em Transe (Land in Torment)	1967	Glauber Rocha
Macunaíma (Jungle Freaks)	1969	Joaquim Pedro de Andrade
Bye Bye Brasil (Bye Bye Brazil)	1979	Carlos Diegues
Pixote, lei do mais fraco (Pixote)	1981	Hector Babenco
A Hora da Estrela (The Hour of the Star)	1985	Suzana Amaral
Terra Estrangeira (Foreign Land)	1995	Walter Salles/Daniela Thomas
Central do Brasil (Central Station)	1998	Walter Salles

There are more recent examples of Brazilian cinema that includes films such as *Cidade de Deus* (City of God) (2002) by directors Fernando Meirelles and Katia Lund, and *Madame Satã* (Madam Satã) (2002) by first-timer Karim Aïnouz. A new breed of filmmakers from the northeast has given Brazilian cinema a decidedly more gritty style. Two very recent examples of this *nordestino* ("northeastern") wave are *Amarelo Manga* (2002) by innovative director Cláudio Assis and *Árido Movie* (2004) by equally creative Lírio Ferreira.

CULTURAL REVIEW: WHAT'S THE WORD?

Think you have a pretty good grasp of the basics of Brazilian culture now? Let's test your knowledge. Match the word with its definition, according to the text you just read. Check your answers in Appendix C.

1. *cinema novo* _____   (a) pig's foot

2. *feijoada* _____   (b) modernist film movement

3. *cachaça* _____   (c) one of the greatest soccer players in the world

4. *caipirinha* _____   (d) lime, sugar, and rum drink

5. *pé de porco* _____   (e) black bean and pork stew

6. *Tetra* _____   (f) squeaky drum

7. *Pelé* _____   (g) sugarcane rum

8. *Il Guarany* _____   (h) tambourine

9. *MPB* _____   (i) classical masterpiece of Gomes

10. *pandeiro* _____   (j) theme samba

11. *cuíca* _____   (l) Brazilian Popular Music

12. *samba enredo* _____   (m) fourth

CHAPTER 19

Means of Communication

Y OU HAVE LEARNED the difference between preterite and imperfect, practiced the subjunctive mood, and learned about Brazilian culture. Now you have enough basic communication skills not only to survive when you're visiting Brazil but also to really engage in meaningful conversations. By the end of this chapter you'll feel much more confident about your language skills!

In Person

You will have lots of opportunities to converse in Portuguese when you get to Brazil, and in this chapter you will review some information that you have already learned but want to sharpen up. First, make sure to greet people correctly when you are in Brazil. Here are some familiar greetings:

TRACK 90

Portuguese	English
Olá, como vai?	Hello, how are you?
Como vai o senhor?	How are you (sir)?
Como vai a senhora?	How are you (ma'am)?
Bem, obrigado.	Fine, thanks. [Obrigada for women speakers]
Oi, tudo bem?	Hi, how's it going?
Tudo bom!	Great!
Tudo legal!/Tudo jóia!	Great! [a little slang]
E aí, tudo bem?	So, how's it going?
Mais ou menos.	So-so.
Tudo em ordem.	Everything is fine [literally "in order"].
Até logo./Até mais.	See you soon./See you later [literally "until..."].
Tchau!	Bye!

One quick note on saying goodbye: Brazilians have adopted the word *tchau* from the Italian *ciao* (bye), pronounced very closely to the Italian, but with a Portuguese spelling. The original word from Portuguese for "good-bye" is *adeus*, which is still very common in European Portuguese. The diminutive *adeuzinho* is also heard among friends. If, however, a Brazilian says *adeus*, it usually has a serious connotation, as in "goodbye forever." So you might want to avoid saying that, especially after you have made some friends!

At a Social Gathering

Learning a language can be so much fun because you are able to make so many new friends from a different culture. In a social gathering, you have to master not only familiar greetings, but also ones that are a bit more formal in nature. The following are some examples of greetings and introductions that will help you with your newly acquired "social skills."

Q: Flávia: *Rodrigo, eu gostaria de te apresentar à Dona Maria.* (Rodrigo, I would like to introduce you to Mrs. Maria.) [The word *Dona* is an honorific, a sign of respect, but it is followed by one's first name.]

A: Rodrigo: *Muito prazer, Dona Maria.* (Nice to meet you, Mrs. Maria.)

Q: Flávia: *Dona Maria, eu gostaria de lhe apresentar ao meu amigo Rodrigo.* (Dona Maria, I would like to introduce you to my friend Rodrigo.)

A: Dona Maria: *Muito prazer, Rodrigo, você é o noivo da Flávia?* (Nice to meet you, Rodrigo, are you Flávia's fiancé?)

Other less formal examples are as follows:

Q: Michele: *Olá pessoal, eu gostaria de apresentar para vocês o meu amigo Robert.* (Hello guys, I would like to introduce you (pl.) to my friend Robert.)

A: Robert: *Prazer!* (My pleasure!)

Q: Felícia: *Oi Robert, tudo bem?* (Hi Robert, how's it going?)

A: Robert: *Tudo bem, mas estou morrendo de calor!* (Great, but I'm dying from this heat!)

Here are some more casual examples:

Q: Flávia: *Este é o meu amigo Patrício.* (This is my friend Patrício.)

A: Sílvio: *Esta é a minha esposa Isaura.* (This is my wife Isaura.)

Q: Flávia: *Encantada.* (Nice to meet you.)

A: Sílvio: *Muito prazer.* (My pleasure.)

Other responses to introductions include the following:
Igualmente. (Likewise.)
O prazer é (todo) meu. (The pleasure is [all] mine.)

Making Conversation in Portuguese

After introductions are done, the real conversation begins. Your host/hostess will probably say bem-vindo (if you are a man) and bem-vinda (if you are a woman). Once you have been introduced to people, you will have to carry on a conversation that goes beyond simple greetings. At times you might want to ask for clarification. Here are some useful guidelines:

Getting into the conversation with polite interruption:

TRACK 91

perdão (excuse me; sorry)
por favor (please)
por obséquio (please [more formal])
por gentileza (please [more formal])

These expressions indicate you are not following the conversation:

Desculpa, não entendi. (Sorry, I didn't understand.)
Não escutei direito. (I didn't hear that well.)
Perdão, não compreendo. (Sorry, I don't understand.)

Here's how to express your confusion with a question:

Como? (What?)
Desculpa, o que o senhor/a senhora falou? (Pardon me, what did you say sir/ma'am?)
O que significa… ? (What does… mean?)
Quando se diz… ? (When do you say… ?)
Por que o senhor/a senhora disse que… ? (Why do you [sir/ma'am] say… ?)

Here's how to request that the speaker repeat what was said:

Por favor, o senhor/a senhora poderia repetir? (Please, could you repeat that [sir/ma'am]?)
Por gentileza, o senhor/a senhora poderia repetir o que disse? (Please, could you repeat what you said [sir/ma'am]?)
O senhor/a senhora poderia me fazer o favor de repetir? (Would the gentleman/the lady do me the favor of repeating that?)

When you are learning a new language, it may seem like people are speaking way too fast. This is because since you are still learning the beginning and ends of words, and they all seem to blend together. So you might want to ask speakers to slow down using the following expressions:

TRACK 92

Desculpe, não falo português fluentemente. Você poderia falar mais devagar? (Sorry, I don't speak Portuguese fluently. Could you speak a little slower?)

Por favor, o senhor/a senhora poderia falar mais devagar? Eu não entendi da primeira vez. (Please, would the gentleman/the lady speak a little slower? I didn't get it the first time.)

Here are some other tips that you might find useful:

- Say *com licença* (excuse me) when you are passing through a crowd and need to get somewhere.
- Say *perdão!* or *desculpa!* (sorry) if you need to apologize for bumping into someone.
- Say *com a sua licença* (excuse me) if you need to excuse yourself from the table.

Conversation Starters

Suppose that you have no idea as to how to start talking. Here are some topics that can help you:

o clima (the weather)
a situação econômica (the economic situation)
a situação internacional (the international situation)
os filmes que estão passando no momento (the movies currently showing)

TRACK 93

Here are some questions to get conversations started with native speakers:
Que clima maravilhoso, não acha? (What wonderful weather, don't you think?)
Que tempo horrível lá fora, não? (What horrible weather outside, right?)
O que você acha? (What do you think?)
Que filmes você gosta de ver? (What movies do you like to see?)

Farewell

Everything must come to an end, and so do conversations. Here are some ways of saying "goodbye" in Portuguese.

> *Até logo!* (See you later!)
> *Até mais!* (See you soon!)
> *Até a próxima.* (Until next time.)
> *Até amanhã.* (Until tomorrow.)
> *Tchau!* (Bye!)

Cultural Differences in Conversations

Brazilians normally like to talk about a variety of topics, such as the weather, fashion, and hotly debated or even controversial topics. The role of the United States in the world, and how this affects Brazilians worldwide, is a favorite among many university students and young people in general. The concept of "Brazilianness" or what it means to be "Brazilian" is another common topic of discussion. In that same vein, be prepared to answer many questions about what it really means to be an "American" or about your views on current world affairs. If talking about these topics makes you uncomfortable, say so! Brazilians will most likely not insist, and then will invite you to a party so you can learn more about their country!

Communication by Mail

Generally, Portuguese speakers write letters in a highly stylized fashion. Here are some guidelines for good letter writing.

As in English, the date is an essential part of the letter. In Portuguese the date usually goes on the top left-hand side of the paper. Take a look at how the dates are expressed in Portuguese.

> *12 de maio de 2006*
> *Boston, 12 de maio de 2006*
> *Boston, 12/6/2006*
> *12/5/2006*

Letter headings depend on purpose and the intended reader. Most of the information will be on the left, unless it is displayed in the letterhead itself. In most formal business letters, the title of the recipient is indicated. If it is not, always start the letter with *Prezado Senhor* (Dear Sir) or *Prezada Senhora* (Dear Madam). If you do not know who the letter addresses, such as all of those in an executive board, you can use *Prezados Senhores* (Dear Sirs). Notice that in Portuguese, abbreviations are not used when addressing the recipient.

For more personal or informal letters, you do not need to include the address, and the salutation is the next printed item. The most common salutations parallel those in English. Here are a few examples:

Meu querido José (My dear José)
Querido José (My dear José)
Meu caro José (My dear José)
Caro José (My dear José)
Minha querida Suzana (My dear Suzana)
Querida Suzana (My dear Suzana)
Minha cara Suzana (My dear Suzana)
Cara Suzana (My dear Suzana)
Meus queridos José e Suzana (My dear José and Suzana)
Queridos José e Suzana (My dear José and Suzana)
Meus caros José e Suzana (My dear José and Suzana)
Caros José e Suzana (My dear José and Suzana)

Common courtesy requires introductions in friendly letters. In business letters, introductions are not expected, since you want to be more efficient and get straight to the point. Here are some frequent introductions, from more informal to more formal:

Olá, Renato. Como vai? (Hello Renato, how are you?)
Eu estou te escrevendo para dizer que... (I am writing to let you know that...)
Desejo lhe comunicar que... (I would like to communicate that...)

The body of the letter is where you get to display your knowledge of Portuguese! There are no preset rules here, but make sure you keep on track, stick to the point, and remember to be consistent with your message.

The farewell of the letter also depends on how you started it. If you are writing a formal letter, stick to formal farewells. But if you are writing to a friend, it's always good to be friendlier at the end too. Here are some examples:

Atenciosamente (literally "Attentively," but better translated as "Cordially")
Saudações cordiais (literally "Cordial salutations," or better "Cordially")
Um forte abraço (literally "A strong hug," or better "A hug," but not too informal)
Com todo meu carinho (With all my affection)
Um abraço (A hug)
Beijos (Kisses)

Exercise: Writing a Letter

Take a look at this letter and see how much you can understand from it. Check the translation in Appendix C.

Minha cara Helena:
Fiquei feliz em receber o seu novo endereço eletrônico. Desculpa não poder ter ido a sua festa de despedida na semana passada. Tenho estado muito cupada com o novo trabalho. Espero que tudo esteja em ordem na sua nova casa! Quem sabe um dia nos encontramos em uma dessas conferências?
Gostaria de manter contato com você, pois lembro com carinho das nossas conversas animadas no centro estudantil.
Um forte abraço,
Diana

Making Phone Calls

Communicating on the telephone is a lot harder for early learners because telephone conversations do not provide the visual clues usually associated with face-to-face conversations. However, learning some new words might help you to decipher what people are saying on the telephone.

Vocabulary: Using the Telephone

Portuguese	English
o aparelho (telefônico)	the telephone set
o gancho	the handset
o orelhão	the telephone booth [literally "the big ear" because of the design of public telephones in Brazil]
desligar o telefone	to hang up the phone
atender o telefone	to answer the phone
deixar um recado	to leave a message
a secretária (eletrônica)	the anwering machine [literally "the electronic secretary"]
fazer um telefonema	to make a phone call
apertar, aperte	to press, press
o telefone sem fio	cordless phone
o sinal, dar sinal	dial tone, to have a dial tone

Here is some vocabulary relating to placing a phone call:

Vocabulary: Making a Phone Call

Portuguese	English
telefonista, ajuda ao assinante	operator, subscriber's assistance
o código de área	the area code
com cartão de crédito	with credit card
interurbano	long distance
ligação direta	direct call, person-to-person call
o catálogo telefônico	the phone book
o número de telefone	the phone number
chamada a cobrar	collect call
o código internacional	the country code

Many public phones still exist in Brazil, usually in an interesting design that looks like a huge yellow ear. To make a telephone call, you must buy a *cartão telefônico* or "phone card" because coins are not used in public phones, in part because the value of Brazilian currency changes constantly due to inflation. You can buy phone cards in *bancas de revistas* or "newsstands."

Here are some useful phrases that will help you to communicate on the phone in Portuguese:

Bom dia! (Good morning!)
Boa tarde! (Good afternoon!)
Boa noite! (Good evening! or Good night!)
Pronto! (Yes?)
Alô! (Hello!)
Quem fala? (Who's speaking?)

Here are some examples of how to introduce yourself:

Eu me chamo Flávia Cavalcanti. (My name's Flávia Cavalcanti.)
Sou o Senhor Silva. (I'm Mr. Silva.)
Meu nome é Madalena Alves. (My name is Madalena Alves.)

If the connection is not clear, and you would like more clarification, you might want to say the following:

Como se escreve (o seu nome)? (How do you write [your name]?)
O senhor/A senhora poderia me dizer como se escreve? (Can the gentleman/ the lady tell me how it is written?)

Remember to spell your name slowly to listeners on the phone. Review how each of the letters are pronounced in Portuguese (refer to Chapter 2 for the alphabet). Also, be sure to describe each letter, in necessary. For example, in order to spell *Flávia* say the following: "*F maiúscula* (capital F)*, l, a com acento agudo* (acute accent)*, v, i, a.*"

After the initial greeting, you might want to speak to someone on the phone. Here is how you do that:

Posso falar com o Senhor Barros? (Could I speak to Mr. Barros?)

Gostaria de falar com o Senhor Barros, por gentileza. (I would like to speak to Mr. Barros, please.)

Você poderia me transferir para a secção de atendimento ao consumidor, por favor? (Could you transfer me to the consumer's desk, please?)

O senhor poderia me fazer a gentileza de informar o Senhor Barros que a filha dele quer falar com ele? (Would you (the gentleman) do me the favor of informing Mr. Barros that his daughter would like to speak to him?)

Here are possible responses to your requests:

É da parte de quem? (Who is calling?)

Sim, pois não. Um momento, por favor. (Yes, of course. One moment, please.)

Desculpe a demora, senhora Ferreira. (Sorry for the wait, Ms. Ferreira.)

Um momentinho, vou fazer a transferência. (A (short) moment, I will make the transfer.)

Sinto muito, mas a doutora Maria Luiza não se encontra. (Sorry, but Dr. Maria Luiza is not in.)

Sinto muito, mas o senhor César está na outra linha. (Sorry, but Mr. César is on the other line.)

Sinto muito, mas a senhora Freitas está com um cliente. (Sorry, but Ms. Freitas is with a client.)

Deseja deixar recado, senhora/senhor? (Would you like to leave a message, ma'am/sir?)

Gostaria de esperar na linha, senhora/senhor? (Would you like to wait on the line, ma'am/sir?)

O senhor/A senhora pode telefonar mais tarde? (Would the gentleman/the lady like to call back later?)

O senhor/A senhora deseja falar com outra pessoa? (Would the gentleman/the lady like to speak to someone else?)

At this point, you may decide to leave a message (say *Posso deixar um recado, por favor?* meaning "Can I leave a message, please?") or call back at another time. Hopefully you will be able to connect and proceed with a conversation!

Vocabulary: *Ficar, Tornar-se, Fazer-se* (to Become)

Part of communicating better has to do with learning idiomatic expressions in the new language. Some of these expressions are seen in familiar verbs that have additional meanings. Three such verbs in Portuguese have the meaning of "to become": *ficar*, *tornar-se*, and *fazer-se*.

Ficar

In addition to meaning "to remain" and "to be located," ficar also can be used to mean "to get [emotion or state]." Here are some examples:

> *Ele ficou achateado com a notícia.* (He got upset with the news.)
> *A rua ficava sempre deserta.* (The street would always get deserted.)
> *Eles ficaram impressionados.* (They became impressed.)

Tornar-se

The additional meaning here is that there some intention on the part of the agent as far as the act of becoming, meaning that the person put some effort in this transformation. Some examples follow:

> *Bill Gates se tornou um dos homens mais rico do mundo.* (Bill Gates become one of the richest men in the world.)
> *De repente elas se tornaram uns anginhos.* (All of a sudden they became little angels.)
> *No final do semestre os alunos se tornam estudiosos.* (At the end of the semester the students become dedicated.)

Fazer-se

This verb is used when referring to occupations, where the person took some time to gather the necessary tools or education to "become" the person with that professional identity. Some examples follow:

Amália se fez cantora de Fado. (Amália became a *Fado* singer.)
Anne e Júlia se fizeram professoras. (Anne and Júlia became professors.)
Depois de seis anos eu me fiz médica. (After six years I became a doctor.)

More Vocabulary: Expressions with *Estar com* and *Ter*

Some of the most important expressions in Portuguese are created with two very simple verbs: *estar com* (to be [emotion/state]) and *ter* (to have). In order to speak this language fluently, you must know these expressions.

Expressions with *Estar com*

Portuguese	English	Example
estar com saudades	to be homesick	*Anne está com saudades de casa.*
estar com pena de	to be sorry for	*Júlia está com pena do gato dela.*
estar com pena que	to be sorry that	*Daniel está com pena que o gato está doente.*
estar com medo de	to be afraid of	*Cláudia está com medo do cachorro.*
estar com medo que	to be afraid that	*Seu irmão está com medo que ela desmaie.*
estar com preguiça	to be feeling lazy	*Eu estou com preguiça de escrever.*
estar com dor de [part of body]	to have a/an [part of body] ache	*Ela está com dor de barriga.*

All of these expressions can be used with the verb *ter* as well. Just substitute the verbal expression *estar com* for the verb *ter* and the meaning is exactly the same. It is just a matter of which verb you would like to use.

However, there are some expressions that can only be used with *ter* (to have). They are as follows:

Expression with *Ter* (to have)

Expression: *ter jeito para* (to have a knack for)

Example: *Ele tem jeito pra desenho.* (He's got a knack for drawing.)

Expression: *ter a ver com* (to have to do with)

Example: *Isso tem a ver com os problemas sociais.* (This has to do with social problems.)

Expression: *não ter nada a ver com* (to have nothing to do with)

Example: *Isso não tem nada a ver com família.* (This has nothing to do with family.)

Expression: *não ter culpa de* [verb] (to [not] be guilty of [verb])

Example: *Ele não tem culpa de ser tão bonito.* (It's not his fault he's so cute. [literally: he's not guilty for being...])

Communication Practice

Now it's time to see what you can remember from the lessons in this chapter. In the first exercise you will decide if the sentences are formal or informal. In the second exercise you'll decide what to say based on the context. Check your answers in Appendix C when you're finished.

EXERCISE: FORMAL OR INFORMAL?

Remember what you learned about communicating formally and informally? Decide if the sentence in the conversation is formal or informal.

1. *Alô!* _____

2. *Sinto muito, mas a doutora não se encontra.* _____

3. *Gostaria de esperar na linha, senhor?* _____

4. *Oi, posso falar com o Luís?* _____

5. *Gostaria de falar com o Senhor Gomes, por gentileza.* _____

EXERCISE: COMMUNICATION PRACTICE

Follow the English directions to decide what to say in Portuguese. Use the context you're given and write your answer in the space.

1. You want to let them know who you are.

   _____

2. You would like to speak to Mr. Barros.

   _____

3. You would like to leave a message.

   _____

4. You want to thank the person on the other line.

   _____

CHAPTER 20

Traveling to *Samba*-Land

CONGRATULATIONS! YOU HAVE almost finished this entire book about Brazilian Portuguese language and culture. Now let's put it all together with important tips before you travel to samba-land. This chapter covers which documents you need before travel, how to find your way around customs and airports, how to get Brazilian currency, and provide an overview of the best spots to visit in Brazil!

Getting Your Papers in Order

Before you can enjoy the wonderful beaches of Brazil, you must complete some paperwork! You will probably need a passport and visa to enter Brazil and to return to the United States. It is illegal to return to your country on an expired passport, even if you are a U.S. citizen.

For a visa, you will need to complete an application form, include a detailed itinerary of your trip, and provide proof of medical insurance, a valid return airline ticket, and proof of accommodations, such as a hotel reservation. You must also carry with you at least two forms of identification, such as your passport or your country's photo ID. Many banks in Brazil require a passport and another ID before cashing traveler's checks.

The U.S. Embassy is located in the capital, Brasília. There is a Consulate General in each large Brazilian urban center, such as São Paulo, Rio de Janeiro, and Recife. In addition, there are consulate agencies around the country. These governmental agencies answer telephone calls around the clock and have Web sites for more information. The addresses and hours of operation for these consulates and their Web information can be found in Appendix D.

Nothing to Declare

Going through customs or a alfândega should not be complicated as long as you have the correct identification. If you have purchased goods and gifts at a duty-free shop, be sure to pay the duty on the value of those items if they exceed the allowance established by the Brazilian government.

"Duty-free" simply means that you do not pay taxes on the goods in the country where you made purchases. But if you buy goods in regular stores, make sure you keep all receipts because you might be able to claim a refund on the added tax.

Where's My Purse?

Even if you are extra careful, sometimes you do lose or misplace items, especially when you are traveling. So you thought you put your passport in your bag, but you had it in another coat pocket. Or worse, your wallet falls out of your coat pocket while you were in a taxi ride in Rio. If you lose your passport, notify the local police immediately, as well as the closest consulate general.

Hotel Reservations

Whether you are staying for a long time or just for a couple of nights, it is best to make reservations at the Brazilian hotel before arrival. Most mid-size hotels have a Web site these days, and you can send an e-mail directly to the reservation desk in order to get the accommodation you want. If even after getting so much better in Portuguese you still decide to send an e-mail message in English, you will be understood, as most hotel Web sites have an English version and someone at the other end who can read your message in English. When you get to your destination, you will notice that hotel clerks are often fluent in English, especially if you're in a big city such as Rio de Janeiro or São Paulo and staying at a flagship hotel. The same is not true for smaller places, away from the urban centers, in which case it would be better to know some basic language, as follows:

Hotel Vocabulary

Portuguese	English
fazer a reserva	make the reservation
número de hóspedes	number of guests
tempo de estadia	length of stay
quarto/apartamento/suite	room
para não-fumantes	non-smoking
para fumantes	smoking
solteiro	single
duplo	double

Hotel Vocabulary

Portuguese	English
triplo	triple
número de confirmação	confirmation number
carteira de identidade	ID card
passaporte	passport
o check-in	the check-in
o check-out	the check-out
não comparecimento	no show
regras de cancelamento	cancellation policy
serviços incluídos	services included
impostos incluídos	taxes included
café da manhã incluído	breakfast included
acesso a Internet	Internet access
acesso para deficientes físicos	handicap accessible
ar condicionado	air conditioner
calefação	heating
cofre	safe
frigobar	mini-bar
hidromassagem	hot tub
radio relógio	clock radio
TV a cabo	cable TV
Central de Atendimento ao Cliente	Customer Service Center

Here is a typical interaction between a client and a hotel reservation specialist:

Q: Hotel staff person: *Bom dia, como posso servi-lo?* (Good morning, how can I help you?)

A: Client: *Bom dia, eu gostaria de fazer uma reserva...* (Good morning, I would like to make a reservation...)

Q: Hotel staff person: *Pois não, senhor, um momento. Para que dia?* (Of course, one moment. For what day?)

A: Client: *Para o dia 15 de dezembro.* (For December 15th.)

Q: Hotel staff person: *Quantas noites?* (How many nights?)

A: Client: *Até o dia 20 de dezembro.* (Until December 20th.)

Q: Hotel staff person: *Cinco noites, para quantos hóspedes?* (Five nights, how many guests?)

A: Client: *Dois hóspedes, um quarto duplo, por favor.* (Two guests, a double room, please.)

Q: Hotel staff person: *Muito bem, o senhor gostaria de um apartamento para fumantes?* (Very well, would you like a smoking room?)

A: Client: *Não, para não-fumantes, por favor!* (No, a non-smoking please!)

Q: Hotel staff person: *Muito bem, qual o cartão de crédito que gostaria de usar para confirmar a reserva?* (Very well, which credit card would you like to use to confirm the reservation?)

A: Client: *Vocês aceitam* American Express? (Do you accept American Express?)

Q: Hotel staff person: *Sim, senhor. Aqui está o número de confirmação da sua reserva no Hotel Ibirapuera.* (Yes, sir. Here's your confirmation number at the Ibirapuera Hotel.)

A: Client: *Obrigado.* (Thank you.)

Q: Hotel staff person: *Não há de que. Algo mais, senhor?* (No problem. Anything else, sir?)

A: Client: *Não, obrigado.* (No, thanks.)

Q: Hotel staff person: *Tenha uma boa viagem e um bom dia!* (Have a great trip and a good day!)

A: Client: *Igualmente.* (Same to you.)

Getting *Real*

The history of the Brazilian currency is marked by constant changes, an unstable economy, and high inflation rates. Because of hyperinflation of past decades,

Brazilian currency lost its value rapidly, and higher bills had to go into circulation. In the eighties and nineties, inflation rates forced the *Banco Central* (the equivalent of the Federal Reserve) to create new denominations, drop zeros from these bills, and redesign and rename the new currency quite a few times.

Because famous historical figures would adorn the bills, and these bills would lose their value so quickly, what was meant to be an honor became a source of ridicule. In later editions of Brazilian currency, images of beautiful species of flowers and native animals have been used.

As far as the name of the Brazilian currency, since 1986 it has gone from *cruzeiro* to *cruzado*, to *cruzado novo*, back to *cruzeiro*, then to *cruzeiro real*. Finally, in 1994 the Brazilian government overhauled its economy and adopted the *real* which, coupled with a more stable economy (the inflation rate is roughly 3 percent a year), has made Brazilians proud of their currency. Check out the site *www.v-brazil.com/information/currency.html* for more information on the history of Brazilian currency and up-to-date exchange rates.

Foreigners cannot buy products or services in Brazil with dollars, so you must exchange your money. In order to get *reais* you can go to a *Casa de Câmbio*, or currency exchange agency, found in many airports and urban centers. Banks will offer the same service, but with an extra fee, a much lower rate, and some disadvantage to the customer.

Here is a typical conversation that might occur at a bank exchange agency:

Q: *Bom dia, senhor.* (Good morning, sir.)
A: *Bom dia, eu gostaria de trocar meus dólares.* (Good morning, I would like to exchange my dollars.)

Q: Pois não, senhor, quanto o senhor gostaria de trocar? (Of course, sir, how much would you like to exchange?)

A: Não sei, acho que uns duzentos dólares. (I don't know, I think about two hundred dollars.)

Q: Pois não, senhor, a nossa taxa de câmbio está em torno de 2,134 reais, no câmbio oficial. (Of course sir, our rate is about 2.134 in the official exchange rate.)

A: Há alguma outra taxa? (Is there another tax or fee?)

Q: Sim, nós temos uma taxa administrativa, mas só de cinco reais por venda. (Yes, we have an administrative fee, but it's only five *reais* per operation.)

A: Está bom, então quero trocar os duzentos. (Okay, so I want to exchange two hundred.)

Q: Muito bem, só preciso do seu passaporte. (All right, I just need your passport.)

A: Aqui está. (Here it is.)

Finally, most banks in Brazil honor your major credit card, so if you don't want to bother with your getting travelers' checks, just use your credit card or ATM card at a local ATM and get *reais*. Your bank in the United States will calculate the withdrawal amount according to the daily posted exchange rates.

Where to Go?

Depending on where you travel to Brazil, there are several activities you will want to do and places you will want to visit. Brazil is a large, continental country, and the weather can be varied, depending if you are in the northeast or in the south. Here are some major cities to visit and activities to do while you are there. The chart on the next page is organized starting from the northernmost part of Brazil going south to the center-west region and back up north again to the Amazon. This list of cultural activities is very far from exhaustive, so be sure to contact the local tourism authority, dress appropriately, and most of all, enjoy the trip!

Region	State	Interesting Sites
northeast	Maranhão	Capital City of São Luis
Activities: watch the Bumba-meu-Boi festival		
northeast	Ceará	Jericoacoara Beach
Activities: drive a buggy on the sandy dunes		
northeast	Rio Grande do Norte	Natal
Activities: visit a mangrove or cashew farm		
northeast	Pernambuco	Recife
Activities: dance with the carnaval troupe Galo da Madrugada		
northeast	Pernambuco	Olinda
Activities: experience the stunning view from the Catedral de Sé located in Olinda's highest hill		
northeast	Bahia	Salvador
Activities: visit the Farol lighthouse, dance at the nearby clubs		
northeast	Bahia	Porto Seguro
Activities: visit the beach purported to be the site of the first Portuguese landing; enjoy restaurant with local flavors		
northeast	Alagoas	Maceió and surroundings
Activities: walk along hundreds of kilometers of white, sandy beaches		
southeast	Rio de Janeiro	Capital City of Rio
Activities: dance with the locals in a escola de samba; walk up the to see the statue of Cristo Redentor on top of Corcovado hill.		
southeast	São Paulo	Capital City of São Paulo
Activities: enjoy the finest European-style restaurants and nightclubs		
south	Rio Grande do Sul	Porto Alegre
Activities: visit a gaúcho restaurant and drink chimarrão, the strong Brazilian tea		
center-west	Minas Gerais	Ouro Preto
Activities: visit the beautiful gold-laden baroque churches and colonial cities		

Region	State	Interesting Sites
center-west	Goiás	Brasília
Activities: visit the amazing modern architecture of the Brazilian capital		
center-west	Goiás	Pantanal
Activities: travel along the natural habitat of hundreds of species of the wetlands ecosystem named Pantanal		
north	Amazonas	Manaus
Activities: walk around the myriad of stands at the famous local market Ver-o-Peso		

In the next few sections we will present important information about some of the key Brazilian cities that make Brazil one of the most beautiful places in South America.

Brasília: The Modern Capital City

Located in the *centro-oeste* or the center-west region of Brazil, this modern capital was planned and constructed in the span of four years, from 1956 to 1960. It was largely the vision of the then President Juscelino Kubischek, who was able to take an idea that started in the nineteenth century and bring it to fruition.

One of the major modernist architects of Brasília was Oscar Niemeyer, who, along with Lúcio Costa's team, envisioned the large vertical structures of the *Palácio do Congresso* (National Congress), as well as the Cathedral of Brasília and many other stunning Modernist buildings throughout the city. Below is a list of buildings that should be visited while you are in Brasília.

Modernist Architecture of Brasília

Portuguese	English
Palácio do Congresso	National Congress
Palácio do Planalto	Executive Branch Offices
Palácio do Itamaraty	Foreign Relations or the Diplomatic Corps Office
Catedral de Brasília	Cathedral of Brasília
Palácio da Alvorada	Alvorada Palace (President's residence)
Esplanada dos Ministérios	Row of Ministries/Departments

The idea behind the city was to create a modern and functional plan that would also reflect the newer vision of a modern, democratic government. Some of the buildings are certainly that, and much more. The beauty of reflective pools, the accompanying sculptures, and the simple vertical and horizontal lines make a stunning city.

> Initially constructed to accommodate about 500,000 people, the city grew beyond its original plan and now has more than 2 million inhabitants, if one counts the so-called "satellite cities" that sprouted up at the very inception of the city.

Most people who live in Brasília enjoy living there, even if there are some typically urban problems. Public transportation can be inefficient, and one probably needs a car to get around the vast expanse of the *Planalto Central* (Central Plains). There might be very little to do on the weekends since it is a "working city" dedicated to the government bureaucracy. On the positive side, the weather is absolutely perfect, there is little pollution and virtually no threat from natural disasters, and the sunsets of the plains are absolutely gorgeous. So, if you visit Brazil, don't forget to stop by its most intriguing capital.

Rio de Janeiro and São Paulo: Big Metropoles

Both Rio and São Paulo are big cities and points of reference for traveling in Brazil. Several weekly flights from Chicago, New York, and Miami go directly to these Brazilian cities, both of which are situated in the southeastern region and are the two largest cities in the country and in South America.

Rio de Janeiro

Also known as Cidade Maravilhosa (Marvelous City), this urban center is marked by the incredible beauty of its surrounding hills and stunning beaches.

The population of Rio is almost 6 million people, and up to 15 million if we count the total metropolitan area. Rio is a great cultural and economic center that boasts several important universities, such as the *Universidade Federal do Rio de Janeiro* or *UFRJ*, the *Universidade do Estado do Rio de Janeiro* or *UERJ*, and the *Pontifícia Universidade Católica do Rio de Janeiro* or *PUC-Rio*, which belongs to the great educational tradition of Catholic universities in Brazil.

Some of the most famous beaches of the world are found in Rio: the famous *Ipanema* and *Copacabana* beaches have been celebrated in songs heard around the world. The view of the *Guanabara Bay* is a natural postcard of Brazil, showing its unique view of mountains and beaches in close proximity.

One of the most famous images of Rio de Janeiro is of *Cristo Redentor* or "Christ the Redeemer," the Art Deco statue of Christ with open arms blessing the city. The Rio de Janeiro beaches attract tourists from around the world, and for native *cariocas* (the name given to those born in Rio) they are part of daily life. Beach culture is almost synonymous with Brazilian culture; it is no wonder that the "Brazilian bikini wax" first became popular among beachgoers in Copacabana, later expanding to California and now the entire world.

One of the most important events in Brazilian culture is the annual *Carnaval* parade in Rio. Every February Brazilians watch hours of footage of dancing performers and intricately decorated floats that cross the *Sambódromo*, the name of the place constructed specifically for the parade.

One of the biggest events in Rio is also the end-of-the-year celebration when Brazilians bring in the New Year on the night of December 31st wearing traditional white and throwing flowers into the ocean, accompanied by intense fireworks and a party that lasts all night, aptly called the *Reveillón*, from the French word *reveiller* or "to wake-up"!

São Paulo

The city of São Paulo has just about 10 million people (17 million if we count the larger metropolitan area). It is the second most populous city in Latin America, losing only to Mexico City. But it is the biggest city in South America, and indeed one of the largest in the world.

São Paulo has welcomed an incredibly diverse international population with immigrants from Italy, China, Japan, and Lebanon, to name a few. The Italian neighborhood of *Bexiga* in São Paulo is larger than the city of Naples. And the neighborhood of *Liberdade*, initially populated by Japanese immigrants, now has a large Asian population, with people from Korea and China, among other countries. In this neighborhood children are taught to speak Asian languages. One of the best places to buy sashimi or to watch a folkloric dance show is in these streets of São Paulo. But new arrivals to São Paulo do not come only from overseas. A large population of people from the north-east of Brazil have significantly contributed to the construction, the economic wealth, and even the cultural make-up of the city.

This financial capital also accommodates the culturally savvy: São Paulo is home to the *Museu de Arte de São Paulo*, also known as the *MASP*, which run internationally recognized exhibitions throughout the year. It has also a highly respected collection of Modern art classics. The famous art exhibition called *Bienal de Artes* is a must-see for art lovers around the world.

São Paulo is also known for its passionate nightlife. Much like New York City, the city never sleeps, and the diversity of venues is truly breathtaking. But if dancing all night is not your cup of tea, São Paulo is home to a beautiful city park called *Ibirapuera* where family and friends gather every morning for a healthy jog or a bike ride.

The Northeast of Brazil: Culture and Tradition

This is one of the most sought-after tourist regions of Brazil. It makes up almost one-fifth of the country and its population is close to 45 million people. The northeast encompasses thousands of miles of white, sandy beaches and perfect tropical weather. The interior of the region is marked by almost untouched forests and more humid weather.

The Portuguese explorer Pedro Álvares Cabral first landed in the region that is now called *Porto Seguro*, located in the northeastern state of Bahia, on April 22, 1500. But the colonization efforts by the Portuguese really started only about fifty years later, with various excursions by the French and Dutch, who also settled in Brazil.

The intrinsic cultural, economic, and geographic variation of the region makes it difficult to talk about the northeast in general terms. Here are some historical and cultural highlights of the most interesting places to visit in the Northeast.

The state of Pernambuco was one of the most prosperous *capitanías* or provinces of the colonial government, with record production of sugarcane in the seventeenth century. The *Quilombo dos Palmares* is the name given to a successful community of ex-slaves who escaped the hardships of working the sugarcane fields. Nowadays you can visit the *Museu do Homem do Nordeste* where you can appreciate historical items such as a collection of porcelain sugar bowls from that time period.

The state of Bahia carries many cultural traditions of Africans, with typical foods sold on the streets by *baianas* (women dressed in typical African garb) and the *capoeira*, a type of martial arts that includes dance and music. The city of Salvador is famous for its colonial architecture and influencing musical styles, especially in the *Pelourinho* district.

The name *Pelourinho* comes from the Portuguese word for the "whipping post" where slaves were tied to and punished. Nowadays the *Pelourinho* refers to several blocks of cobblestone streets in the hills of the city of Salvador where artists, musicians, and community activists have established themselves. A city within a city, the *Pelourinho* is where you will find restaurants with local Afro-Brazilian foods, dance studios, and many arts and crafts stores.

The state of Maranhão is known for its forests and mineral production, as well as for one of the most beautiful capital cities in the northeast. São Luis do Maranhão is the only state capital originally started by the French in the early seventeenth century. The name of the city is in honor of King Louis XII of France. The city was later taken over by the Dutch and eventually the Portuguese.

Recife, the capital city of Pernambuco, is also known as the "Brazilian Venice" because it was built in between two rivers, the Capibaribe and the Beberibe Rivers, and its many bridges resemble the Italian city. It is also one of the largest cities in the northeast (with a population of about 1.5 million people) and a well-known cultural center.

Just north of Recife there is the city of Olinda, a beautiful town of colonial architecture that has been designated as a World Heritage Site by UNESCO in 1982 due to the preservation of its original colonial buildings. During *Carnaval*, many revelers parade on its old streets dancing the *frevo* and the *maracatu*.

Fortaleza, the capital city of the state of Ceará, has one of the liveliest beach-front nightlife of the northeast regions. The *Praia de Iracema* or Iracema Beach is famous for its warm waters.

The northeast region has one of the most interesting arts-and-crafts traditions of the country. Some of the most beautiful handmade clothing can be found in many northeastern markets. As you plan your vacation to Brazil, do not hesitate to visit at least one of these northeastern states. If you are interested in water sports, colonial architecture, or simply relaxing at the beach without big crowds, the northeast is for you!

Florianópolis and Other Southern Belles

The south of Brazil also has its charm. One of the most beautiful sites in the south of Brazil is the city of Florianópolis, charmingly referred to its inhabitants as *Floripa*. The city is the capital of Santa Catarina and it is located on an island surrounded by other smaller islets. It has a population of a bit more than 800,000 inhabitants and a beauty of its own.

The city was originally settled by Azorean Portuguese, but the influence of Germans and Italians is clearly seen by the architecture and the presence of immigrant communities.

One of the largest and most important cities in the south of Brazil is Curitiba, with more than 1.5 million people living in the larger metropolitan area. In this city, you will be able to enjoy one of the most efficient and environmentally friendly transportation systems in Latin America. Buses stop near clear elevated tubes where people get in once and can ride for the entire day. The city is also one of the "greenest" in Brazil, with well-kept parks.

The city of Porto Alegre is one of the largest cities of the south, and the closest big city to the South American countries of Argentina, Uruguay, Paraguay, and Chile. It is a large urban, industrialized center that is important to the *Mercosul*, the Brazilian version of the NAFTA. Business people from South American often stop first in Porto Alegre to conduct business and trade with Brazilians. Porto Alegre is the capital of Rio Grande do Sul and the home of the *gaúcho*, or Brazilian cowboy, culture. There you can also find many *churrascarias* or restaurants that serve the typical Brazilian barbecue, a never-ending feast of different meats that are brought to the table in long spears. These types of restaurants are becoming increasingly popular in big American cities such as Miami, Boston, New York, and Los Angeles.

More to the south of Porto Alegre you will find the small city of Gramado, located in the hills of the *Serra Gaúcha*, an area heavily influenced by the German settlers. Gramado is home to the Gramado Film Festival, one of the most influential festivals of avant-garde films in South America. An interesting mix of Brazilian and European culture can be found in these "Southern Belles."

Survival Phrases: Don't Leave Home Without Them

You have finally gone full circle in your study of Portuguese that you need to review some basic "survival" Portuguese in order to take that first step in getting acquainted with Brazilian culture. You may not remember all the lessons on the subjunctive or the preterite and the imperfect as you attempt to speak fluent Portuguese. But you should at least commit the following phrases to memory, as they will be essential in your quest for making friends with Brazilians or other Portuguese speakers.

Até amanhã! (Until tomorrow!/See you tomorrow!)
Até logo! (Until soon!/See you soon!)
Bom dia (Good morning)
Boa tarde (Good afternoon)
Boa noite (Good evening/Good night)
Como é seu nome? (What's your name?)
Faz uma semana que estou aqui. (I've been here for a week.)
Oi! (Hi!)
Prazer! (A pleasure!/Nice to meet you!)
Tudo bem? Tudo jóia? Tudo legal? (How's it going?)

The "Travel to Brazil" Quiz

Test your expert knowledge of the land of *bossa nova* before you travel. Fill in the blanks with the most appropriate word. Check your answers in Appendix C.

1. What is the name of the Brazilian currency?

   _____

2. Where can you exchange currency in Brazil?

   _____

3. Which city can you see the *Bumba-meu-Boi* festival?

   _____

4. How do you greet people informally?

   _____

5. How do you thank people?

   _____

English-to-Portuguese Glossary

A

a lot
muito

abdominal
abdominal

able
capaz

absolutely not!
absolutamente!

abstinence
abstinência

acceptable
aceitável

accessible
accesível

accident
acidente

accommodating
acomodável

accountant
contador, contadora

achieve, to
conseguir

action
ação

actor
ator

actress
atriz

acute accent
acento agudo

address
endereço

admissible
admisível

adolescence
adolescência

adorable
adorável

affable
afável

affection
carinho

against
contra

airplane
avião

all
todos, todas

all, entire
todo, toda

allow, to
permitir

already
já

also
também

always
sempre

American
americano, americana

anaconda
sucuri

and
e

angel
anjo

Angola
Angola

Angolan
angolano, angolana

animal
animal

annex
anexo

anniversary
aniversário

annual
anual

answer the phone, to
atender o telefone

answer, to
responder

anwering machine
secretária (eletrônica)

anxious
ansioso, ansiosa

any
qualquer

applaud, to
aplaudir

apple
maçã

approve, to
passar

April
abril

apron
avental

architect
arquiteto, arquiteta

ardor
ardor

area code
código de área

Argentina
Argentina

Argentinian
argentino, argentina

armadillo
tatu

aroused
excitado, excitada

arrest, to
prender

arrive, to
chegar

arrive, to
vir

art
arte

artist
artista

as much as
tanto... quanto

as... as
tão... quanto

ask for, to
pedir

asleep
dormindo

astral
astral

at the same time
ao mesmo tempo

atheist
ateu, atéia

athlete
atleta

athleticism
atletismo

attack
ataque

attend, to
assistir (a)

attention
atenção

attentively, cordially
atenciosamente

auditor
auditor

August
agosto

aunt
tia

Australia
Austrália

Australian
australiano, australiana

Austria
Áustria

Austrian
austríaco, austríaca

author
autor

automobile
automóve

autumn, fall
outono

average height
estatura mediana

avoidable
evitável

awake
acordado, acordada

B

backpack
mochila

bad
ruim

bag
bolsa

baggage
bagagem

bakery
padaria

bald
careca

bank
banco

bank teller
bancário

barbershop
barbeiro

basketball
basquetebol

bath
banho

be (situated), to
ficar

be able to, to
poder

be afraid, to
ter medo

be surprised, to
surpreender-se com

be windy, to
ventar

be, to
estar, ser

beans
feijão

beautiful
lindo, linda

beauty salon
salão de beleza

because
porque

become, to
ficar

beef
carne de boi

beer
cerveja

before
antes

behind
atrás, detrás de

Belgian
belga

Belgium
Bélgica

believe, to
acreditar

belt
cinto

better
melhor

big
grande

bill, account
conta

billfold
carteira

billion
bilhão

biodegradable
biodegradável

bird
pássaro

birthday
aniversário

black pepper
pimenta do reino

blasphemous
blasfemável

blind
cego

blond
louro, loura

blouse
blusa

blue
azul

board
quadro

boat, ship
nau, navio

bonbon
bombom

book
livro

bookstore
livraria

boring
chato, chata

both
ambos, ambas

bowsprit
proa

boy
menino

boyfriend
namorado

Brazil
Brasil

Brazilian
brasileiro, brasileira

bread
pão

brevity
brevidade

bride
noiva

bring, to
trazer

British
britânico, britânica

brother
irmão

brother-in-law
cunhado

brown
marrom

brush/comb (oneself), to
pentear-se

building
prédio

business partner
sócio, social

busy
ocupado, ocupada

but, however
porém

butcher shop
açougue

buy, to
comprar, fazer compras

bye
tchau

C

cake
bolo

calculating
calculável

call oneself, to
chamar-se

call, to
chamar, ligar

call (someone or something a name), to
chamar de

calm
tranqüilo, tranqüila

Canada
Canadá

Canadian
canadense

capital
capital

captain
capitão

car
carro

cardiac
cardíaco

cards
cartões

care
cuidado

careful (exclamation)
cuidado

cashew fruit
caju

cat
gato

catch, to
pegar

cathedral
catedral

celebrated
comemorado, comemorada

celebrity
pessoa famosa

censor
censor

center
centro

central
central

central-west
centro-oeste

chaos
caos

chapter
capítulo

chapter
capítul

cheap
barato, barata

cheese
queijo

chess
xadrez

chest
baú

child
criança

Chile
Chile

Chilean
chileno, chilena

China
China

Chinese
chinês, chinesa

chocolate
chocolate

choose, to
escolher

Christmas
Dia de Natal

church
igreja

circumflex accent
acento circunflexo

city
cidade

clarinet
clarinete

clarity
claridade

class
aula

classroom
sala de aula

clean
limpo, limpa

clearly
claramente

client
consumidor

climax
clímax

clinic
clínica

close, nearby
perto

clothes designer
costureiro, costureira

clothing store
loja de roupa

cloudy
nublado

club, gym
clube

coat
casaco

code
código, senha

coffee
café

cold
frio

cold cuts
frios

collect call
chamada a cobrar

Colombia
Colombia

Colombian
colombiano, colombiana

color
cor

comb
pente

come back, to
voltar

come, arrived
vindo

come, to
vir

comedian
comediante

comedy
comédia

comfortable
confortável

commercial
comercial

communicate, to
comunicar

communication
comunicação

compete, to
competir

competitors
concorrentes

complain about, to
queixar-se de

complete, to
completar

complex
complexo

compose, to
compor

composer
compositor

comprehend, to
compreender

comprehensible
compreensível

computer
computador

concert
concerto

conductor
condutor

conference
conferência

congested (by a cold)
constipado

conspirer
conspirador

consulate
consulado

consultant
consultor, consultora

consumed
consumido, consumida

consumer
consumidor

contruct, to
construir

conversation (colloquial)
bate-papo

convertible
conversível

convince oneself of, to
convencer-se de

cordial
cordial

cordially
saudações cordiais

cordless phone
telefone sem fio

corner
esquina

correct
certo

correct, to
corrigir

Costa Rica
Costa Rica

Costa Rican
costa-riquenho

cotton
algodão

counting
contagem

country code
código internacional

couple
casal

cousin (female)
prima

cousin (male)
primo

covered
coberto

cradle
berço

crazy
louco, louca

creature
criatura

credit
crédito

crime
crime, delito

cruel
cruel

Cuba
Cuba

cultural
cultural

culture
cultura

cup
xícara

curable
curável

curious
curioso

currency exchange
agency
casa de câmbio

customer
freguês, freguesa

customs
alfândega

cycle, ring
ciclo

cyclist
ciclista

Czech
checo, checa

Czech Republic
República Checa

D

dad, daddy
papai

dance, to
dançar

dark-skinned
moreno, morena

daughter
filha

daughter-in-law
nora

day
dia

day after tomorrow
depois de amanhã

day before yesterday
anteontem

dear (formal)
prezado, prezada

dear (informal)
caro, cara, querido, querida

December
dezembro

decide to, to
decidir-se a

dedicate (oneself to), to
dedicar-se a

demand, to
exigir

dentist
dentista

desire, to
desejar

destroyer
destruidor

detector
detector

development
desenvolvimento

dial tone
sinal

dice
dado

dictionary
dicionário

died, dead
morto

dierisis
trema

difficult
difícil

digestable
digestível

direct call
ligação direta

director
diretor, diretora

dish
prato

divided
dividido

divorced
divorciado, divorciada

do, to
fazer

doctor
médico

document
documento

dog
*cachorro, cão (male);
cachorra, cadela (female)*

dollars
dólares

domino
dominó

door
porta

dream
sonho

dress (oneself), to
vestir-se

dressmaker
costureiro, costureira

drink coffee, to
tomar café

drink, to
beber, tomar

drop
gota

drug, drugs
droga

drugstore
drogaria, farmácia

drunk
bêbado, bêbada

dry cleaners
lava a seco

duck
pato

durable
durável

Dutch
holandês, holandesa

dynasty
dinastia

E

early
cedo

earth, land
terra

easy
fácil

eat, to
comer

economic
econômico, econômica

Ecuador
Ecuador

Ecuadorian
equatoriano, equatoriana

editor
editor

educational
educacional

egg
ovo

Egypt
Egito

Egyptian
egípcio, egípcia

eight
oito

eight hundred
oitocentos, oitocentas

eighteen
dezoito

eighth
oitavo, oitava

eighty
oitenta

elderly
idoso, idosa

electric guitar
guitarra

electronic
eletrônico, electrônica

elegance
elegância

elegant
elegante

elementary school
escola primária

elephant
elefante

eleven
onze

eleventh
*décimo-primeiro,
décima-primeira*

embarassed
*envergonhado,
envergonhada*

embassy
embaixada

emotional
emocional

employee, maid
empregado, empregada

engineer
engenheiro, engenheira

England
Inglaterra

English
inglês, inglesa

enjoy, to
aproveitar

enjoy, to (slang)
curtir

enter, to
entrar em

entertain (oneself), to
divertir-se

envelope
envelope

error, mistake
erro

escape
fuga

essay, rehearsal
ensaio

essential
essencial, imprescindível

Europe
Europa

ever, never
jamais

exam
exame

excellent
excelente

exceptional
excepcional

excited
animado, animada

exclude, to
excluir

excuse me, sorry
com licença

exercise, to
fazer exercícios

exist, to
haver

exotic
exótico

expensive
caro

explain, to
explicar

explainable
explicável

explanations
explicações

eyeglasses
óculos

F

facing, in front of
defronte de

factory worker
operário, operária

falsifiable
falsificável

familiar,
pertaining to family
familiar

family
família

famous
famoso, famosa

far from
longe de

fast
rápido, rápida

fat
gordo, gorda

fatal
fatal

father
pai

father-in-law
sogro

favor
favor

feat
façanha

February
fevereiro

federal
federal

fervor
fervor

few
poucos, poucas

fiancé
noivo

fiancée
noiva

fifteen
quinze

fifth
quinto, quinta

fifty
cinqüenta

find
arrumar

find, to
encontrar

find, to
achar

find (oneself), to
encontrar-se

finish, to
acabar, terminar

first
primeiro, primeira

five
cinco

five hundred
quinhentos, quinhentas

fix
arrumar

fluently
fluentemente

fly (insect)
mosca

fog
neblina

food
comida

forget to, to
esquecer-se de

fork
garfo

forklift
grúa

fortunately
felizmente

forty
quarenta

fossil
fóssil

four
quatro

four hundred
quatrocentos, quatrocentas

fourteen
catorze

fourth
quarto, quarta

France
França

French
francês, francesa

frequency
freqüência

Friday
sexta-feira

friend, partner
companheiro, companheira

frog
sapo

fundamental
fundamental

funny
engraçado, engraçada

future, future tense
futuro

G

garage
garagem

garlic cloves
dente de alho

German
alemão, alemã

Germany
Alemanha

gesture
gesto

get married, to
casar-se

get together, to
reunir-se

get used to, to
acostumar-se com

get, to
conseguir

gift
presente

girl
menina

girlfriend
namorada

give, to
dar

go on a short trip, to
dar uma volta

go on strike, to
fazer greve

go out (leave), to
sair

go to bed
deitar-se

go up, to
subir

go, to
ir

god
deus

goddaughter
afilhada

godfather
padrinho

godmother
madrinha

godson
afilhado

going-away party
festa de despedida

good
bom, boa

good afternoon
boa tarde

good evening
boa noite

good luck
boa sorte

good morning
bom dia

grammar
gramática

granddaughter
neta

grandfather
avô

grandma, granny
vovó

grandmother
avó

grandpa
vovô

grandson
neto

grave accent
acento grave

great
ótima

Great Britain
Grã-bretanha

great-grandfather
bisavô

great-grandmother
bisavó

Greece
Grécia

Greek
grego, grega

groom
noivo

guide
guia

gym
ginásio

H

hairdresser
cabelereiro

Haiti
Haiti

Haitian
haitiano, haitiana

ham
presunto

handed, given
entregue

handset
gancho

hang up the phone, to
desligar o telefone

hangover
ressaca

happiness
felicidade

happy
contente, feliz

have a good trip
boa viagem

have breakfast, to
tomar café

have dinner, to
jantar

have fun, to
divertir-se

have lunch, to
almoçar

have, to
haver

have, to
ter

to have a dial tone
dar sinal

he
ele

hear, to
escutar, ouvir

heart
coração

Hebrew
hebreu, hebréia

hello
alô

help
socorro

help, to
ajudar

her (possessive)
dela

here
aqui

hey!
opa!

hi
oi, olá

himself/herself
si

his (possessive)
dele

Hindu
hindu

Holland
Holanda

homework
dever de casa

horrible
horrível

hospital
hospital

hot
calor

hot pepper sauce
pimenta malagueta

hotel
hotel

hour
hora

house
casa

how many
quantos, quantas

how much
quanto, quanta

hug
abraço

humid
húmido, húmida

humor
humor

hunt
caça

hurt (oneself), to
machucar-se

husband
marido

I

I
eu

idea
idéia

ideal
ideal

idealism
idealismo

identical
idêntico

identification tag
crachá

identity
identidade

illegal
ilegal

image
imagem

immediately
imediatamente

impede, to
impedir

importance
importância

important
importante

impose, to
impor

impossible
impossível

impressed
*impressionado,
impressionada*

in
em

in front of
em frente de

in love
apaixonado, apaixonada

include, to
incluir

included
incluído, incluída

Independence Day
Dia da Independência

India
India

Indian
indiano, indiana

indoor soccer
futebol de salão

inevitable
inevitável

inferior
inferior

inform, to
informar

information
informação

inside
dentro de

insistence
insistência

inspector
inspetor

instructor
instrutor

intelligent
inteligente

international
internacional

Internet café
cyber café

introduce, to
apresentar

invent, to
inventar

inventor
inventor

invest, to
investir

Iran
Irã

Iranian
iraniano, iraniana

Iraq
Iraque

Iraqi
iraquiano, iraquiana

Ireland
Irlanda

Irish
irlandês, irlandesa

irritated
irritado, irritada

Israel
Israel

Israeli
israelense

Italian
italiano, italiana

Italy
Itália

J

Jamaica
Jamaica

Jamaican
jamaicano, jamaicana

January
janeiro

Japan
Japão

Japanese
japonês, japonesa

jealousy
ciúme

judge
juiz, juíza

July
julho

June
junho

K

kennel
canil

key
chave

king
rei

kiss
beijo

kiss (one another), to
beijar-se

knife
faca

know (information, skills), to
saber

know (people, places), to
conhecer

L

lack, to
fazer falta

lamentable
lamentável

last week
na semana passada

late
tarde

Latin America
América Latina

laugh, to
rir

laugh (at), to
rir-se de

lawyer
advogado, advogada

learn, to
aprender

leave a message, to
deixar um recado

leave, to
deixar

leave, to
partir

legume
legume

less
menos

lesson
lição

liberty
liberdade

library
biblioteca

lie, to
mentir

lightening
relâmpago

like, to
gostar de

likewise, same here
igualmente

liqueur
licor

Lisbon
Lisboa

listen, to
escutar, ouvir

live, to
viver

live, to (reside)
morar

local
local

long distance
interurbano

look like, to
parecer-se com

look (at oneself), to
olhar-se

look (at), to
olhar para

lose, to
perder

lotion
loção

love
amor

love, to
amar

luggage, baggage
bagagem

M

ma'am, lady
senhora

macaw
arara

made, done
feito

make, to
fazer

magazines
revistas

make a phone call, to
fazer um telefonema

make peace, to
fazer as pazes

mall
shopping

manager
gerente

map
mapa

March
março

married
casado, casada

match
fósforo

May
maio

may
poder

May I help you?
Pois não?

mechanic
mecânico

medicine, medication
medicina, remédios

melon
melão

mentor
mentor

Merry Christmas
Feliz Natal

message
recado

Mexican
mexicano, mexicana

Mexico
México

midnight
meia-noite

milk
leite

million
milhão

millionaire
milionário

minus
menos

mirror
espelho

miserable
miserável

miss, to
fazer falta

mister, sir
senhor

modern
moderno, moderna

mom, mommy
mamãe

moment
momento

Monday
segunda-feira

money
dinheiro

more
mais

mother
mãe

mother-in-law
sogra

motor, engine
motor

movie
filme

movies, cinema
cinema

Mozambique
Moçambique

multiple choice
múltipla escolha

museum
museu

music
música

musician
músico, música

my
meu, minha
(plural: meus, minhas)

N

naked
nu, nua

name
nome

nap
cuchilo

napkin
guardanapo

national
nacional

natural
natural

nature
natureza

necklace
corrente, colar

need, to
precisar de

negotiable
negociável

neighbor
vizinho, vizinha

neighborhood
bairro

neither
também não

neither... nor
nem... nem

nephew
sobrinho

nervous
nervoso, nervosa

never
nunca

new
novo, nova

newspaper
jornal

newspaper seller
jornaleiro

newsstand
banca de revista

Nicaragua
Nicarágua

Nicaraguan
nicaragüense

nice
simpático

nice to meet you
encantado, encantada

nice to meet you
muito prazer

niece
sobrinha

nine
nove

nine hundred
novecentos, novecentas

nineteen
dezenove

ninety
noventa

ninth
nono, nona

no
não

nobody
ninguém

noise
barulho

noon, midday
meio-dia

normal
normal

north
norte

North America
América do Norte

northeast
nordeste

not one
nenhum, nenhuma

not yet
ainda não

notebook
caderno

nothing
nada

November
novembro

number
número

O

obvious
óbvio

October
outubro

office
escritório

official
oficial

official meeting
audiência

old
velho, velha

on top
em cima de

one
um, uma

one hundred and one
cento e um, uma

onion
cebola

open, to
abrir

opened
aberto

operator,
directory assistance
*telefonista, ajuda
ao assinante*

opposing
opositor

orange
laranja

organ
órgão

organizable
organizável

original
original

orphan
órfão

ostensible
ostensível

other
outro, outra

our
nosso, nossa

outside
fora

over, on top
sobre

overcome, to
passar

P

page
página

paid
pago

pain
dor

paintbrush
pincel

pale
pálido, pálida

Panama
Panamá

Panamenian
panamenho, panamenha

paper
papel

paper
trabalho

pardon, sorry
perdão

park
parque

partial
parcial

party
festa

pass, to
passar

passable
passável

past
passado, passada

pastor
pastor

patience
paciência

pay, to
pagar

peach
pêssego

pediatrician
pediatra

pen
caneta

pencil
lápis

people
gente

perfume
perfume

persistent
persistente

personal infinitive
infinitivo pessoal

pharmacist
farmacêutico, farmacêutica

phenomenal
fenomenal

Philippines
Filipinas

phone book
catálogo telefônico

phone card
cartão telefônico

phone number
número de telefone

photographer
fotógrafo, fotógrafa

phrase
frase

physical
físico

physicist
físico

pianist
pianista

pig's ear
orelha de porco

pig's foot
pé de porco

pig's tail
rabo de porco

pilot
piloto

pineapple
abacaxi

piranha
piranha

pity
dó

place
lugar

place, to
colocar, pôr

plane, leveled
plano

planet
planeta

play (a sport or game), to
jogar

play (an instrument), to
tocar

please
por favor

please (formal)
por gentileza, por obséquio

pleasure
prazer

Poland
Polônia

police
polícia

policeman
guarda

Polish
polonês, polonesa

poor
pobre

popular
popular

populated
populoso, populosa

pork
carne de porco

Portugal
Portugal

possible
possível

postcard
cartão postal

poster
cartaz

potent
potente

power
potência

presentable
presentável

president
presidente

press, to
apertare

pretend, to
fazer de conta

preterite tense
pretérito

pretty
bonito, bonito

problem
problema

profession
profissão

program
programa

progressive present
presente contínuo

proposal
proposta

protector
protetor

psychotherapist
analista

pub
barzinho

purple
roxo

purse
bolsa

purse
bolsa

put in jail
pôr na cadeia

put, set
posto

put, to
colocar, pôr

Q

question
pergunta

R

radio
rádio

rain, to
chover

ranking
ranking

rational
racional

raw
cru, crua

react, to
reagir

read, to
ler

receive, to
receber

recognized
reconhecido, reconhecida

red
vermelho, vermelha

redhead, redheaded
ruivo, ruiva

reflect, to
refletir

reflector, reflecting
refletor

remember, to
recordar

remember to, to
lembrar-se

remembrance, souvenir
lembrança

reporter, journalist
jornalista

reptile
réptil

Republican
republicano, republicana

respectable
respeitável

rest, to
descansar

restaurant
restaurante

rested
descansado, descansada

retire, to
deitar-se

rice
arroz

rich
rico, rica

ride a bike, to
andar de bicicleta

rifle
fuzil

right, indeed
pois é

river
rio

root
raiz

rumor
rumor

run, to
correr

S

sad
triste

said
dito

saint
santo

Saint Patrick's Day
Dia de São Patrício

salesperson
vendedor, vendedora

salt
sal

same
mesmo

sandwich
sanduíche

satisfied
satisfeito, satisfeita

Saturday
sábado

say (imperative)
diga

say, to
dizer

scared
amedrontado, amendrontada

scheme, plan
esquema, complô

school
escola

sea, ocean *mar*	serve, to *servir*	since *desde*	size *tamanho*
second *segundo, segunda*	service *atendimento*	sing, to *cantar*	sky *céu*
secretary *secretária*	set, to *pôr*	singer *cantor, cantora*	slave quarters *senzala*
section *seção*	seven *sete*	single *solteiro, solteira*	sleep, to *dormir*
seductor *sedutor*	seven hundred *setecentos, setecentas*	sinister *sinistro*	slowly *devagar*
see, to *ver*	seventeen *dezessete*	sister *irmã*	snow *neve*
see you later *até mais*	seventh *sétimo, sétima*	sister-in-law *cunhada*	snow, to *nevar*
see you soon *até breve, até logo*	seventy *setenta*	sit, to *sentar-se*	so *assim*
see you tomorrow *até amanhã*	shave, to *fazer a barba*	sit, to *sentar-se*	so many *tantos, tantas*
seen *visto*	she *ela*	situation *situação*	so much *tanto, tanta*
sell, to *vender*	shoe store *sapataria, loja de sapatos*	six *seis*	sober *sóbrio, sóbria*
sensational *sensacional*	short *baixo, baixa*	six hundred *seiscentos, seiscentas*	soccer *futebol*
separated *separado, separada*	sick *doente*	sixteen *dezesseis*	socialist *socialista*
September *setembro*	sick, bored, boring *enjoado, enjoada*	sixth *sexto, sexta*	sofa *sofá*
serious *sério, séria*	simple *simples*	sixty *sessenta*	some, something *algum, alguma*

someone
alguém

son
filho

song
música

song
canção

son-in-law
genro

sorry
desculpe, desculpa

so-so
mais ou menos

soup
sopa

south
sul

South America
América do Sul

southeast
sudeste

speak, to
falar

specialist
especialista

speech, language
fala

spend, to
gastar

sport
esporte

spouse
esposo, esposa

spring
primavera

stairs
escadas

start, to
começar

state
estado

statement
afirmação

stationary store
papelaria

stay, to
ficar

stepfather
padrasto

stepmother
madrasta

storage facility
armazém

store
loja

street
rua

street market
feira

street vendor
*vendedor,
vendedora ambulante*

strong, stocky
forte

student
estudante

student center
centro estudantil

studious
estudioso, estudiosa

study, to
estudar

stunned
estupefato, estupefata

stupid
burro, burra

such
tal

suddenly, all of sudden
de repente

sugarcane rum
cachaça

summer
verão

sun, sunny
sol

Sunday
domingo

superior
superior

supermarket
supermercado

Sure!, Of course!
Pois não!

surprising
surpreendente

Sweden
Suécia

Swedish
sueco, sueca

sweet
doce

Swiss
suíço, suíça

Switzerland
Suíça

systems analyst
analista de sistemas

T

table
mesa

take advantage of, to
aproveitar

take, to
tirar

talent
talento

talk (n.), conversation
conversa

tall
alto, alta

task, homework
tarefa

taxi
táxi

tea
chá

teacher, professor
professor, professora

telephone
telefone

telephone booth
orelhão

telephone call
telefonema

telephone set
aparelho (telefônico)

television
televisão

ten
dez

tennis player
tenista

tenor
tenor

tenth
décimo, décimo

test
prova

Thai
tailandês, tailandesa

Thailand
Tailândia

thank you
obrigado, obrigada

that
aquele, aquela

that (neutral, abstract)
aquilo

the
o, a, os, as

theirs
deles, delas

then
então

then, that
que

there, over there
lá

these
esses, essas

they, them
eles, elas

thin
magro, magra

think
achar

think, to
refletir

third
terceiro, terceira

thirteen
treze

thirty
trinta

this
esse, essa, este, esta

this (neutral, abstract)
isso

thorax
tórax

those
aqueles, aquelas

thousand
mil

three
três

three hundred
trezentos, trezentas

thunder
trovoada

Thursday
quinta-feira

tilde
til

time, climate
tempo

times (occasions)
vezes

tired
cansado, cansada

title
título

to
para

to you, him, her
(indirect pronoun)
lhe

today
hoje

together
juntos, juntas

tomorrow
amanhã

too much
demais

touch, to
tocar

traditional
tradicional

traffic
trânsito

train
trem

transfer
transferência

transfer, to
transferir

trash
lixo

travel, to
viajar

traveler's checks
cheques de viagem

tree
árvore

trip
viagem

truck
caminhão

truth
verdade

Tuesday
terça-feira

turkey
peru

twelfth
décimo-segundo,
décima-segunda

twelve
doze

twentieth
vigésimo, vigésima

twenty
vinte

twenty-one
vinte e um, vinte e uma

twenty-three
vinte e três

twenty-two
vinte e dois, vinte e duas

two
dois, duas

two hundred
duzentos, duzentas

type
tipo

U

ugly
feio, feia

uncle
tio

uncomparable
incomparável

under
debaixo de, embaixo de

understand, to
entender

understand, to
compreender

usual
usual

V

vacation
ferias

Valentine's Day
Dia dos Namorados

valor
valor

value
valor

vegetable oil
óleo

vegetables
verduras

Venezuela
Venezuela

Venezuelan
venezuelano, venezuelana

very
muito

vinegar
vinagre

virgin
virgem

visit, to
visitar

voluntary, volunteer
voluntário

W

wait on, to
atender

waiter
garçom

waitress
garçonete

walk, to
andar

want, to
querer

war
guerra

wash, to
lavar

wash (oneself), to
lavar-se

watch, to
assistir (a)

way
jeito

we
nós

we (the people)
a gente

weak
fraco, fraca

weather
clima, tempo

Wednesday
quarta-feira

week
semana

weekend
fim de semana

welcome
bem-vindo, bem-vinda

well
bem

what, which
qual

what
que

when
quando

where
onde

where to, to where
aonde

while
enquanto

white
branco

who
quem

why
por quê

widow
viúva

widower
viúvo

wife, spouse
mulher

will
vontade

window
janela

wine
vinho

winter
inverno

wish, to
desejar

with
com

with credit card
com cartão de crédito

with you (pl.) (archaic)
convosco

won
ganho

wonder
maravilha

wonderful
maravilhoso, maravilhosa

wood
pau

work
trabalho

work, to
trabalhar

worried
preocupado, preocupada

worry about, to
preocupar-se com

worse, the worst
pior

Wow!
Nossa!

write, to
escrever

written
escrito

Y

year
ano

yellow
amarelo, amarela

yes
sim

yesterday
ontem

yet
ainda

you
tu, você, vocês

you (pl.) (archaic)
vós

young
jovem

young boy (pejorative)
moleque

young man
rapaz

youngest offspring
caçula

youngster
jovem

your (familiar)
teu, tua, teus, tuas

your (formal)
seu, sua, seus, suas

yours (archaic)
vosso

Z

zinc
zinco

Zulu
zulu

Portuguese-to-English Glossary

A

a, as
the (fem.)

a gente
we (the people)

abacaxi
pineapple

abdominal
abdominal

aberto
opened

abraço
hug

abril
April

abrir
to open

absolutamente!
absolutely not!

abstinência
abstinence

acabar
to finish

açaí
acai fruit, a wild berry found in the Amazon

ação
action

acesível
accessible

aceitável
acceptable

acento agudo
acute accent

acento circunflexo
circumflex accent

acento grave
grave accent

achar
to find, to think

acidente
accident

acomodável
accommodating

acordado, acordada
awake

Açores
also called the Azores, an archipelago or group of islands that belongs to Portugal

acostumar-se com
to get used to

açougue
butcher shop

acreditar
to believe

admisível
admissible

adolescência
adolescence, teenage years

adorável
adorable

advogado, advogada
lawyer

afável
affable

afilhada
goddaughter

afilhado
godson

afirmação
statement

agogô
two bells together, struck with a stick or squeezed together

agosto
August

ainda
yet

ainda não
not yet

ajudar
to help

Alemanha
Germany

alemão, alemã
German

alfândega
customs

adorável
adorable

algodão
cotton

alguém
someone

algum, alguma
some, something

almoçar
to have lunch

alô
hello

alto, alta
tall

amanhã
tomorrow

amar
to love

amarelo, amarela
yellow

Amazonas
a state in the north of Brazil

ambos, ambas
both

amendrontado, amen- drontada
scared

América do Norte
North America

América do Sul
South America

América Latina
Latin America

americano, americana
American

amor
love

analista
psychotherapist

analista de sistemas
systems analyst

andar
to walk

andar de bicicleta
to ride a bike

anexo
annex

Angola
Angola

angolano, angolana
Angolan

animado, animada
excited

animal
animal

aniversário
birthday, anniversary

anjo
angel

ano
year

ansioso, ansiosa
anxious

anteontem
day before yesterday

antes
before

anual
annual

ao mesmo tempo
at the same time

aonde
where to, to where

apaixonado, apaixonada
in love

aparelho (telefônico)
telephone set

apertare
to press

aplaudir
to applaud

aprender
to learn

apresentar
to introduce

aproveitar
*to take advantage of,
to enjoy*

aquele, aquela
that

aqueles, aquelas
those

aqui
here

aquilo
that (neutral, abstract)

arara
macaw

ardor
ardor

Argentina
Argentina

argentino, argentina
Argentinian

armazém
storage facility

arquiteto, arquiteta
architect

arroz
rice

arrumar
fix, find

arte
art

artista
artist

árvore
tree

às
to the (a + as contraction)

assim
so

assistir (a)
to attend, to watch

astral
astral

ataque
attack

até amanhã
see you tomorrow

até breve
see you soon

até logo
see you soon

até mais
see you later

atenção
attention

atenciosamente
attentively, cordially

atender
*to answer the phone,
to wait on*

atender o telefone
to answer the phone

atendimento
service

ateu, atéia
atheist

atleta
athlete

atletismo
athleticism

ator
actor

atriz
actress

atrás
behind

audiência
official meeting

auditor
auditor

aula
class

Austrália
Australia

australiano, australiana
Australian

Áustria
Austria

austríaco, austríaca
Austrian

automóvel
automobile

autor
author

avental
apron

avião
airplane

avó
grandmother

avô
grandfather

azul
blue

B

bagagem
baggage, luggage

bairro
neighborhood

baixo, baixa
short

bambuzal
plantation of bamboo trees

banca de revista
newsstand

bancário
bank teller

banco
bank

Banco Central
Central Bank (the equivalent of the Federal Reserve)

banho
bath

barato, barata
cheap

barbeiro
barbershop

barulho
noise

barzinho
local pub

basquetebol
basketball

bate-papo
conversation, friendly chat (colloquial)

baú
chest

bêbado, bêbada
drunk

beber
to drink

beijar-se
to kiss one another

beijo
kiss

belga
Belgian

Bélgica
Belgium

bem
well

bem-vindo, bem-vinda
welcome

berço
cradle

berimbau
one-string African instrument

biblioteca
library

bilhão
one billion

biodegradável
biodegradable

bisavó
great-grandmother

bisavô
great-grandfather

blasfemável
blasphemous

blusa
blouse

boa noite
good evening

boa sorte
good luck

boa tarde
good afternoon

boa viagem
have a good trip

bolo
cake

bolsa
bag, purse

bom
good

bom dia
good morning

bombom
bonbon

bonito, bonito
pretty

Boniwa
*indigenous language
of Brazil*

bonzinho, boazinha
very nice (about a person)

bossa nova
*jazzy musical style
that originated in the
sixties in Brazil*

branco
white

Brasil
Brazil

brasileiro, brasileira
Brazilian

brevidade
brevity

britânico, britânica
British

burro, burra
stupid

C

Caatinga
*desert-like region of
northeast Brazil*

cabelereiro
hairdresser

caça
hunt

cachaça
sugarcane rum

cachorra
female dog

cachorro
dog

caçula
youngest offspring

caderno
notebook

café
coffee

caipirinha
*a Brazilian cocktail
made with limes, sugar,
and sugarcane rum*

caixa
*a small drum with strings
in the bottom that creates
a sound like a snare drum*

caju
cashew fruit

calculável
calculating

calor
hot

caminhão
truck

Canadá
Canada

canadense
Canadian

canção
song

caneta
pen

canil
kennel

cansado, cansada
tired

cantar
to sing

canto
I sing (present)

cantor, cantora
singer

cão
dog

caos
chaos

capaz
able

capital
capital

capitanias
*territories awarded to
Portuguese officials in
the sixteenth century*

capitão
captain

capítulo
chapter

capoeira
*martial art that
incorporates African dance*

cardíaco
cardiac

careca
bald

carinho
affection

Carnaval
*the equivalent of Mardi
Gras, a week of festivities
before Lent*

carne de boi
beef

carne de porco
pork

carne seca
Brazilian beef jerky

caro, cara
expensive; dear (informal)

carro
car

cartão de crédito
postcard

cartão postal
postcard

cartão telefônico
phone card

cartaz
poster

cartões
cards

casa
house

casa de câmbio
currency exchange agency

casaco
coat

casado, casada
married

casal
couple

casar-se
to get married

castanho
brown, chestnut color

catálogo telefônico
phone book

catar (inf.)
to look for (colloquial)

catedral
cathedral

catorze
fourteen

cavaquinho
a small, four-string guitar-like instrument created in Portugal that later inspired the ukulele

cebola
onion

cedo
early

cego, cega
blind

cem
one hundred

censor
censor

cento e um, cento e uma
one hundred and one

central
central

centro
center

centro estudantil
student center

centro-oeste
central-west

certo
correct

cerveja
beer

céu
sky

chá
tea

chamada a cobrar
collect call

chamar
to call

chamar de
to call (someone or something a name)

chamar-se
to call oneself

chato, chata
boring

chave
key

checo, checa
Czech

chegar
to arrive

cheques de viagem
traveler's checks

Chile
Chile

chileno, chilena
Chilean

China
China

chinês, chinesa
Chinese

chocolate
chocolate

chover
to rain

chucalho
a shaker instrument made by putting metal cans together and filling it with rocks, sand, or beans

churrasco
Brazilian barbecue

ciclista
cyclist

ciclo
cycle, ring

cidade
city

cinco
five

cinema
movies, cinema

cinema novo
Brazilian cinematic movement

cinqüenta
fifty

cinto
belt

ciúme
jealousy

claramente
clearly

claridade
clarity

clarinete
clarinet

clima
weather

clímax
climax

clínica
clinic

clube
club, gym

coberto
covered

código
code

código de área
area code

código internacional
country code

colocar
to put, to place

Colombia
Colombia

colombiano, colombiana
Colombian

com
with

com licença
excuse me, sorry

começar
to start

comédia
comedy

comediante
comedian

comemorado,
comemorada
celebrated

comer
to eat

comercial
commercial

comida
food

companheiro,
companheira
friends, partners

competir
to compete

completar
to complete

complexo
complex

complô
scheme

compor
to compose

compositor
composer

comprar
to buy

compreender
*to understand, to
comprehend*

compreensível
comprehensible

computador
computer

comunicação
communication

comunicar
to communicate

concerto
concert

concorrentes
competitors

condutor
conductor

conferência
conference

confortável
comfortable

conhecer
to know (people, places)

conseguir
to achieve, to get

conspirador
conspirer

constipado
congested (by a cold)

construir
to contruct

consulado
consulate

consultor, consultora
consultant

consumido, consumida
consumed

consumidor
consumer, client

conta
bill, account

contador, contadora
accountant

contagem
act of counting

contente
happy

contra
against

conversa
conversation, talk (n.)

conversível
*convertible, capable
of being converted*

convosco
with you (pl.) (archaic)

Copacabana
famous Brazilian beach located in Rio de Janeiro

cor
color

coração
heart

cordial
cordial

corrente, colar
necklace

correr
to run

corrigir
to correct

Costa Rica
Costa Rica

costa-riquenho
Costa Rican

costureiro, costureira
clothes designer, dressmaker

convencer-se de
to convince oneself of

crachá
identification tag

crédito
credit

criança
child

criatura
creature

crime
crime

cru, crua
raw

cruel
cruel

Cuba
Cuba

cuchilo
nap

cuíca
drum-like instrument with a stiff string upon which the player slides his fingers up and down to produce a squeaky sound

cuidado
care; (be) careful (exclamation)

cultura
culture

cultural
cultural

cunhada
sister-in-law

cunhado
brother-in-law

curável
curable

curioso
curious

curtir
to enjoy (slang)

Curupira
human-like creature whose feet are backwards; brings bad luck or death to those who see him

cyber café
Internet café

D

D. Pedro I
Dom Pedro I, the Emperor of Brazil

D. Pedro II
Dom Pedro II, son of D. Pedro I and Emperor of Brazil

dado
dice

dançar
to dance

dar
to give

dar sinal
having a dial tone

dar uma volta
to go on a short trip

de repente
suddenly, all of sudden

debaixo de
under

decidir-se a
to decide to

décimo, décimo
tenth

décimo-primeiro, décima-primeira
eleventh

décimo-segundo, décima-segunda
twelfth

dedicar-se a
to dedicate oneself to

defronte de
facing, in front of

deitar-se
to go to bed, to retire

deixar
to leave

deixar um recado
to leave a message

dela
her

dele
his

deles, delas
theirs

delito
crime

demais
too much

dente de alho
garlic cloves

dentista
dentist

dentro de
inside

depois de amanhã
day after tomorrow

descansado, descansada
rested

descansar
to rest

desculpe, desculpa
sorry

desde
since

desejar
to wish, to desire

desenvolvimento
development

desligar o telefone
to hang up the phone

destruidor
destroyer

detector
detector

detrás de
behind

deus
god

devagar
slowly

dever de casa
homework

dez
ten

dezembro
December

dezenove
nineteen

dezesseis
sixteen

dezessete
seventeen

dezoito
eighteen

dia
day

Dia da Independência
Independence Day

Dia de Natal
Christmas Day

Dia de São Patrício
Saint Patrick's Day

Dia dos Namorados
Valentine's Day

dicionário
dictionary

difícil
difficult

digestível
digestable

dinastia
dynasty

dinheiro
money

diretor, diretora
director

dito
said

divertir-se
*to entertain oneself,
to have fun*

dividido
divided

divorciado, divorciada
divorced

dizer
to say

dó
pity

doce
sweet

documento
document

doente
sick

dois, duas
two

dólares
dollars

domingo
Sunday

dominó
domino

Dona
*a title of respect for
women, as in Dona Maria*

dor
pain

dormindo
asleep

dormir
to sleep

doze
twelve

droga
drug, drugs

drogaria
drugstore

durável
durable

duzentos, duzentas
two hundred

E

e
and

econômica
economic

Ecuador
Ecuador

editor
editor

educacional
educational

egípcio, egípcia
Egyptian

Egito
Egypt

ela
she, her

ele
he, him

eles, elas
they, them

elefante
elephant

elegância
elegance

elegante
elegant

eletrônico, eletrônica
electronic

em
in

em cima de
on top

em frente de
in front of

embaixada
embassy

embaixo de
under

emocional
emotional

empregado, empregada
employee, maid

encantado, encantada
a pleasure, nice to meet you

encontrar
to find

encontrar-se
to find oneself

endereço
address

engenheiro, engenheira
engineer

engraçado, engraçada
funny

enjoado, enjoada
sick, bored, boring

enquanto
while

ensaio
essay, rehearsal

então
then

entender
to understand

entrar em
to enter

entregue
handed, given

envelope
envelope

envergonhado,
envergonhada
embarassed

equatoriano, equatoriana
Ecuadorian

erro
error, mistake

escadas
stairs

escola
school

escola primária
elementary school

escolher
to choose

escrever
to write

escrito
written

escritório
office

escutar
to hear, to listen

especialista
specialist

espelho
mirror

esporte
sport

esposo, esposa
spouse

esquecer-se de
to forget to

esquema
scheme, plan

esquina
corner

esse, essa
this

essencial
essential

esses, essas
these

estado
state

estar
to be

estatura mediana
average height

este, esta
this

estudante
student

estudar
to study

estudioso, estudiosa
studious

estupefato, estupefata
stunned

eu
I

Europa
Europe

evitável
avoidable

exame
exam

excelente
excellent

excepcional
exceptional

excitado, excitada
aroused

excluir
to exclude

exigir
to demand

exótico
exotic

explicações
explanations

explicar
to explain

explicável
explainable

F

faca
knife

façanha
feat

fácil
easy

Fado
Portuguese musical style

fala
speech; language

falar
to speak

falsificável
falsifiable

família
family

familiar
familiar, pertaining to family

famoso, famosa
famous

farmacêutico, farmacêutica
pharmacist

farmácia
drugstore

fatal
fatal

favor
favor

fazer
to do, to make

fazer a barba
to shave

fazer as pazes
to make peace

fazer compras
to buy

fazer de conta
to pretend

fazer exercícios
to exercise

fazer falta
to miss, to lack

fazer greve
to go on strike

fazer um telefonema
to make a phone call

federal
federal

feijão
beans

feijoada
Brazilian black bean and pork stew

feio, feia
ugly

feira
street market

feito
made, done

felicidade
happiness

feliz
happy

Feliz Natal
Merry Christmas

felizmente
fortunately

fenomenal
phenomenal

ferias
vacation

fervor
fervor

festa
party

festa de despedida
going-away party

fevereiro
February

ficar
to be (situated), to become, to stay

filha
daughter

filho
son

Filipinas
Philippines

filme
movie

fim de semana
weekend

físico (adj.)
physical

físico (n.)
physicist

fluentemente
fluently

fora
outside

forte
strong, stocky

fósforo
match

fóssil
fossil

fotógrafo, fotógrafa
photographer

fraco, fraca
weak

França
France

francês, francesa
French

frase
phrase

freguês, freguesa
customer

freqüência
frequency

frio
cold

frios
cold cuts

fuga
escape

fundamental
fundamental

futebol
soccer

futebol de salão
indoor soccer

futuro
future, future tense

fuzil
rifle

G

gancho
handset

ganho
won

garagem
garage

garçom
waiter

garçonete
waitress

garfo
fork

gasto
spent

gato
cat

genro
son-in-law

gente
people

gerente
manager

gesto
gesture

ginásio
gym

gordo, gorda
fat

gostar de
to like

gota
drop

Grã-bretanha
Great Britain

gramática
grammar

grande
big

Grécia
Greece

grego, grega
Greek

grúa
forklift

Guanabara
beach/locality in Rio de Janeiro

guaraná
a tropical berry found in the Amazon; the main ingredient in a Brazilian soft drink

guarda
policeman

guardanapo
napkin

guerra
war

guia
guide

guitarra
electric guitar

guri
young boy; indigenous origin word

H

Haiti
Haiti

haitiano, haitiana
Haitian

haver
to exist, to have

hebreu, hebréia
Hebrew

hindu
Hindu

hoje
today

Holanda
Holland

holandês, holandesa
Dutch

hora, horas
hour, hours

horrível
horrible

hospital
hospital

hotel
hotel

húmido, húmida
humid

humor
humor

hundred
cem

I

ideal
ideal

idealismo
idealism

idéia
idea

idêntico, idêntica
identical

identidade
identity

idoso, idosa
elderly

igreja
church

igualmente
likewise, same here

ilegal
illegal

imagem
image

imediatamente
immediately

impedir
to impede

impor
to impose

importância
importance

importante
important

impossível
impossible

imprescindível
essential

impressionado, impressionada
impressed

incluído, incluída
included

incluir
to include

incomparável
uncomparable

India
India

indiano, indiana
Indian

inevitável
inevitable

inferior
inferior

infinitivo pessoal
personal infinitive

informação
information

informar
to inform

Inglaterra
England

inglês, inglesa
English

insistência
insistence

inspetor
inspector

instrutor
instructor

inteligente
intelligent

internacional
international

interurbano
long distance

inventar
invent, to

inventor
inventor

inverno
winter

investir
to invest

Ipanema
famous beach in Rio de Janeiro

ir
to go

Irã
Iran

iraniano, iraniana
Iranian

Iraque
Iraq

iraquiano, iraquiana
Iraqui

Irlanda
Ireland

irlandês, irlandesa
Irish

irmã
sister

irmão
brother

irritado, irritada
irritated

Israel
Israel

israelense
Israeli

isso
this (neutral, abstract)

Itália
Italy

italiano, italiana
Italian

J

já
already

Jacarepaguá
locality in São Paulo

Jamaica
Jamaica

jamaicano, jamaicana
Jamaican

jamais
ever, never

janeiro
January

janela
window

jantar
to have dinner, dinner (n.)

Japão
Japan

japonês, japonesa
Japanese

jeito
way

joelho de porco
defumado
smoked ham hocks

jogar
to play (a sport or a game)

jornal
newspaper

jornaleiro
newspaper seller

jornalista
reporter, journalist

jovem (adj.)
young

jovem (n.)
youngster

juiz, juíza
judge

julho
July

junho
June

juntos, juntas
together

L

lá
there, over there

lambada
*African-inspired dance
and musical style*

lamentável
lamentable

lápis
pencil

laranja
orange

lava a seco
dry cleaners

lavar
to wash

lavar-se
to wash oneself

legume
legume, vegetable

leite
milk

lembrança
remembrance, souvenir

lembrar-se
to remember to

ler
to read

lhe
*to you, him, her
(indirect pronoun)*

liberdade
liberty

lição
lesson

licor
liqueur

ligação direta
direct call

ligar
to call

limpo, limpa
clean

lindo, linda
beautiful

lingüiça
*Brazilian chorizo
or pepperoni*

Lisboa
Lisbon

livraria
bookstore

livro
book

lixo
trash

local
local

loção
lotion

loja
store

loja de roupa
clothing store

loja de sapatos
shoestore

longe de
far from

louco, louca
crazy

louro, loura
blond

lugar
place

M

maçã
apple

machucar-se
to hurt oneself

Madeira
island in the Atlantic Ocean belonging to Portugal

madrasta
stepmother

madrinha
godmother

mãe
mother

magro, magra
thin

maio
May

mais
more

mais ou menos
so-so

mamãe
mom, mommy

Manaus
city in the north of Brazil, capital of the state of Amazonas

mapa
map

mar
sea, ocean

maravilha
wonder

maravilhoso, maravilhosa
wonderful

março
March

marido
husband

marrom
brown

mecânico
mechanic

medicina
medicine

médico
doctor

meia-noite
midnight

meio-dia
noon, midday

melão
melon

melhor
better, best

menina
girl

menino
boy

menos
minus

menos
less

mentir
to lie

mentor
mentor

mesa
table

mesmo
same

meu, minha
(plural: meus, minhas)
my

mexicano, mexicana
Mexican

México
Mexico

mil
one thousand

milionário
millionaire

Minas Gerais
a state in the south-east of Brazil

miserável
miserable

Moçambique
Mozambique

mochila
backpack

moderno, moderna
modern

moleque
young boy; pejorative

momento
moment

morar
to live (reside)

moreno, morena
dark-skinned

morto
died

morto, morta
dead

mosca
fly (insect)

motor
motor, engine

MPB, Música Popular Brasileira
Brazilian Popular Music

mucama
young slave girl who fetches things

muito
a lot, very

muito prazer
nice to meet you

mulher
wife, spouse

múltipla escolha
multiple choice

museu
museum

música
music, song

música sertaneja
Brazilian country music

músico, música
musician

N

na semana passada
last week

nacional
national

nada
nothing

namorada
girlfriend

namorado
boyfriend

não
no

natural
natural

natureza
nature

nau, navio
boat, ship

neblina
fog

negociável
negotiable

nem… nem
neither… nor

nenhum, nenhuma
not one

nervoso, nervosa
nervous

neta
granddaughther

neto
grandson

nevar
to snow

neve
snow

Nheengatu
indigenous language of Brazil

Nicarágua
Nicaragua

nicaragüense
Nicaraguan

ninguém
nobody

noiva
fiancée, bride

noivo
fiancé, groom

nome
name

nono, nona
ninth

nora
daughter-in-law

Nordeste
northeast

normal
normal

norte
north

nós
we

Nossa!
Wow!

nosso, nossa
our

nove
nine

novecentos, novecentas
nine hundred

novembro
November

noventa
ninety

novo, nova
new

novo, nova
new

nu, nua
naked

nublado
cloudy

número
number

número de telefone
phone number

nunca
never

O

o, os
the (masc.)

obrigado, obrigada
thank you

óbvio
obvious

óculos
eyeglasses

ocupado, ocupada
busy

oficial
official

oi
hi

oitavo, oitava
eighth

oitenta
eighty

oito
eight

oitocentos, oitocentas
eight hundred

olá
hi

óleo
vegetable oil

olhar para
to look at

olhar-se
to look at oneself

onde
where

ontem
yesterday

onze
eleven

opa!
hey!

operário, operária
factory worker

opositor
opposing

orelha de porco
pig's ear

orelhão
telephone booth

órfão
orphan

organizável
organizable

órgão
organ

original
original

ostensível
ostensible

ótima
great

outono
autumn, fall

outro, outra
other

outubro
October

ouvir
to hear, to listen

ovo
egg

P

paciência
patience

padaria
bakery

padrasto
stepfather

padrinho
godfather

pagar
to pay

página
page

pago
paid

pagode
type of backyard samba typical of Rio

pai
father

pálido, pálida
pale

Panamá
Panama

panamenho, panamenha
Panamanian

pandeiro
large tambourine that is played fast and sometimes spun on one finger for show

pão
bread

papai
dad, daddy

papel
paper

papelaria
stationary store

para
to

parcial
partial

parecer-se com
to look like

parque
park

partir
to leave

passado, passada
past

passar
to pass, to overcome,
to approve

pássaro
bird

passável
passable

pastor
pastor

pato
duck

pau
wood

pé de porco
pig's foot

pediatra
pediatrician

pedir
to ask for

pegar
to catch

pente
comb

pentear-se
to brush/comb oneself

perdã
pardon, sorry

perder
to lose

perfume
perfume

pergunta
question

permitir
to allow

Pernambuco
state in northeast Brazil

persistente
persistent

perto
close, nearby

peru
turkey

pêssego
peach

pessoa famosa
celebrity

pianista
pianist

piloto
pilot

pimenta do reino
black pepper

pimenta malagueta
hot pepper sauce

pincel
paintbrush

pior
worse, the worst

piranha
piranha

planeta
planet

plano
plane, leveled

pobre
poor

poder
to be able to, can, may

pois é
right, indeed

Pois não!
Sure!

Pois não?
May I help you?

polícia
police

polonês, polonesa
Polish

Polônia
Poland

popular
popular

populoso, populosa
populated

pôr
to put, to place

por favor
please

por gentileza
please (formal)

pôr na cadeia
put in jail

por obséquio
please (formal)

por quê
why

porém
but, however

porque
because

porta
door

Portugal
Portugal

possível
possible

posto
put, set

potência
power

potente
potent

poucos, poucas
few

prato
dish

prazer
pleasure

precisar de
to need

prédio
building

prender
to arrest

preocupado, preocupada
worried

preocupar-se com
to worry about

presentável
presentable

presente
gift

presente contínuo
progressive present

presidente
president

presunto
ham

pretérito
preterite tense

prezado, prezada
dear (formal)

prima
cousin (female)

primavera
spring

primeiro, primeira
first

primo
cousin (male)

proa
bow, front part of the ship

problema
problem

professor, professora
teacher, professor

profissão
profession

programa
program

proposta
proposal

protetor
protector

prova
test

punha
he/she would put (imperfect tense)

Q

quadro
board

qual
what, which

qualquer
any

quando
when

quanto, quanta
how much

quantos, quantas
how many

quarenta
forty

quarta-feira
Wednesday

quarto, quarta
fourth

quatro
four

quatrocentos, quatrocentas
four hundred

que
then, that, what

queijo
cheese

queixar-se de
to complain about

quem
who

querer
to want

querido, querida
dear (informal)

quilombo
village of marooned slaves

quinhentos, quinhentas
five hundred

quinta-feira
Thursday

quinto, quinta
fifth

quinze
fifteen

R

rabo de porco
pig's tail

racional
rational

rádio
radio

raiz
root

ranking
ranking

rapaz
young man

rápido, rápida
fast

reagir
to react

real, reais
Brazilian currency

recado
message

receber
to receive

Recife
a city in northeast Brazil

reconhecido, reconhecida
recognized

recordar
to remember

refletir
to reflect, to think

refletor
reflector, reflecting

rei
king

relâmpago
lightening

remédios
medicines, medication

repenique
a medium-size drum, larger than a snare-drum, played with a stick and one hand

réptil
reptile

República Checa
Czech Republic

respeitável
respectable

responder
to answer

ressaca
hangover

restaurante
restaurant

reunir-se
to get together

revistas
magazines

rico, rica
rich

rio
river

Rio Capibaribe
Capibaribe River, a river in the state of Pernambuco

Rio Grande do Sul
a state in the south of Brazil

rir
to laugh

rir-se de
to laugh at

roxo
purple

rua
street

ruim
bad

ruivo, ruiva
redhead, redheaded

rumor
rumor

S

sábado
Saturday

saber
to know (information, skills)

sair
to go out, leave

sal
salt

sala de aula
classroom

salão de beleza
beauty salon

samba
a distinctly Brazilian musical style heavily influenced by the African drumming tradition

samba canção
also called the samba song, a slower samba piece with romantic lyrics put to music

samba enredo
fast, highly rhythmic samba with words and lyrics sung during Carnaval

Sambódromo
the place where samba schools parade every year in Rio de Janeiro

sanduíche
sandwich

Santa Catarina
a state in the south of Brazil

santo
saint

sapataria
shoe store

sapo
frog

satisfeito, satisfeita
satisfied

saudações cordiais
cordially

seção
section

secretária
secretary

secretária (eletrônica)
answering machine (literally "the electronic secretary")

sedutor
seductor

segunda-feira
Monday

segundo, segunda
second

seis
six

seiscentos, seiscentas
six hundred

semana
week

sempre
always

senha
code

senhor
mister

senhora
ma'am, lady

sensacional
sensational

sentar-se
to sit

sentar-se
to sit oneself

senzala
slave quarters

separado, separada
separated

ser
to be

sério, séria
serious

servir
to serve

sessenta
sixty

sete
seven

setecentos, setecentas
seven hundred

setembro
September

setenta
seventy

sétimo, sétima
seventh

Seu
abbreviation for senhor, a title of respect

seu, sua
(plural: seus, suas)
your

sexta-feira
Friday

sexto, sexta
sixth

shopping
mall

si
himself/herself

sim
yes

simpático
nice

simples
simple

sinal
dial tone

sinistro
sinister

sinto muito
I am terribly sorry

situação
situation

sobre
over, on top

sobrinha
niece

sobrinho
nephew

sóbrio, sóbria
sober

socialista
socialist

sócio, social
business partner

socorro
help

sofá
sofa

sogra
mother-in-law

sogro
father-in-law

sol
sun, sunny

solteiro, solteira
single

sonho
dream

sopa
soup

subir
to go up

sucuri
anaconda

sudeste
southeast

Suécia
Sweden

sueco, sueca
Swedish

Suíça
Switzerland

suíço, suíça
Swiss

sul
south

superior
superior

supermercado
supermarket

surdo
a large drum with a low but loud sound ("surdo" means deaf in Portuguese)

surpreendente
surprising

surpreender-se com
to be surprised

T

tá
short for está

tailandês, tailandesa
Thai

Tailândia
Thailand

tal
such

talento
talent

tamanho
size

também
also

também não
(not) either, neither

tamborim
a small, short drum played very fast with a stick

tanga
short bikini or loincloth

tanto, tanta
so much

tanto… quanto
as much as

tantos, tantas
so many

tão… quanto
as… as

tarde
late

tarefa
task, homework

tatu
armadillo

táxi
taxi

tchau
bye

telefone
telephone

telefone sem fio
cordless phone

telefonema
telephone call

telefonista, ajuda ao assinante
operator, directory assistance

televisão
television

tempo
time, climate

tempo
weather

tenista
tennis player

tenor
tenor

ter
to have

ter medo
to be afraid

terça-feira
Tuesday

terceiro, terceira
third

terminar
to finish

terra
earth, land

Tetra
fourth soccer championship

teu, tua
(plural: teus, tuas)
your

tia
aunt

Tijuca
locality in Rio de Janeiro

til
tilde

tio
uncle

tipo
type

tirar
to take

título
title

tocar
to play (an instrument), to touch

todo, toda
all, entire

todos, todas
all

tomar
to drink

tomar café
to have breakfast, to drink coffee

tórax
thorax

trabalhar
to work

trabalho
work, paper

tradicional
traditional

tranqüilo, tranqüila
calm

transferência
transfer

transferir
to transfer

trânsito
traffic

trazer
to bring

trem
train

trema
dierisis

três
three

treze
thirteen

trezentos, trezentas
three hundred

trinta
thirty

triste
sad

Tropicália
psychedelic musical style created by Caetano Veloso and others in the seventies

trovoada
thunder

tu
you

Tukano
indigenous language of Brazil

Tupã
supreme being of the Tupi people

Tupi Guarani
indigenous language of Brazil

U

um milhão
one million

um, uma
one

usual
usual, or an extension of use

V

valor
value, valor

velho, velha
old

vendedor, vendedora
salesperson

vendedor, vendedora ambulante
street vendor

vender
to sell

Venezuela
Venezuela

venezuelano, venezuelana
Venezuelan

ventar
to be windy

ver
to see

verão
summer

verdade
truth

verduras
vegetables

vermelho, vermelha
red

vestir-se
to put on clothes, to dress oneself

vezes
times

viagem
trip

viajar
to travel

vigésimo, vigésima
twentieth

vinagre
vinegar

vindo
come, arrived

vinho
wine

vinte
twenty

vinte e dois, vinte e duas
twenty-two

vinte e três
twenty-three

vinte e um, vinte e uma
twenty-one

vir
to come, to arrive

virgem
virgin

visitar
to visit

visto
seen

viu
he/she saw (Preterite)

viúvo
widower

viúva
widow

viver
to live

vizinho, vizinha
neighbor

você
you

você, vocês
you

voltar
to come back

voluntário
voluntary, volunteer

vontade
will

vós
you (pl.) (archaic)

vosso
yours (archaic)

vovó
grandma, granny

vovô
grandpa

X

xadrez
chess

xícara
cup

Y

Yara
proper name; Tupi divinity

Z

zinco
zinc

zulu
Zulu

Answer Key

Chapter 1

Exercise: Suffixes

1. *incidente (incident)*
2. *mecânico (mechanical)*
3. *identidade (identity)*
4. *infelizmente (unfortunately)*
5. *resistência (resistance)*

Chapter 2

Listening Practice 1

1. *avô (grandfather)*
2. *ganho (I gain/earn)*
3. *hesitar (hesitate)*
4. *chá (tea)*
5. *cancão (song)*
6. *ríspido (rude)*
7. *pingo (drop)*
8. *broa (type of bread)*

Listening Practice 2

1. *dor (pain)*
2. *guia (guide)*
3. *the sound [sh]*
4. *the sound [ks]*
5. *the sound [s]*

Listening Practice 3

1. *cinto (belt)*
2. *cato (I look for [colloquial])*
3. *ajo (I act)*
4. *sim (yes)*
5. *fuga (flight, escape)*

Chapter 3

Exercise: What to Say?

1. *nome (name)*
2. *chamo/prazer (I call/pleasure)*
3. *onde (where)*
4. *Eu (I)*

Exercise: Goodbye!

1. *como (how)*
2. *obrigada (thank you)*
3. *Tudo (Everything)*
4. *mais or logo (later or soon)*

Exercise: Chapter Review

1. *Desculpe! or Perdão!*
   (Sorry or Pardon)
2. *Com licença. (Excuse me.)*
3. *Obrigada or Obrigado (Thank you)*
4. *Poderia repetir, por favor?*
   (Can you repeat, please?)
5. *Falo um pouquinho (de português).*
   (I speak a little [Portuguese].)
6. *Como se diz isso em português? (How do you say this in Portuguese?)*

Chapter 4

Practice with Gender

1. *o caderno (notebook)*
2. *a contagem (act of counting)*
3. *o caminhão (truck)*
4. *o armazém (storage facility)*
5. *o amor (love)*
6. *a ação (action)*
7. *o/a socialista (socialist)*
8. *o avental (apron)*
9. *o crachá (identification tag)*
10. *a alfândega (customs)*
11. *o esquema (scheme, plan)*
12. *a liberdade (liberty)*

Exercise: Addressing Others

1. *você (tu in some regions)*
2. *o senhor*
3. *o senhor*
4. *você (tu in some regions)*
5. *você (tu in some regions)*
6. *a senhora*

Exercise: Definite or Indefinite?

1. *. . . um lápis, um caderno e uma caneta.*
2. *. . . um livro de português.*
3. *. . . as suas canetas?*
4. *. . . chamaram o José. . .*
5. *. . . ter um ataque cardíaco!*

Exercise: Contractions

1. *Eu sou dos Estados Unidos.*
2. *Eu moro na residência estudantil.*
3. *Ela é de Cuba.*
4. *Eles são da Ilha da Madeira.*
5. *Eu estudo na universidade grande.*

Chapter 5

Exercise: Name the Nationalities

1. *Ela é alemã.*
2. *Ele é brasileiro.*
3. *Eles são russos.*
4. *Eles são italianos.*
5. *Ele é japonês.*

Exercise: Name That Profession!

1. *Ele é pianista. (He is a pianist.)*
2. *Ela é professora. (She is a professor.)*
3. *Ele é bancário. (He is a bank teller.)*
4. *Ela é juíza. (She is a judge.)*
5. *Ela é vendedora. (She is a salesperson.)*

Chapter 6

Exercise: Choosing *Ser* or *Estar*

1. *Clarice está no hospital.*
2. *Ela é médica pediatra.*
3. *Ela é uma pessoa contente por natureza.*
4. *Clarice e Kadu são brasileiros.*
5. *Agora estão no Rio de Janeiro.*
6. *Kadu é estudante de medicina.*
7. *Ele está nervosa com os exames.*

Exercise: Now You Conjugate!

1. *Meus pais estão na Europa. (My parents are in Europe.)*
2. *O vermelho é uma cor linda. (Red is a beautiful color.)*
3. *Meu amigo Jonas é engenheiro civil. (My friend Jonas is a civil engineer.)*
4. *O livro de Português está encima da mesa. (The Portuguese book is on top of the table.)*

5. *Fortaleza fica (or está) no Nordeste do Brasil. (Fortaleza is in Northeast Brazil.)*
6. *São sete horas da noite. (It's seven at night.)*
7. *Nós estamos muito contentes com os nossos filhos. (We are very happy with our children.)*

Exercise: Time to Translate

1. *Ela está magra. (She is skinny.)*
2. *Eles são professores. (also: Elas são professoras.) (They are professors.)*
3. *Ele está furioso. (He is mad.)*
4. *Nós somos cubanos. (also: Nós somos cubanas.) (We are Cuban.)*
5. *Você está na cidade. (You are in the city.)*

Exercise: What's the Plural Form?

1. *corações (hearts)*
2. *canis (dog shelters)*
3. *pincéis (brushes)*
4. *pães (breads)*
5. *órfãos (orphans)*
6. *difíceis (difficult) [plural adjective]*
7. *cantores (singers)*
8. *tórax (thorax) [plural is written the same as singular]*

Chapter 7

Exercise: Transforming Adjectives

1. *francês (French): francesa*
2. *indiano (Indian): indiana*
3. *nu (naked): nua*
4. *ateu (Atheist): atéia*
5. *jornaleiro (newspaper seller): jornaleira*
6. *japonês (Japanese): japonesa*
7. *israelense (Israeli): (same as masculine)*
8. *colombiano (Colombian): colombiana*

Exercise: Put It All in Order

1. *um carro vermelho (a red car)*
2. *umas casas novas (some new houses)*
3. *todos (os) meus amigos (all my friends)*
4. *o aluno inteligente (the intelligent student)*
5. *uma blusa laranja (an orange blouse)*
6. *ambos os livros (both of the books)*
7. *a minha amiga ([the] my friend)*
8. *um carro novo (a new car)*

Exercise: Comparing Unequal Elements

1. *Rita é mais inteligente que Teresa (also: Teresa é mais burra que Rita.)*
2. *Marta é mais nova que Rodrigo (also: Rodrigo é mais velho que Marta.)*
3. *Amaro é mais baixo que Cláudio (also: Cláudio é mais alto que Amaro.)*
4. *Jorge é mais gordo que Maria. (also: Maria é mais magra que Jorge.)*
5. *Bill é mais rico que Donald. (also: Donald é mais pobre que Bill.)*

Exercise: Comparing Equal Elements

1. *Jorge é tão feio quanto Vicente.*
2. *Martha é tão rica quanto Donald.*
3. *O Porsche tem tanta potência quanto o Ferrari.*
4. *Meu computador tem tantos problemas quanto o seu.*
5. *Gilberto tem tanto talento quanto Chico.*

Exercise: Fill in the Superlative

1. *O futebol é o esporte mais popular do Brasil.*
2. *Brasília é a capital mais moderna da América Latina.*
3. *Amália Rodrigues é a melhor cantora de Fado de Portugal.*

Exercise: Write Superlative Sentences (possible answers)

1. *O MacIntosh é o computador mais caro do mundo.*
2. *Conan é o comediante mais engraçado dos Estados Unidos.*
3. *A feijoada é a comida mais famosa do Brasil.*

Exercise: Who Owns It?

1. *my pen: minha caneta*
2. *your book: seu caderno*
3. *my friends: meus amigos (also: minhas amigas)*
4. *our parents: nossos pais*
5. *your backpack: sua mochila*
6. *our house: nossa casa*
7. *your notebooks: seus cadernos*
8. *my sisters: minhas irmãs*

Exercise: Translation

1. *Their (female) classes: as aulas delas*
2. *His computer: o computador dele*
3. *Her pencil: o lápis dela*
4. *Their (male) house: a casa deles*
5. *Her books: os livros dela*
6. *Their (female) car: o carro delas*
7. *His glasses: os óculos dele*
8. *Her purse: a bolsa dela*

Chapter 8

Exercise: Translation Using Numbers

1. *15 notebooks: quinze cadernos*
2. *83 books: oitenta e três livros*
3. *379 professors: trezentos e setenta e nove professores*
4. *761 female students: setecentas e sessenta e uma alunas*
5. *1.006 cars: mil e seis carros*
6. *432.578 people: quatrocentas e trinta e duas mil, quinhentas e setenta e oito pessoas*

Exercise: Using Ordinal Numbers

1. *A sétima maravilha do mundo (the seventh wonder of the world)*
2. *O quarto ciclo do inferno (the fourth ring of hell)*
3. *A primeira lição (the first lesson)*
4. *A quinta dinastia (the fifth dinasty)*
5. *O vigésimo tenista do ranking mundial (the twentieth tennis player of the world)*

Exercise: Do You Have the Time?

1. *2:30*
2. *7:20*
3. *17:10*
4. *12 A.M.*

Exercise: What Is the Date?

1. *01/04*
2. *11/08*
3. *06/07*
4. *31/03*

Exercise: Holidays

1. *O Dia da Indenpendência dos Estados Unidos: 4 (quatro) de julho.*
2. *O Dia dos Namorados (Valentine's Day): 14 (catorze) de fevereiro*
3. *O Dia de São Patrício (Saint Patrick's Day): 17 (dezessete) de março.*
4. *O (Dia de) Natal (Christmas Day): 25 (vinte e cinco) de dezembro.*

Chapter 9

Exercise: Fill in the Blank

1. *A criança joga futebol. (The child plays soccer.)*
2. *Os jovens tocam clarinete. (The youngsters play clarinet.)*
3. *Nós falamos português e inglês. (We speak Portuguese and English.)*
4. *Você compra pão todo dia? (Do you buy bread every day?)*
5. *Vocês moram no Brasil? (Do you (pl.) live in Brazil?)*

Exercise: Make a Match

1. *O concerto (e) começa às cinco horas.*
2. *Você (c) joga basquetebol?*
3. *Nós (d) moramos em Ipanema.*
4. *Eu (b) pago a conta, sempre!*
5. *Os alunos (a) estudam muitas horas por dia.*

Exercise: Conjugate the Verb

1. *Ele precisa do dicionário. (He needs the dictionary.)*
2. *Você chama essa fruta de laranja? (You call this fruit an orange?)*
3. *Eles gostam da comida. (They like the food.)*
4. *Os alunos entram na biblioteca. (The students enter the library.)*
5. *Eu não entro num banco sem documentos. (I don't go in a bank without documents.)*

Exercise: Where Can I Buy...?

1. *pão (bread): padaria, supermercado, mercearia*
2. *revistas (magazines): banca de revistas, livraria*
3. *leite (milk): supermercado, padaria*
4. *frutas (fruit): feira, supermercado*
5. *bolos (cakes): pastelaria, padaria, supermercado*

Exercise: Put Them in Order

1. *Anne almoça com os amigos. (3)*
2. *Anne brinca com os gatos. (5)*
3. *Anne volta para casa. (4)*
4. *Anne trabalha na universidade. (2)*
5. *Anne se acorda as 8 da manhã. (1)*

Exercise: What Is Your Schedule Like? (Answers will vary.)

1. *Eu (me) acordo às 8:30 da manhã.*
2. *Eu trabalho seis horas por dia.*
3. *Eu almoço em casa com minha esposa.*
4. *Eu volto para casa às 6 da noite.*
5. *Eu brinco com os meus cachorros.*

Chapter 10

Exercise: Fill in the Verb

1. *A criança come o sanduíche. (The child eats the sandwich.)*
2. *Os jovens assistem o filme. (The youngsters watch the movie.)*
3. *Nós dormimos oito horas por dia. (We sleep eight hours a day.)*
4. *Você vive nos Estados Unidos? (Do you live in the United States?)*
5. *Vocês respondem às perguntas? (Do you (pl.) answer the questions?)*

Exercise: The Right Match

1. *Minha amiga (e) atende o telefone imediatamente.*
2. *Essa livraria (d) vende livros e revistas?*
3. *Nós sempre (a) comemos neste restaurante.*
4. *Eu (b) parto amanhã para o Rio!*
5. *Os amigos (c) riem muito com a comédia.*

Exercise: Regular and Special Verbs

1. *O garçom serve a cerveja no restaurante, e eu sirvo vinho em casa.*
2. *Eu subo as escadas, e a secretária sobe pelo elevador.*
3. *Meus amigos dormem oito horas por dia, mas eu só durmo seis horas.*
4. *A aluna repete as frases, e eu repito a tarefa de casa.*
5. *Eu não minto muito, mas minha irmã mente demais!*

Exercise: Using Ir and Vir

1. *Eu vim do cabelereiro. (I come from the hairdresser.)*
2. *As garotas vão para a casa. (The girls go/are going home.)*

3. *Nós vimos do banco. (We come from the bank.)*
4. *Meus amigos vão para a escola todo dia. (My friends go to school every day.)*
5. *Eu vou para o trabalho de carro. (I go to work by car.)*
6. *Os vizinhos vêm do parque. (The neighbors come from the park.)*

Exercise: Using Ter
1. *Eu tenho dois carros. (I have two cars.)*
2. *Minha amiga tem pouca paciência. (My friend has little patience.)*
3. *Nós temos uma casa no Rio. (We have a house in Rio.)*
4. *Eles não têm aula na sexta. (They don't have class on Friday.)*
5. *O menino tem olhos azuis. (The boy has blue eyes.)*
6. *Tem duas janelas na sala. (There are two windows in the room.)*

Exercise: I Have To... (possible answers)
1. *Eu tenho que fazer exercícios.*
2. *Eu tenho que sair menos.*

Exercise: Who Is It?
1. *O filho do meu filho é o meu neto.*
2. *A irmã da minha mãe é a minha tia.*
3. *Os filhos dos meus tios são os meus primos.*
4. *A mãe da minha mãe é a minha avó.*
5. *Os pais dos meu pai são os meus avós.*
6. *O marido da minha irmã é o meu padrastro.*

Exercise: Write a Description (possible answer)
Oi, meu nome é Júlia. Minha família é pequena. Geraldo é o meu pai, Cristina é a minha mãe, e Orlando é o meu irmão. Eu não tenho irmãs.

Meu primo favorito é Cláudio, e a minha tia favorita é Roseane. Eu também adoro minha avó Ritinha.

Hi, my name is Julia. My family is small. Geraldo is my dad, Cristina is my mom, and Orlando is my brother. I don't have sisters. My favorite cousin is Cláudio, and my favorite aunt is Roseane. I also love my grandma Ritinha.

Chapter 11

Exercise: Multiple Choice
1. The workers are getting very low wages, so...
   a. *Eles fazem greve.*
2. My nephew is having all of his friends over for a party.
   c. *Ele faz anos.*
3. He has that five o'clock shadow, so...
   d. *Ele decide fazer a barba.*
4. Maria has practically nothing in the fridge, so...
   b. *Ela vai fazer compras.*
5. They were mad at each other, but not anymore. That means that...
   b. *Eles fizeram as pazes.*

Exercise: Choose the Verb
1. *Elas conhecem bem a capital do Brasil. (They know Brazil's capital really well.)*
2. *Você sabe andar de bicicleta? (Do you know how to ride a bike?)*
3. *Nós conhecemos os nossos vizinhos. (We know our neighbors.)*
4. *Vocês conhecem aquela música do Gil? (Do you guys know that song by Gil?)*
5. *Maristela sabe que Magdale é atriz. (Maristela knows that Magdale is an actress.)*

Exercise: Fill in the Blank
1. *Eu conheço Lisboa, a capital de Portugal.*
2. *Vocês conhecem o Rio Capibaribe?*
3. *Minha esposa e eu sabemos dirigir muito bem.*
4. *Eu sei que preciso estudar mais.*
5. *Os nossos amigos sabem que estamos juntas.*

Exercise: Translate
1. She loses the keys frequently. *Ele perde as chaves freqüentemente.*
2. Mário always asks for guaraná at the restaurant. *Mário sempre pede guaraná no restaurante.*
3. Sabrina never tells the truth. *Sabrina nunca diz a verdade.*
4. We bring the books to school. *Nós trazemos os livros para a escola.*
5. Mário and Maria put the cups on the table. *Mário e Maria poem as xícaras na mesa.*

Exercise: Make a Match
1. *Eu (f) perco as chaves do carro.*
2. *Eu (d) ouço música muito alto.*
3. *Eu (e) trago os livros para a aula.*
4. *Eu (b) digo a verdade à mamãe.*
5. *Eu (c) ponho o lápis na mesa.*
6. *Eu (a) saio de casa muito cedo.*

Chapter 12

Preterite or Imperfect? Exercise A
1. *Quando eu era criança, comia muito chocolate.*
2. *Ontem nós vimos um filme interessante.*
3. *Chovia um pouco quando saímos do cinema.*
4. *Meu pai sempre nos levava para o parque.*
5. *Estava no banho e de repente minha irmã me ligou.*
6. *Em Illinois fazia um frio horrível.*

Preterite or Imperfect? Exercise B

1. *No mês passado eu fui a Aruba.*
2. *Todos as manhãs, minha irmã e eu íamos à praia.*
3. *Na adolescência, nós nos acordávamos muito cedo.*
4. *Anteontem nós nos acordamos tarde.*
5. *Minha esposa cozinhou ontem à noite.*
6. *Minha avó cozinhava todos os dias.*

Future and Conditional Verbs: Exercise A

1. *I'm going to call you tomorrow. Eu vou chamar você amanhã.*
2. *We are going to visit Brazil in the summer. Nós vamos visitar o Brasil no verão.*
3. *You are going to write a book? Você vai escrever um livro?*

Future and Conditional Verbs: Exercise B

1. *O advogado solicitará uma audiência amanhã.*
2. *A prova terá cinco perguntas de ensaio.*
3. *Nós acompanharemos as crianças até o parque.*

Future and Conditional Verbs: Exercise C

1. *Se fosse mais cedo, nós sairíamos para dar uma volta.*
2. *Ele disse à Maria que chegaria tarde.*
3. *As meninas levantariam mais cedo se pudessem.*

Chapter 13

Using Two Verbs Together: Exercise A

1. *A minha irmã quer ir para a Inglaterra no ano que vem. (My sister wants to go to England next year.)*

2. *Eu tenho vontade de comer doce depois das quatro da tarde. (I feel like eating sweets after four in the afternoon.)*
3. *Os meus primos quiseram visitar o Museu de Arte Moderna de São Paulo. (My cousins wanted to visit the Modern Art Museum in São Paulo.)*
4. *A minha amiga Júlia e o marido querem sair para jantar na sexta-feira à noite. (My friend Júlia and her husband wants to go out to eat on Friday night.)*
5. *Nós os brasileiros sempre temos vontade de ir à Disneylândia de férias. (We Brazilians always feel like going to Disneyland for vacation.)*

Using Two Verbs Together: Exercise B (Answers will vary.)

1. *Eu quero sair com os meus amigos. (I want to go out with my friends.)*
2. *Eu tenho vontade de assistir à televisão. (I feel like watching TV.)*

Using Two Verbs Together: Exercise C

1. *Elvis has just left the building. Elvis acabou de sair do prédio.*
2. *May I go now? Posso ir agora?*
3. *Maria can run for a long time. Maria pode correr por muito tempo.*
4. *The teacher has to correct the tests. O professor (or A professora) tem que corrigir as provas.*
5. *We have just finished reading the paper. Nós acabamos de ler o jornal.*
6. *Can you go out tonight? Você pode sair hoje à noite?*
7. *They can come in. Eles podem entrar.*

Using Two Verbs Together: Exercise D (Answers will vary.)

1. *Eu tenho que estudar português.*
2. *Eu tenho que visitar o Brasil.*

Exercise: Past Participles

1. *As portas estavam abertas. (The doors were open.)*
2. *O mecânico está muito ocupado. (The mechanic is very busy.)*
3. *O que está escrito ali? (What is written there?)*
4. *A mesa está posta para o jantar. (The table is set for the dinner.)*
5. *Os bancos estão cob-ertos de neve. (The benches are covered with snow.)*

Exercise: Passive Voice

1. *The two men were seen near here. Os dois homens foram vistos aqui perto.*
2. *The money was spent very fast. O dinheiro foi gasto muito rapidamente.*
3. *What was said yesterday? O que foi dito ontem?*
4. *The food was consumed by the birds. A comida foi consumida pelos pássaros.*

Reflexive and Reciprocal Verbs: Exercise A

1. *Eles (f) se casaram na igreja.*
2. *Nós (c) nos divertimos muito na festa.*
3. *Minha amiga (b) se preocupa com a família.*
4. *Meu irmão (e) se parece com meu pai.*
5. *Os alunos (d) se queixam do livro sempre.*
6. *Eu (a) me deito às 11 da noite.*

Reflexive and Reciprocol Verbs: Exercise B

1. *The professor dedicates herself to teaching. A professora se dedica à educação.*
2. *Our neighbor was surprised with the visit. Nosso vizinho se surpreendeu com a visita.*

3. *The man laughed at the situation.*
   O homem se riu da situação.
4. *I look like my father. Eu me*
   pareço com o meu pai.

Chapter 14

Exercise: Practice with Negatives

1. *Eu não me lembro de ninguém da escola primária. (I don't remember anyone from elementary school.)*
2. *A minha amiga Júlia nunca se acorda antes das dez da manhã. (My friend Julia never gets up before ten in the morning.)*
3. *Sofia não tem nada contra seus colegas de trabalho. (Sofia has nothing [or: doesn't have anything] against her coworkers.)*
4. *Nós não fizemos nenhum exercício hoje. (We did not do any exercises [or: not one exercise] today.)*
5. *Os escritores não completaram nenhuma página nesta semana. (The writers did not complete any pages [or: not one page] this week.)*

Exercise: Positive to Negative

1. *Eu já fui no banco. (I already went to the bank.) > Eu ainda não fui ao banco. (I did not go to the bank yet.)*
2. *Você ainda tem medo de avião. (You are still afraid of airplanes.) > Você não tem mais medo de avião. (You are not afraid of planes anymore.)*
3. *Tem alguém na sala. (There is someone in the room.) > Não tem ninguém na sala.*
4. *Eles estão fazendo alguma coisa. (They are doing something.) > Eles não estão fazendo nada.*
5. *Elas sempre vão ao supermercado. (They always go to the supermarket.) > Elas nunca vão ao supermercado.*

Exercise: Negative to Positive

1. *Eles não encontraram nada em casa. (They did not find anything at home.) Eles encontraram alguém em casa. (They found someone at home.)*
2. *Eu não vi ninguém na festa. (I didn't see anybody at the party.) Eu vi alguém na festa.*
3. *Nós não o vimos em lugar nenhum. (We did not see him anywhere.) Nós o vimos em algum lugar. (We saw him somewhere.)*
4. *Você jamais telefona à noite. (You never call at night.) Você sempre telefona à noite.*
5. *Eu ainda não terminei o capítulo. (I did not finish the chapter yet.) Eu já terminei o capítulo.*

Chapter 15

Exercise: Is It a Question?

1. *[voice]: A casa é ali? (Is the house there?) uma afirmação*
2. *[voice]: O carro é aquele? (The car is that one?) uma pergunta*
3. *[voice]: Vocês vêm conosco? (You guys coming with us?) uma pergunta*
4. *[voice]: Eles vão com vocês. (They're going with you (pl.).) uma afirmação*
5. *[voice]: Você me faz um favor? (You do me a favor?) uma pergunta*

Exercise: Interrogative Words

1. *Quando é seu aniversário? (... is your birthday?)*
2. *Quanto custa essa blusa? (... is this blouse?)*
3. *Aonde você quer ir hoje? (... do you want to go today?)*
4. *Por que ele foi tão cedo? (... he left so early?)*
5. *Onde você mora? (... you live?)*

6. *Como se diz em português? (... you say it in Portuguese?)*
7. *O que você acha disso? (... do you think of that?)*

Exercise: Asking Questions

1. *Como você se chama? Eu me chamo Daniel.*
2. *Onde você mora? Eu moro no Rio de Janeiro.*
3. *Quantos irmãos você tem? Eu tenho três irmãos.*

Exercise: Translate Exclamations

1. *What a pretty girl she is! Que menina linda (que) ela é!*
2. *What an excellent hotel! Que hotel excelente!*
3. *How badly he drives! Como ele dirige mal!*
4. *What horrible cold weather! Que frio horrível!*
5. *How interesting! Que interessante!*

Chapter 16

The Personal Infinitive: Exercise A

1. *Eu lembro dos nomes dos alunos. (I remember the names of the students.) > É importante eu lembrar os nomes dos alunos. (It's important I remember the names of the students.)*
2. *Vocês dizem a verdade. (You (pl.) tell the truth.) > É essencial vocês dizerem a verdade. (It's essential you (pl.) tell the truth.)*
3. *Elas trazem os livros para a escola. (They bring the books to school.) > É imprescindível elas trazerem os livros para a escola. (It's indispensable that they bring the books to school.)*
4. *Nós visitamos nossos avós. (We visit our grandparents.) > É necessário nós visitarmos nossos avós. (It's necessary that we visit our grandparents.)*

5. *Você e o Roberto põem a mesa.
(You and Robert set the table.) >
É bom você e o Roberto (vocês)
porem a mesa. (It's good that
you and Robert set the table.)*
6. *As meninas dormem cedo. (The young
girls sleep early.) > É importante
as meninas dormirem cedo. (It's
important that the girls sleep early.)*

The Personal Infinitive: Exercise B

1. *Antes de eu ligar, eu procurei o
número. (Before calling, I looked
for the number.)*
2. *Até eles chegarem, nós esperamos.
(Until arriving (they), we waited.)*
3. *Depois de vocês comerem, podem
lavar os pratos. (After eating,
you [pl.] can wash the dishes.)*
4. *Para você receber os presentes, é
preciso ser um bom menino. (In
order for you to receive the presents,
you must be a good boy.)*

Exercise: What's the Weather Like?

1. *It's really hot in the Amazon. Faz
muito calor na Amazônia.*
2. *It does not snow in Brazil.
Não neva no Brasil.*
3. *It's hot in the North of Brazil.
Faz muito calor no Norte do Brasil.*
4. *There is some fog on the road.
Tem um pouco de neblina na estrada.*
5. *The weather is nice today.
O tempo está bonito hoje.*

Exercise: What Would You Wear?
(Answers will vary.)

1. *Faz muito sol, a temperatura
é de 38 graus Celsius. shortes,
camiseta sem manga, sandálias*
2. *Chove muito! impermeável*
3. *Está nevando. botas, casaco
de frio, xale, luvas*

4. *Está um pouco frio, a temperatura
é de 15 graus Celsius. jaqueta*
5. *Você está em Copacabana!
óculos de sol, biquíni*

Chapter 17

Exercise: Subjunctive Forms

1. *Eu preciso que vocês me respondam.
(I need you to answer to me.)*
2. *Ela deseja que você lhe dê o livro.
(She wants you to give her the book.)*
3. *Nós gostaríamos que ele viesse mais
cedo. (We wanted him to come
earlier.)*
4. *Eles se surpreenderam que ela
estivesse/fosse tão magra. (They
were surprised that she was so
skinny.) [Note: use estivesse for
a recent change of state and fosse
for a permanent condition.]*
5. *Se não for muito tarde, vou
pegar o ônibus. (If it is not too
late, I will take the bus.)*
6. *Enquanto ele precisar de mim,
eu vou ajudá-lo. (While he
needs me, I will help him.)*

Subjunctive Forms: Exercise B

1. *Se eu me lembrasse de tudo, seria
mais fácil. (If I remembered everything, it would be much easier.)*
2. *Elas não se esquecem de nada.
(They do not forget anything.)*
3. *Nós gostaríamos que eles
trousessem a cerveja. (We would
like them to bring the beer.)*
4. *É bom que eles comam tudo. (It's
nice that they eat everything.)*

Exercise: Using the Verb Dar

1. *I made breakfast but it didn't turn
out well.
Fiz o café mas não deu certo.*

2. *This is just not right!Assim não dá!*
3. *I'll call a friend and we'll find
a solution.
Eu chamo um amigo e nós damos um
jeito. Also: ... a gente dá um jeito.*
4. *The new venture fell through.
O negócio novo não deu em nada.*

Chapter 18

Cultural Review: What's the Word?

1. *cinema novo
(b) modernist film movement*
2. *feijoada(e) black bean and pork stew*
3. *cachaça (g) sugarcane rum*
4. *caipirinha (d) lime, sugar,
and rum drink*
5. *pé de porco (a) pig's foot*
6. *Tetra (m) fourth*
7. *Pelé (c) one of the greatest soccer
players in the world*
8. *Il Guarany (i) classical masterpiece of Gomes*
9. *MPB (l) Brazilian Popular Music*
10. *pandeiro (h) tambourine*
11. *cuíca (f) squeaky drum*
12. *samba enredo (j) theme samba*

Chapter 19

Exercise: Writing a Letter
*Minha cara Helena:
Fiquei feliz em receber o seu novo
endereço eletrônico. Desculpa não poder
ter ido a sua festa de despedida na semana
passada. Tenho estado superocupada com
o novo trabalho. Espero que tudo esteja
em ordem na sua nova casa! Quem sabe
um dia nos encontramos em uma dessas
conferências? Gostaria de manter contato
com você, pois lembro com carinho das
nossas conversas animadas no centro
estudantil.*

Um forte abraço,
Diana

My dear Helena:
I was so happy to receive your new
e-mail address. Sorry for not being able
to attend your farewell party last week.
I have been so busy with the new job. I
hope everything is all right with the new
home! Who knows, one of these days we
may meet at one of those conferences?
I would like to keep in touch with you,
as I remember our happy conversations
at the student center fondly.
A big hug,
Diana

Exercise: Formal or Informal?

1. *Alô! informal*
2. *Sinto muito, mas a doutora*
   não se encontra. formal
3. *Gostaria de esperar na*
   linha, senhor? formal
4. *Oi, posso falar com o Luís? informal*
5. *Gostaria de falar com o Senhor*
   Gomes, por gentileza. formal

Exercise: Communication Practice

1. *You want to let them know who*
   you are. Alô, meu nome é...
   (Hello my name is...) OR *Alô,*
   eu sou... (Hello, I'm ...)
2. *You would like to speak to Mr.*
   Barros. Por favor, eu gostaria de
   falar com o senhor Barros. (I would
   like to speak to Mr. Barros, please.)
3. *You would like to leave a message.*
   Posso deixar uma mensagem,
   por gentileza? (Can I leave
   a message, please?)
4. *You want to thank the person on*
   the other line. Muito obrigado!
   (Thank you!) [Use Muito
   obrigada! if you are a woman].

Chapter 20

The "Travel to Brazil" Quiz

1. *What is the name of the Brazilian*
   currency? Reais
2. *Where can you exchange currency*
   in Brazil? Casa de câmbio or banco
3. *Which city can you see the*
   Bumba-meu-Boi festival?
   São Luis do Maranhão.
4. *How do you greet people informally?*
   Oi, tudo bem?
5. *How do you thank people? Obrigado!*

Index